# LOVE

# ROBERT C. SOLOMON

# LOVE

## EMOTION, MYTH, & METAPHOR

PROMETHEUS BOOKS ⊞ Buffalo, New York

Published 1990 by Prometheus Books
700 East Amherst Street, Buffalo, New York 14215

Library of Congress Cataloging-in-Publication Data

Solomon, Robert C.
   Love : emotion, myth, and metaphor / by Robert C. Solomon.
      p.    cm. Includes index
   ISBN 0-87975-569-5
   Reprint. Originally published: Garden City, N.Y.:
Anchor/Doubleday, 1981.
   1. Love. I. Title.
BD436.S63    1990
128'.4—dc20                                  89-39922
                                                CIP

Printed in the United States of America

# CONTENTS

For K.H.

Do you know what it is like to be a self-centered not unhappy man who leads a tolerable finite life, works, eats, drinks . . . sleeps, then one fine days discovers that the great starry heavens have opened to him and that his heart is bursting with it. It? She. Her. Woman. Not a category, not a sex, not one of two sexes, a human female creature, but an infinity. . . . What else is infinity but a woman become meat and drink to you, life and your heart's own music, the air you breathe? Just to be near her is to live and have your soul's own self. Just to open your mouth on the skin of her back. What joy just to wake up with her beside you in the morning. I didn't know there was such happiness.

WALKER PERCY, *Lancelot,* p. 129

# PREFACE TO THE
# PAPERBACK EDITION

Rereading this book, for me, is like looking back over an old love. A flush of delight punctuated by pangs of embarrassment, inebriated memories of "falling" happily in love interrupted by sober thoughts about what really constitutes love and loving. But memories of happiness are not irrelevant to happiness, and memories of foolishness are not irrelevant to wisdom. Accordingly, I have resisted the obvious temptations to revise and rewrite and, except for the always awkward business of a dedication, I have decided not to change a word of the original text. It expresses, as well as I could at the time, the philosophical giddiness, the romantic sensibility, and the somewhat frivolous sense of humor inspired by the emotion of erotic love, and if since then I have had ample opportunity to explore its other and sometimes darker dimensions, I see no reason to deny or try to reinterpret that original enthusiasm. Today, I make much more of the "identity theory," herein developed only briefly in Part II, and I take much more seriously the consequences of that theory for the difficulties and ruptures that seem to me to be just as much a part of love as its delights. It does not surprise me that my views have changed along with my life, and I have never thought that consistency over time at the expense of experience was much of a philosophical virtue. But for now, it is a delight for me, and I hope for the reader, to relive this exploration of what I continue to believe is one of our most profound emotions, together with the myths and metaphors that have shaped its history. I am much gratified that Prometheus has given new life to this book and is supporting its reappearance with such enthusiasm.

# PREFACE

# "FALLING IN" LOVE

*Locate* I
love you *some-*
*where in*
*teeth and*
*eyes . . .*

*Words*
*say everything,*

*I*
love you
*again,*

*then what*
*is emptiness for. . . .*

ROBERT CREELEY, *The Language*


We'd known each other for years; and for months, we were—
what?—"seeing each other" (to choose but one of so many silly
euphemisms for playful but by no means impersonal sex). We
reveled in our bodies, cooked and talked two or three times a
week, enjoying ourselves immensely, but within careful
bounds, surrounded by other "relationships" (another euphemism), cautiously sharing problems as well as pleasures, ex-
orcising an occasional demon and delighting each other with
occasional displays of affection, never saying too much, or revealing too much, or crossing those unspoken boundaries of intimacy and independence.

Then, we "fell in" love. What happened?

There was no "fall," first of all. Why do we get so transfixed with that Alice-in-Wonderland Heideggerian metaphor, and not just that one but a maze of others, obscuring everything; what is a "deep" relationship, for example? And why is love "losing" yourself? Is "falling for" someone really "falling for"— that is, getting *duped?* Where do we get that imagery of tripping, tumbling, and other inadvertent means of getting *in*-volved, *im*-mersed and *sub*-merged in love, "taking the plunge" when it really gets serious? If anything, the appropriate image would seem to be openness rather than "depth," flying rather than "falling." One "makes" love (still another euphemism, this one with some significance), but our entire romantic mythology makes it seem as if it "happens," as if it is something someone "suffers" (enjoying it as well), as if it's entirely "natural," a "need" and something all but unavoidable.

In our case, it was clear. Love was a *decision,* a mutual decision—fully conscious, conscientious, deliberate. In particular, it was the decision to say a word.

It is often said, particularly by psychiatrists, that love is a *need.* (Why are so many books on love written by psychiatrists?) But our sense of need *followed,* rather than preceded, our decision to love. Before that moment there was no need, no sense of urgency, nothing missed when we were not together. In fact we later confessed that we were each wholly agreeable, not resigned but almost indifferent, to the likelihood of our not seeing each other again. Our decision was in part a decision *that* we would "need" one another, and to create that need we rearranged our world, seeing ourselves in terms of each other. But "need" is too static a term, a sense of *deficit* in the satisfactions of life. In that sense, we surely didn't need love at all. This was a luxury, not a necessity, not one of the requirements of human nature but a passion most *un*-natural, however "natural" it is (wrongly) supposed to be.

Nothing had changed. We had long been comfortable together, seemingly satisfied with our thrice weekly intimacy rituals, showing none of those unwelcome signs of boredom or encroaching indifference, no sense of need or nagging anxiety; and yet we can pinpoint the moment when we *decided* to love. I remember rehearsing five possible consequences and conversations, weighing the not inconsiderable risks and then *leaping*, not falling, into that vast indeterminacy. It was anything but a "commitment," that overused, much-abused, quasi-marital legalistic existential pretension that is supposed to be definitive of love but in fact only substitutes for *lack* of passion. What I said was "I-love-you"—not a description or confession of feelings already felt but the *creation* of an emotion, a work of conceptual art, the shared fabrication of an experience.

So, I believe, do we construct our grandest—and our pettiest —passions, from words, concepts and judgments. Not from nothing, of course. She was there, and so was I. The time was evidently "ripe" for both of us. We already had our own brief history, our excitement, our fantasies. And, of course, our desires. Who knows what else? (In a brilliant but ephemeral film a few years ago, Claude Lelouch used three hours and three generations to set up, at the last moment of his story, a young man and woman meeting "by accident" on a plane, "love at first sight," with the whole of history behind them.) But whatever else may have been there, the love itself was a decision, a choice, a leap. There was nothing "right" about it. We did it. That's all. I said the word, and after a moment's surprise ("I never thought I'd hear that from you"), she said it too. (How would I have responded if she had said it first? I'm not so sure.)

It is often said that love is a feeling. And, indeed, we were weeping, choking, shaking, bordering on incontinence—much like the symptoms of our annual flu. But none of this was the cause of our emotion, much less its essential nature. At most, it was an uncomfortable distraction, a mere effect, not cause but consequence. How could anyone confuse *that* with love, regardless of the circumstances?

Once we had decided, there was nothing more to be said or wondered about whether it was "real." Decisions are like that. They make themselves true. Sometimes they even feel as if they "happen" to you. But they never do.

It was then that everything changed. The way we looked at each other—constantly, searchingly, obsessively. Now we did indeed feel a "need" to be together, to imagine a future (at least dinner), as if to confirm and reconfirm our decision of the night before. There was that sense that "making love" was no longer physical but *meta*-physical, whatever that means. Something *profound* seemed to be happening. Words like "forever" began to creep into our thinking, but luckily not into our speech. Should they be taken seriously? Even as we feared a disaster at every moment?

What could "forever" mean in a moment of passion? (A high school girl friend once pleaded, "Tell me you love me forever, if only tonight.") Why does a moment of emotion have to be justified, as if its "truth" consisted only in its duration? Why is "true" love supposed to be eternal? Or could the whole of Western metaphysics be but the slippery slope toward God and marriage, nailing the moment onto the cross of eternity?

We wanted a word, a name that would clarify everything. But "love," once said, could no longer provide it. First it had opened a door, but now a thousand repetitions brought us no further; they were assurances, but they failed to clarify, they failed to express, they failed to *do* anything any more. Why? Because the emotion itself was that grand sense of indeterminacy, a burst of freedom. Two lifetimes of proud resolutions and fears forgotten. (Was it really only last month that I said I'd never do this again?) We were inventing a universe, as if for the first time. The great poet Goethe was simply wrong when he said "only the first love is true." (Every love is first love, and "the best," "the most," etc.) And if names seemed wholly inadequate, if love seemed "mysterious" and "indescribable" (amor-fuss?), that was only because love was first this sense of being *open*, creative. Nothing fixed and finished existed yet to be named or finally described.

So we turned to poetry and metaphor, clumsily trying to express in our painfully limited language—no, to give shape to—this new half-invented world, as if some image—any image —or even a sound, might make it comprehensible. And so, "love." A cheap linguistic trick, rendering common an experience we knew to be unique. But without the word, would there have been the emotion? Then why was it that, in our uniqueness, we found ourselves mouthing the words of a hundred popular songs? Once I even caught myself thinking, "You light up my life"—surely one of the more mawkish musical hits of the seventies. So much for both uniqueness and imagined profundity.

Love is "letting go," we hear, even a loss of control. But "letting" is an *act*, something done deliberately, rather than simply *losing* control. In fact we were in total control, with all the complexities of our mutual uncertainty. We enjoyed a new and passionate recklessness, making new rules only to break them. We shut ourselves off from the world, arrogant, terrified. Our terror was not fear—fear of falling, fear of "being hurt," fear of being foolish—so much as anxiety—*angst* to the professionals. Fear is being afraid of what will happen to you; anxiety is uncertainty about what you will *do*. True anxiety is not the merely neurotic and pathetic paralysis discussed by psychiatrists; it is rather a quite ordinary—yet extraordinary—sense of power, an awareness of risk, a kind of enthusiastic fatalism. It was not an unpleasant feeling—even exhilarating—the beginning, or at least the possibility, of a whole new world. *Amor fati*, the philosopher Nietzsche called it—love of fate, living on the edge, in the heights, being vulnerable, "open," excited. Our love was an adventure, a risk, the emotional equivalent of exploring—a rebellion, against the banal authorities of reasonableness and sensibility, against the stale dictates of propriety and tired rules and duties—all of those little lists and obligations that made up our lives. All these small vanities—being on time, afraid of being missed at the meeting, keeping the respect of those one despises—became but little jokes, along with words like "responsible," "sensible" and "respectable." We floated free from the world with our affection and our foolishness, not oblivious to but only amused by how others came to view us—suspiciously, of course. We risked our friends and our careers—we, two so careful people—redefining our world as it suited us at the moment, and only on our own frivolous terms. We were exiles and outcasts, in our own little world, making guerrilla excursions, when it suited us, into a hostile but harmless public world.

("The one thing your friends will never forgive you," writes Camus in *The Fall*, "is your happiness.")

As in all revolutions, we were driven to excesses by the sheer indeterminacy of our newly declared freedom, by the breakdown of normal restraint and formal courtesies. Nowhere was this more evident than in the very substance of our wholly unreasonable and utterly obsessive *lust*. Now it is often said, with no small amount of self-righteous piety by those who neither love nor lust, that love and lust are two different worlds, the first sacred and "spiritual," the second "profane." Ever since the twelfth century the ideal of love without lust has even had a special name, "platonic love," for which Plato should not wholly be blamed. Desire is degraded and an emasculated concept of love is elevated to the status of a religion, with endless litanies on cardinal sins, lust, greed, gluttony and the virtues of impotence. But if there was one thing that was utterly obvious to us, it was the *sanctity* of sex. Sex as a ritual. Sex as expression. Sex as creative desire, not a need, not "satisfaction." The more we had, the more we wanted, the more dissatisfied we became, the less sex was "sex" and the less we even knew *what* we wanted. What once seemed obvious now became a bewildering question: what do we want when we "want" someone?

We seemed insatiable, always wanted more; not sex itself but certainly something *through* sex. How silly it seemed, thinking of Freud's view that love is but sublimated lust; how could that even make sense, when we were making love all day? Sex and love, in love, are as inseparable as a word and its meaning. But what, in this case, was the meaning?

Strangely enough, Plato (my primary antagonist in this book) caught this in his *Symposium* (but, significantly, through the voice of Aristophanes, not Socrates):

> The intense yearning which lovers have toward each other does not appear to be the desire for sexual intercourse, but for something else which the soul of each desires and cannot tell, and of which he/she has only a dark and doubtful presentiment.
>
> *Symposium*, Jowett trans., p. 192

It is this continuing sense of something more to come, this "dark and doubtful presentiment," that introduces the metaphysical element of love. Love is philosophy, a certain view of the world, not merely a "feeling." The ominous word "metaphysical," however, does *not* mean that love is a cosmic process, the union of the Eternal genitalia or any of the other erotic allegories that love theorists prefer to discuss instead of love itself.

Love, Plato warns, is never satisfied. But satisfaction isn't the point, since what defines the emotion is not the quest for satisfaction, not even for "happiness," but its very opposite, this continuing reckless frenzied sense of dissatisfaction, which expressed itself so clearly in our sexual excesses, excitement as its goal, not contentment. It was the desire that we desired, not its satisfaction, the emotion and not its reasonable resolution.

If I wrote in my diary, "I've never been happier," that was a superfluous surprise, a fringe benefit, for, as Aristotle rightly argued, you can never *aim* for happiness. And as for those who would reduce the whole of metaphysics to the mere search for pleasure, it must be said that we never even noticed how much we were enjoying ourselves—perhaps the true test of pleasure. Satisfaction, happiness and pleasure—those are the results of small desires, desires too easily answered, desires devoid of passion. We would have none of that. All we wanted—at least for a while—was love.

# AUTHOR'S NOTE

I have tried to write a book appropriate to its subject:
too often serious
overly playful, in compensation
irresponsible
repetitious
not always consistent
contentious, but (I hope)
entertaining.

Its virtues—and vices too—I owe to my friends, who have given me ideas, encouragement, solace, delusions and, not least, love. I owe a special debt of gratitude to my editor, Loretta Barrett, particularly for her patience, to my agent, Molly Friedrich, for her encouragement and support, to Shelby Hearon for her prompting and friendship, and, of course, much more than gratitude to Kristine Hanson, the book's original inspiration.

# INTRODUCTION

### *Romantic Love*

*I heard of a man and woman recently who had fallen in love. "Hopelessly in love" was the woman's antique phrase for it. I hadn't realized people still did that sort of thing jointly. Nowadays the fashion is to fall in love with yourself, and falling in love with a second party seems to be generally regarded as bad form.*

SShipFrags RUSSELL BAKER, *New York Times Magazine*, March 1978

Adults dismiss it as adolescent. Adolescents are embarrassed by it and deride it as childish. Children are bored by it. Therapists try to cure it. "True" men regard it as feminine. Feminists attack it as oppressive. Radicals demean it as frivolity. Frivolous people see it as absurdly serious. Christians call it "profane." Libertines mock it as "pious." Biological realists accept it as "Nature's way of telling us what to do." Social realists tolerate it as Western society's slippery slope to marriage. Businessmen sell it. Consumers voraciously buy it. (Master Charge and Visa are now accepted.) Cynics sneer at it, a nasty gloss over timid sexual lust. Puritans are appalled by it, a timid gloss over nasty sexual lust. Self-styled romantics, of course, think it's "divine," but they make such fools of themselves that they only confirm what everyone else suspected all along—that romantic love is like a disease, perhaps "incurable."

It is appropriate to horny Victorians, Shakespearean tragedies, afternoon soap operas and adolescents.

It is acceptable—briefly—in middle-aged men and recent divorcees, frowned upon but tolerated in people over forty-three.

For some, love is a game, often ending in marriage (which is emphatically *not* a game) or in "heartbreak," which is a metaphor.

In any case, love is a passion. But what is a passion but a passing obsession, not to be taken seriously except as a "passage," or a joke, or a literary device, or perhaps an experience we all *ought* to go through? (A bit of moralizing is sure to take the wind out of its sails.)

It is romantic love that one "falls into," that resembles a kind of terror, or an illness, marked by fever, loss of appetite, shaky knees, nervous twittering and a certain looseness in the brain and bowels. It is romantic love that, as the Spanish philosopher Ortega y Gasset describes it, "is a state of mental misery which has a restricting, impoverishing and paralyzing effect upon the development of consciousness." And yet we not only enjoy this but we consider it the richest experience of all. (Isn't this odd?) It is romantic love for which men and women wreck careers and abandon families and obligations, which provides plots for soaps and operas, which Plato called a kind of madness and which so infuriated St. Paul, which inspired Shakespeare if not also Dante and led to the downfall of Antony, Juliet, Romeo, Samson, Emma Bovary and King Kong.

We are obsessed by it, this passion. We are *the* romantic society, for whom all of our successes sometimes seem but distractions, inessential periods of happiness, during our search for our "one true love." We do indeed have a *moral* view of this passion. To accuse someone of being "incapable of love" is an indictment, as if he or she is less than wholly human. Not to have ever been in love is a matter of grave concern, as if one has not yet really lived, or as if one might have some probably fatal flaw in his or her moral character. Christian love has long been said to be the highest *duty* of humanity, even a gift from God. Psychiatrists refer to our "tragic incapacity to love," the "disintegration" and the "banalization" of love, leaving no doubt about their own role as the new high priests of a still unearthly and inaccessible God.

> They had always known, they say, that they could only be cured by love, and before the treatment began they had expected that through this relation they would at last be granted what life had hitherto withheld from them.
>
> FREUD, *Introductory Lectures*, p. 441

There is no topic that has inspired more garbled and wishful thinking than love, or more garbage to be written about it. ("Garbage is garbage," said the logician Burton Dreben of Harvard, "but the history of garbage is scholarship.") We are treated to our daily dose of off-the-cuff witticisms, such as "Love means never having to say you're sorry," and a monthly best seller with the message that love, though rare, is the answer to all of our problems. "All you need is love," sang the Beatles fifteen years ago. "Only love is real" is the recurrent cosmological theme and, in a slightly more Newtonian vein, "Love makes the world go round." This unqualified cosmic praise has been repeated by some of the greatest minds in history in their weaker moments. Benjamin Disraeli, for example, a hardheaded realist in his politics if not in his affairs with women, declared, "Love is the principle of existence and its only end." Konrad Lorenz, the great biologist for whom evolution became something of a religion, called love "the most wonderful product of ten million years of evolution." Several philosophers, Jesus and Hegel among them, have believed that society could and should be ruled through love alone, and Mozart, in his *Magic Flute*, musically tried to make it happen, "happily ever after" of course. From the Bible comes the simplest piety, "God is love" (I John 4:8), but Gertrude Stein, as usual, wins the prize for succinctness. "Love IS," she insists, and who can disagree with her?

Whether they are as oratorical and edifying as Rollo May or

as mellow and dramatic as Erich Segal, these are more than harmless valentines, thoughtless praises for a grand and beautiful passion. They reflect a *dangerous* view of love, and everything we say about it, think about it, write about it, wish about it and especially *do* about it betrays our confusion. We are taught that love is everything, the key to happiness, that love is "the answer," the way to God, the keystone of human nature, that everyone not only can but ought to love, and that those who do not are less than wholly human. In the midst of our passion we say, "I'll always love you," but we don't. And so, of course, we are disappointed—not in love but in ourselves. These seemingly harmless valentines are sadistic, manipulative epigrams on the death of a feeling. They announce ideals and set up expectations which no experience can possibly match. They make us feel impoverished with the experiences that we do have. They demand sacrifices that no one in his or her right mind would ever make. They turn an emotion into a religion, and when it can't bear its own solemnity, it is made to look foolish, adolescent, irresponsible or childish by contrast. It is then said to be "not the real thing." We have killed love, by bloating our expectations with cosmic praise, by obscuring love and turning it into a weapon. And just in case we have our doubts, we are told that love is "ineffable," beyond the realm of explanation and, most assuredly, beyond suspicion.

Now you might say, "No one really believes all this stuff. In our enthusiasm, we—shall we say—stretch the truth a bit." But why such unbridled enthusiasm, which so often turns to embarrassment? And what we say—even in love—is a good indication of what we believe—or hope. Everywhere we turn, we learn, from Plato to St. Paul, from comic books to the *Cosmo* quiz-of-the-month, that love is the most important ingredient in human life, that we cannot do without it, and in any case we would not want to. And not surprisingly we find ourselves believing it.

Perhaps they were right putting love into books. . . . Perhaps it could not live anywhere else.

WILLIAM FAULKNER, *Light in August*

Against this backdrop of bloated love, this bladder filled with hot air and piety, it is easy to understand the bitter disillusionment of the cynic.

If love is so obviously not what it has so long and so loudly been said to be—the answer to everything, the key to being "human" as well as happy—then, the cynic concludes too quickly, love must be an illusion, a bad joke or a conspiracy. First Marx and Freud, then Marxists and feminists, started to suspect the sinister effects of this bloated and pious view of love. Freud once suggested that romance was nothing but lust, "plus the ordeal of civility." Marx and Engels hypothesized that romantic love was a rationalization of (lifelong) prostitution, and an entire generation of feminists have rightly complained that they find themselves caught between feeling that love is inescapable and all-important and the realization that it is political manipulation and degrading. The miracle of love becomes a myth, and the religion becomes but an extravagant façade for lust, an opiate more powerful than religion precisely because it is entirely personal; we must always blame its failures on ourselves.

The two sides of the schizoid view play against each other, piety against cynicism, and the result is our curious confusion about love. We snicker at love as children, only to be told that it is the most important thing in life. We praise love to the heavens as adults, worry endlessly about finding it, keeping it, losing it, not being able to feel it, getting trapped by it and getting over it, only to make ourselves miserable, disappointed and ultimately cynical. Our confusion is promoted by our pop psychotherapists, who play off an ethereal ideal in order to make what we actually feel seem pathetic—or worse—by comparison. Thus Erich Fromm, for example, defends his quasi-

religious "art of loving" to the millions by contrasting this with
the "neurotic" love he holds in such contempt, the same emotion that most of us experience with such satisfaction. The idea
that love is a need gets coupled with the idea that we moderns
("modern man") have made it impossible; thus Rollo May, for
instance: "Where love was once considered the answer, it now
is the problem." "*What* problem?" we should ask, and leave
open the possibility that Dr. May may be himself the problem,
with his cosmic view of *eros* and his persistent accusations
that we are failing to live up to *his* ethereal ideal of love.

One asks a simple question, "What is it to fall in love?" or
"Why is love so important to us?" and in return what we get
are murky allegories and the mythological heroes of ancient
Greece and Rome, biological studies of the mating habits of in-
sects, fish, birds and monkeys, "how to" and "how not to"
books about almost everything, surveys, interviews and confessions, bad poetry and volumes of vacuity the only point of
which seems to be to impress us with the author's own sensitivity. We get greeting-card platitudes, and voyeuristic anthropology (1001 ways the savages and the French make love and
the curious things they believe about it) and, of course, psychi-
atric diagnoses and advice, often bemoaning the perennial
"tragedy of modern man's inability to love." Everything but an
answer.

So why another book on love? I haven't discovered that love
prevents, or causes, cancer, hemorrhoids or heart disease. I see
no need once again to repeat the same tired and inevitably in-
accurate Greek allegories, or intimate along with so many religious leaders and psychiatrists in recent years, that I know
what true love is and you do not—much to your disadvantage,
of course.

What I want to contend in this book, although it is hard to
say it with quite the piety or flamboyance of those who praise
love along with the Lord or condemn it as a capitalist conspiracy, is this: love is an emotion, just an ordinary, non-cosmic,

luxurious but not essential emotion. It is not divine, much less eternal, it is not a part of human nature or the key to the gates of happiness or any kind of "answer" (to questions mostly unasked and unknown). It is an emotion long surrounded by myths and metaphors, motivated by false hopes and the desire for a guarantee that, somehow, a miserable life can be turned into happiness at a single stroke, that love once found will last, even "forever," that one will be loved, "no matter what." These are illusions, and much of what has been said about love is nothing but illusion, in Freud's sense—a kind of wishful thinking, even when it parades as poetry—or psychiatry. But it does not follow that love itself is an illusion, as many Marxists, feminists and Freudians (not Freud) have insisted. And my purpose in this book is precisely to separate the passion from the illusions, to explode the myth without in any way demeaning or denying the importance of the emotion. Indeed, it is the importance of this emotion that itself has to be explained, but in so doing one makes clear its limitations as well.

The reader has a right to know what to expect in the following pages, to be on guard and ready with objections in mind, because there is nothing more infuriating—to me anyway—than those grand tomes on the magnificence of love, whose titles promise some great revelation but, 462 pages later, not a single theme has emerged. So what I want to argue, in blunt and clumsy summary, is this:
• Much of what we believe about love is a confusion of myths and metaphors, some quaint, some innocent, some amusing, some vulgar, some nuts-and-bolts and matter-of-fact, and some insidious. The most insidious myth begins with Plato, who defended a view of love in his dialogue *Symposium* which de-emphasized sex and turned *eros* to the service of impersonal knowledge. It is Plato who begins the march of love toward divinity and away from simple personal relationships, who takes love out of the realm of ordinary emotions and

friendship and pretends that it is something spectacular, our psychic introduction to an ideal world, beyond mere emotion, which is eternal. It is a myth picked up and fostered by Christianity, by St. Paul in particular, who so vehemently condemns love that is "profane" (that is, what we know as love) and praises love divine, sacred love, indeed so sacred that he tells us over and over again that it is a love of which we are not even capable. And the myth is picked up again in different guise in the twelfth century, during which a group of poets called "troubadours" wandered around France "devoting" themselves to singing mediocre love songs to women—usually married—who rarely gave them the favors they so desired. And it was this longing, the *languor*, the protracted but intentional sexual frustration that came to be identified by scholars as the origins of "romantic" love as such. And in Italy, about the same time, Plato's heritage was fully recognized by a number of monks who canonized "Platonic love," ideal love without sexual expression or desire, which is, ultimately, aimed only at God and therefore lasts, happily, forever.

Now there may well be some poetic pleasure in protracted sexual self-denial, and I do not doubt that there is that peculiar religious experience that Freud called "oceanic," which one might call "love." (Why not?) But none of this has anything to do with romantic love, nor is it in any way necessarily opposed to it, an alternative to it, or (as in Plato) an improvement upon it. Romantic love, unlike the love of God and the languor that comes of frustration, is essentially sexual, secular, personal and always tentative, tenuous, never certain. Love is not inhuman, or superhuman, or in any way impossible, but then too, there are no metaphysical guarantees.

• Love is an emotion, nothing else. But emotions are not— traditional linguistic usage and certain current popular songs aside—"feelings." Our emotions are neither primitive nor "natural," but rather intelligent constructions, structured by concepts and judgments that we learn in a particular culture, through which we give our experience some shape and meaning. And it is not only love that gives meaning to life but all emotions—hatred, anger and envy too. But if emotions are primarily judgments, ways of shaping the world, then one might say that we do not "fall in" love at all. Quite to the contrary, the fall is rather a creation, which we have been taught to make by a thousand movies, stories and novels; its most essential ingredient—too often hidden in the language of "spontaneity" and "chance"—is personal *choice*. This in turn raises the question, "Why?" Why choose love at all? And why choose to love this particular person? (All the more urgent a question when the choice continues to be disastrous.) Love does not prick us from behind (we've had enough of the metaphor of Cupid's arrows). We choose it, and if we often choose badly or desperately, that does not prove that love is irrational. People are irrational.

• If emotions are learned and purposeful ways of structuring our experience, it follows that what emotions one has or can have depend in part upon the particular culture one belongs to. Having a certain emotion is restricted to those who share certain concepts, or speak a certain language, and make certain kinds of judgments about themselves and the world. A great many writers on the topic of love assume, without argument, that the features they recognize in themselves and their friends (or patients) are, to borrow a phrase from Rollo May, "universal human characteristics." But love is not the keystone of "human nature" (if there is any such thing, which I would deny). The English sailors under Captain Cook may have had a grand time in Tahiti—followed by the fictional characters on His Majesty's good ship *Bounty*—but they found no romantic love there, except what they brought with them (along with syphilis). Anthropologists who have spent years with certain Eskimo communities may or may not have seen the proverbial nose rubbings, but they did not find romantic love. In fact the number of societies that would recognize or would have recognized romantic love at all, at least as anything more than Western foolishness, is extremely small throughout history. (The number is no doubt exploding now, with the invasion of American television even onto the islands of Micronesia and the systematic destruction of traditional community bonds.) Romantic love is a cultural artifact, something along the lines of cooked carrots and kosher butchers. There is nothing "natural" about it. (Sex, of course, is quite "natural," but even this is extremely misleading: what sex *means* is not natural and, in particular, sex as an "expression" of love is a highly specific—and peculiar—cultural invention.)

• What kind of society makes romantic love possible? (This is not yet to ask what kind of society makes this emotion desirable, much less an obsession which is said to "make the world go round.") My answer, briefly, is that it is a society which places extraordinary emphasis on the concept of individuality and individual self-identity, a society which distinguishes more or less plainly between public positions and personal roles, a society which places a premium on individual idealization, fantasy and fiction, and, perhaps most importantly, a society that grants a high degree of mobility and flexibility in relationships in general, places personal choice at the core of mating and marriage rituals and the idea of what we call "intimacy" (again, not a global concept) at the very center of interpersonal relationships. But if this is what is necessary to make romantic love *possible*, what more is needed to make it seem like a need, a *necessity*? What kind of society would make this one emotion, among a hundred other emotions no less moving, no less complex, no less "human," so enormously important, so urgent, so crucial to one's very conception of oneself and "who I am"? It is a society in which independence and mobility are celebrated even at the cost of massive loneliness and the systematic destruction of almost all seemingly "natural" bonds. Family ties, community bonds, ethnic identity and tribal membership have all been sacrificed to "making it" and "finding oneself." It is a society in which the family is a nest to be kicked *out* of, and "home town" is the place where you are *from*. In such a society, where long-term bonds no longer serve as a source of constant familiarity and intimacy, an emotion whose primary purpose is the rapid formation of interpersonal ties and intimacy serves an all-important purpose. Romantic love provides a transient sense of "belonging" in a society that is self-consciously in perpetual disarray. And what could serve as a better medium for this emotion than sex? It is as universal as any human attribute, as intrinsically enjoyable as any other human activity and readily available as a bond of intimacy, personal tastes and choice aside. It is sudden "spontaneous" intimacy—in our culture symbolized and synthesized by sex—that forms the structural core of romantic love.

• Even so, love is not everything, and not for everybody. Love is a luxury, not a need. It is not the only emotion to play this role, even in our society. We have not yet done away with friendship and family, colleagues at work and the boys in the band, shared oppression and the company of misery. Romantic love is just one option among many. Even within a couple in love, there are a hundred other emotional bonds of no less significance, if considerably less melodrama: shopping together at the same old Safeway and putting together the rent, trying to be on time and deciding between Werner Herzog and *The Muppet Movie*. And if these admittedly unromantic connections do not find their way into our epic love sagas, that may not be so much because they are irrelevant as because our conception of the exclusive importance of love is so exaggerated and our conception of the alternatives so impoverished. Romantic love is not for everyone, and there may be good reasons for rejecting it. The intimacy of love may violate a person's sense of individuality and solitude—and it should not be concluded that he or she "is afraid of intimacy" any more than an aversion to brussels sprouts should be automatically considered akin to anorexia. And, on the other side, the privacy and exclusivity of romantic love may well offend a person's sense of the larger community or interfere with friendship and tribal camaraderie. It is said that lovers love the world, but a more accurate description would be that love systematically reduces a couple's concern to "their own little world." For good reason, all the world does not love a lover.

• I have said that intimacy is the core of romantic love, but it is not all that obvious what intimacy is. Let me begin by saying what it is *not:* intimacy has nothing to do with telling your lover your "innermost secrets"; and yet, in almost all of the scientific literature that exists on the subject, such "disclosure" is the definition of intimacy. What I shall argue here, though it is impossible to summarize in a paragraph, is that intimacy—and love—consist in *shared identity,* a redefinition of self which no amount of sex or fun or time together will add up to. Most of the final parts of the book, in fact, are dedicated to working out this somewhat paradoxical notion—how two people in a society with an extraordinary sense of individuality and individual identity mutually fantasize, verbalize and act their way into a relationship that can no longer be understood as a mere conjunction of the two but only as a complex one.

• But even this would be too simple. (It always is.) Television preachers often tell us that the couple (heterosexual and married, of course) form a "union" (pronounced "*yewn-*yon"), but this is only half true. If romantic love presupposes a strong sense of individuality and individual identity, but also requires a sense of shared identity, it is not hard to see that the dynamics of romantic love are inevitably going to be *tension,* the assertion of individuality coupled with the mutual sense of identity. Early in a relationship the exhilaration of the newly created sense of unity may be overwhelming; later on the sense of unity or worse, "being stuck with one another," may manifest itself in that all too familiar scenario of two people, who claim without a twitch of doubt that they love each other, devoting every comment and gesture to the annoyance or embarrassment of one another, as if to prove to themselves and all who see them that they are, after all, two distinct people, locked in what appears to be lifelong mortal combat. But in between the exhilarating initiation period and the hopefully avoidable epoch of *kvetch* and humiliation is a sequence of moves that a philosopher will recognize as a *dialectic,* the constant interplay of words and roles through which two (or more) people define themselves and each other *both* as individuals and as a shared identity. A sense of shared identity alone, without a dialectic, is not romantic love, whatever else it might be. But neither is mere companionship, a partnership, in effect, the same as romantic love. And when a couple of friends of yours, fighting it out all the time, inevitably end up in bed for a bout of (what they describe as) "incredible" love-making, they might in fact be a better example of romance than all the unrequited Romeos and tragic Juliets and hopeful, junior psychology students who populate the literature on the subject. But are two people fighting still in love? Of course. The tune might be in the key of B♭ but a dissonant A is still part of the melody.

• One point which will lie at the basis of virtually everything I say in this book deserves explicit mention, if only occasional discussions as such. Romantic love need have nothing to do with *gender.* There is romantic love between men and men and between women and women in no sense different from the more usual paradigm case (which it was not for the ancient Greeks) between man and woman. The precise significance of the male and female genitalia is of at most incidental interest to love as such, but this is not to deny that a *particular* relationship might well be defined in terms of male and female sexuality or—what is entirely different—masculine and feminine roles. (One need not be female to be feminine, or a man to be masculine, and one need be neither to be in love.) But this point is more than a bow to liberalism, for if romantic love were anything like what some people have thought it is—a distinctive set of gender roles—then one could not define the emotion at all without distinguishing explicitly male and female, and co-ordinately masculine and feminine roles, much to the detriment of the female. If that were true, love might well turn out to be indefensible.

• What I have just said about the gender of people in love also applies to the *concept* of love. It is being said with some frequency today that our concept of romantic love—and even the whole system of our concepts of science, knowledge, philosophy and culture—is a purely male fabrication, foisted upon females who accept it under duress or pretend to accept it to satisfy the foolish male ego. There are indeed aspects of our conception of love roles that lend themselves to this charge, particularly the idea that a woman's love requires "submissiveness" and the like. But it is hard to know what to make of the claim that men and women's *concepts* of love are so different that they are mutually unrecognizable. For the most part, we share our concepts as we share our language and culture: *Wuthering Heights* and even *The Second Sex* and *The Women's Room* are part of *our* literature. There is no such thing as a "woman's novel" any more than there is such a thing as "a man's magazine." If men and women think about love differently, it is essentially one and the same concept of love about which they disagree. If not, what is it that they disagree about?

There may be—I cannot deny it—some unchecked male bias in my theory. If so, that is a flaw in it. But the concept I am trying to understand is not itself biased, whatever inequities and asymmetries have been promoted in its name and continue to color our judgments about it. It may be that we have different expectations and hopes, sometimes contradictory fears and demands. But the current insistence that "men are incapable of love" or, conversely, that (romantic) love is only a male invention, clarifies nothing and leads to no understanding of any kind. Indeed its effect as well as its intention is precisely the opposite, to fortify mutual misunderstanding and declare, once and for all, that nothing better will ever take its place.

• Love is not a "commitment," has nothing to do with commitment, indeed is the very antithesis of commitment, as that term is used so much today. Love is an emotion; a commitment is a promise (whether to oneself or someone else) to do something—or continue to do something—*whatever* one's feelings. If you're in love, you don't need to make a commitment; if you need a commitment, it has nothing to do with love.

• One last point of no small importance: along with the idea that one would like to be loved "forever" often goes the desire to be loved "no matter what." Sometimes this is an excuse for discourtesy and slovenliness; after all, it does tend to be a bother to keep up the appearances which made one seem so lovable in the first place, to maintain conversation at such an exalted level ("When was the last time we talked about the importance of Proust for the existentialists?"), and just to be so concerned, to listen so carefully, to watch so closely, to behave so respectfully. "No matter what" has a way of sneaking out of the bottom drawer, like an old pair of comfortable pajamas, as if, now that we've "hooked" ourselves a lover, he or she is bound to love us whatever we do. Indeed, some people call this the "test" of love. In modern humanist parlance, this is expressed as the love of the "total person," in all of his or her "uniqueness and individuality" (the phrase is from psychologist Victor Frankyl). Against this, I want to argue that the idea of the unqualified, unspecified, open-ended and totally tolerant love of "the individual human being" is just another part of the love myth, derived, perhaps, from the Christian concept of the "soul"—that essential spiritual pit that lies at the core of each of us, beneath our clothes and our manners and our bodies and our genitals and our intelligence and accomplishments. But this is motivated, as usual, by our childish desire for a guarantee, as if hard-earned love, once "won," will not be so easily lost. But love always has its "reasons." Every

love has its built-in limitations, and the question then, both in
the abstract and in every particular relationship, becomes,
"What are these reasons, and these limits?" Is money a legitimate reason for loving someone? (If not, why not?) Personality? Sexual performance? A chance to get ahead? The fact
that he/she loves me? Her legs? His arms? But in no case the
"total person." This adds an additional kink to the traditional
mythological picture of love: if one loves a person "for reasons," what about someone else, someone new, who satisfies
those same reasons, perhaps even more so, and in any case adds
a bit of novelty? Are lovers replaceable? Is love exclusive? Indeed, perhaps romantic love not only fails to last "forever" but
has the faults of its own collapse already built right into its
structure.

My aim in this book is to attempt what might be called a
philosophical reconstruction of our conception of romantic
love. It is, on the one hand, a rather harsh and sometimes belligerent attack on the nonsense that has been perpetrated—
often with the most benign of intentions—in praise of this much-
praised emotion, but it is also an attempt to describe the experience of love and its place in our lives from the point of view
of an enthusiast. It is an attempt to take account of the sense
within the nonsense and look once again at the very tangible
facts of our collective experience, not least our literature and
late night conversations, separating out the wishful thinking
from the nature of the experience itself. It is looking at some of
the seemingly "obvious" features of love with an eye to peer-
ing beneath the surface and seeking out the not so obvious
and trying to make sense of what most of us would agree to be
at one and the same time the most seemingly simple and tor-
tuously complex emotion in the Western world.

At the end of *Annie Hall*, Woody Allen tells us a bad joke: a
man complains that his brother imagines that he's a chicken.
"Why don't you take him to a psychiatrist?" asks a well-mean-

ing friend. "Because we need the eggs" is the answer. "Relationships are like that," Allen explains—they are necessary illusions. What I want to do here, philosophically, is to distinguish the chicken from the eggs.

# PART I:
## *Emotion, Myth and Metaphor*

# IN THE BEGINNING, THE WORD 1

*There are many people who would never have been in love, had they never heard love spoken of.*

LA ROCHEFOUCAULD, *Maxim* 136

W hat is love?
Or should we rather begin by asking, What is "love"? for it is an open question—or should be— whether we are ultimately concerned more with a word than a feeling. We use one and the same word to refer to so many different sensibilities; we love our country as well as our friends, one loves chocolate cheesecake as well as the sun and a day on the beach. And even limiting ourselves to the love be- tween two people, there is the love of a mother, the love of a brother, the love one feels for an old teacher, the love of a friend, the love of a hero as well as the love of a lover. And even love between lovers seems so varied and in many cases unique that it is only with some hesitancy and in haste that we cover them with the same word. Thus Albert Camus, in his *Myth of Sisyphus*, writes, "We call love what binds us to cer- tain creatures only by reference to a collective way of seeing for which books and legends are responsible. But of love I know only that mixture of desire, affection and intelligence that binds me to this or that creature. That compound is not the same for another person. I do not have the right to cover all these experiences with the same name" (p. 55).

Consider, by way of contrast, the wealth of meticulous and

fine distinctions we make in describing our feelings of hostility: hatred, loathing, scorn, anger, revulsion, resentment, envy,
abhorrence, malice, aversion, vexation, irritation, annoyance,
disgust, spite and contempt, or worse, "beneath" contempt.
And yet we sort out our positive affections for the most part
between the two limp categories, "liking" and "loving." We
distinguish our friends from mere acquaintances and make a
ready distinction between lovers and friends whom we love
"but not that way." Still, one and the same word serves to
describe our enthusiasm for apple strudel, respect for a distant father, the anguish of an uncertain romantic affair and
nostalgic affection for an old pair of slippers. One begins to
wonder if "love" means anything more than "warm affection,"
occasionally, enthusiasm.

The vagueness of this word and its expansive domain have
been pointed out by virtually every writer on love or "love,"
but what is remarkable is how rarely this has raised an eye-
brow, much less inspired some serious re-evaluation of our favorite word, if not also our favorite emotion. If it is true, as our
linguists tell us, that a language tends to make distinctions in
proportion to the importance of the subject matter (thus the
Eskimos and their fifty-one words for "snow"), then the poverty of our language of love, compared to the exquisite richness of our language of hostility, should make us suspicious indeed. The French, by contrast again, have a dozen categories
where we have but one. Thus one wonders whether it is only a
word, a grab-bag category for feelings not important enough
to deserve their own special name. Or perhaps one wonders
why a word that works so hard for us ought still to remain so
obscure, unless it is hiding something, serving some function
not readily admitted, perhaps giving the appearance of a concrete and specific feeling when in fact there are a multitude of
feelings, including even those of envy, hostility and jealousy,
mutual bitterness and protracted annoyance, sanctified by a
word, "love."

"Love" is a *political* word. It does not just name an emotion;
it is itself emotive. It is not so much a "sign" that refers as a
sigh that applauds, a sound that transforms; it does not describe so much as congratulate. To be in love, writes Rollo
May of the Victorians, was to be one of the elect, with a sense
of salvation and a right to be self-righteous (*Love and Will*,
pp. 13–14). But it is the right to use the word, rather than the
discovery of any particular emotion, that bestows this
confidence. Everyone knows at least one unhappy couple who,
despite the fact that they have spent every day for the past ten
years bickering and suffering mutual self-abasement, consider
themselves the very model of love. Every word and gesture
signals contempt; some of them, according to Dr. John L.
Schimel of New York University, cannot remember a time
when either of them has ever said anything complimentary or
positive. They wrangle from breakfast until bedtime, and they
insist that they "love" one another. Grant them that word, acknowledge that they do indeed love one another, and all will
be well. Deny them the word, and you have crushed them, accused them of a meaningless and mean-spirited life. But this is
the power of "love," not love. As Romeo says, "Call me but
love, and I'll be new baptized."

The word "love" is so full of praise and self-congratulation
that just to use it is already a sign of character; to use it to
describe one's own feelings—no matter how complex or confused those feelings might actually be—is to display one's enthusiasm, to grant oneself an exalted status in the world of
emotions, to prove oneself a "loving person," as Erich Fromm
would say, regardless of whom or what one loves, or how.
Twenty-five hundred years ago Plato had the first speaker in
his classic *Symposium* praise love or *eros* by arguing its successful effects in battle, and St. Paul and his successors half a
millennium later saw quite clearly how effective a weapon
love could be. Or rather, "love" (as *agape*), the Word, for it
was not by loving their enemies that the early Christians suc-

ceeded in opposing them. They battered down their defenses
with the Word. For who could fight against "love"? It was the
Word that became invincible, irrefutable, like the word "freedom," with which it shares many similarities. Both mean so
much that they might well be thought to mean nothing. In fact
both are words so hallowed that no one could possibly be
against them. "Even the Nazis said they were for freedom,"
writes philosopher Frithjof Bergmann. And who would not
also be "for" love?

Given the varieties of affection that can count as love, and
the variety of "objects" that can be loved, it is easy to understand how it is that, even restricting themselves to love between peers and excluding motherly love and the like, those
who write about love end up talking about very different phenomena, choosing very different paradigms and arguing very
different political positions as well. A happily married couple
quite understandably take themselves as an example and look
with compassion or contempt on those who are too "unsettled"
or "immature" to enjoy the same. Wise old Socrates praised
wisdom itself as the only "true" love, and the novelist Stendhal, in justification of his amorous but often troubled adven-
tures in Italy, celebrated love only as passionate, desperate
yearning. Psychoanalysts naturally tend to emphasize motherly
love, feminists often choose to point out those cases in which
love is primarily overidealization and disillusion, and writers
with an aesthetic bent (including Plato) often tend to take
love to be intense admiration. The Spanish philosopher Ortega y Gasset, for example, calls love "gravitation toward a
beautiful object." But then, is there any significant difference
between loving a lover and loving a sports car or a painting?
Or, for that matter, wouldn't a little boy passing a pastry shop
come to count as the consummate lover? The examples are
most revealing.

If we push past the ordinary toward the gruesome, it becomes even more obvious how elastic and political the word

can become. A man murders his lover "because of love." A couple radiate mutual loathing but stay together—"where else would we go?" They insist that they "love" each other. A woman sacrifices her career for her husband and calls it "love." We then start to wonder, what could *not* be called "love," at least by way of *an excuse?* Thus deprived of determinate content, we can easily understand why some recent critics, in conjunction with Camus, have insisted that "love" is *just* a word and nothing more.

> There are so many sorts of love that one does not know where to seek a definition of it.
>
> VOLTAIRE

Of course the word "love," given a suitable context, does have a meaning. A woman asks a man if he loves her, and it will not do, for even so odd a character as Meursault in Camus's *The Stranger*, to say, "The question doesn't mean anything." We know what it means, and we know its importance. The problem is how to be clear about the meaning and also capture the importance, since clarity in such matters often succeeds only at the expense of significance.

In order to both clarify and glorify love, the bookkeepers of the love-chat industry have developed two complementary and by now well-established methods to minimize confusion and avoid the unwanted conclusion that love is something quite ordinary. First, they have learned to routinely separate different "kinds" of love. Thus motherly and brotherly love are distinguished from romantic love and friendship. My love of New York cheesecake is safely insulated from the tragic love of Romeo and Juliet, and our wild weekend in the Bahamas is distinguished from the calm comfortable "conjugal" love of an old married couple. And all of these, in turn, are to be sharply (and usually unflatteringly) distinguished from those more abstract "kinds" of love, the love of humanity, the love of God, love *as* God, sometimes called "Platonic." This would be unob-

jectionable if the various "kinds" of love were not so immediately confused with one another, set to war against one another to see which of them is most "true," reduced one to
another as if romantic love were "nothing but" sublimated
Oedipal motherly love, for example, or conjugal love, ultimately, nothing but the love and grace of God. What begins as
an attempt at clarification soon becomes a muddy battlefield,
much more confused than before.

The second bookkeeping gambit is often linked to the first,
but its efforts lie in the direction of turning what might otherwise be a prosaic routine into a task that requires enormous
learning and sensitivity. It consists, quite simply, of obscuring
the word "love" further by translating it into Greek.

> "I am not very well versed in Greek," said the giant.
> "Nor I either," replied the philosophical mite.
> "Why then do you quote Aristotle in Greek?" resumed
>     the Sirian.
> "Because," answered the other, "it is but reasonable
>     we should quote what we do not comprehend in a
>     language we do not understand."
>                                   VOLTAIRE, *Micromegas*

To see how this technique works, we might turn to one of
the recent classics of the genre, Rollo May's much-read treatise
on *Love and Will*. He begins his discussion by flatly listing, as
if in a dictionary or a Burpee seed catalogue, "four kinds of
love in Western tradition." They are: sex, *eros*, *philia* and
*agape*. Sex is the only word not translated back into the Greek
(it comes from the Latin *secare*, to divide), but to call sex a
"kind of love" is already highly suspicious, particularly since
May defines the central dilemma of his book as "the separation
of sex and love." *Eros*, as May defines it, is "the drive to pro-
create or create—the urge, as the Greeks put it, toward higher
forms of being and relationship." *Philia* is friendship, "broth-

erly love." And *agape* "is devoted to the welfare of the other, the prototype of which is the love of God for man."

Now the first thing to say about this is that the terms are *archaic;* their etymology is confused even in ancient Greek and they can mean almost anything a scholar wants them to mean. *Eros,* for instance, is a term with an extremely varied and unsettled history (which becomes so obvious in the arguments in Plato's *Symposium*) and, in any case, it was invented by an all-male warrior society for whom relationships with women were considered "vulgar" and for whom pederasty was the accepted practice and a good time was knocking the genitals off Athenian statues and Persians. *Agape,* on the other hand, is a later concept, promoted particularly by St. Paul and the early Christians (sometimes in the Latin, as *caritas*). It is not, as May suggests, a complement, "blended in various proportions" with *eros,* but rather an explicit verbal rejection of *eros* and "pagan" love, that is, sexual, sensual, personal love. *Agape* tends to be abstract, impersonal and distinctly unromantic. It is sometimes called "the love of humanity," often identified with the love of God, or the love that is appropriate to God. Much of the history of Western love, written primarily by theological scholars and German philologists, has consisted in the mock battle between these two Greek words, complete with shifting definitions which, in any case, would not be recognizable to the Greeks who used them in the first place. Needless to say, the battle usually gets resolved in favor of the "higher" love, *agape,* much to the detriment of *eros.* But all of this has nothing to do with love, or "love"; it is rather a technique to indulge in scholarship and avoid looking at any actual experience or emotion. Indeed, rather than clarify the issues, this scholarly piddling is itself another political move, a way of making an ordinary emotion sound impressively profound— and of making us sound pathetic by comparison.

The second thing to say about *eros* and *agape,* and *philia* too, is that love in the West doesn't come so neatly packaged. Indeed, one should ask very critically, for example, why *eros* and *philia* should be so distinguished, since many Greek writers (Aristotle, for example) used them more or less interchangeably, and since—to return to ordinary English—it is a very real question why we are so adamant about distinguishing friendship from romantic love, that is, apart from the initially obvious fact that the latter is intrinsically sexual and the former is not. But why should this be the case? Perhaps we place an excessive emphasis on sexual relationships? Or maybe we have an emasculated notion of friendship. Anyway, why distinguish sex from *eros* unless, perhaps, one means by "sex" mere physical intercourse and by *eros*—as we find in *Love and Will*—everything Good, True, Spiritual, Inspiring, Creative, Healthy, Courageous and Beautiful. There have been attempts to make the distinction between *eros* and *agape* more compatible; Paul Tillich (May's teacher), for example, defined them as "possessiveness" and "giving" respectively, but are these in any sense "kinds of love"? And to make this classic-minded list of four even far less palatable, one need only point out that "motherly love," the "kind" of love that would seem most obvious to Dr. May, who is a Freudian of sorts, does not even appear on the list. That would be news to Oedipus, and also to Erich Fromm, also a Freudian and keen on reducing love to variations of motherly love. Indeed, one need not be a gung-ho Freudian to appreciate the tenuousness of the distinction between motherly and romantic love, at least in some fairly familiar relationships.

One could pursue the "kinds of love" game probably endlessly. (Is the love of an old uncle the same as the love of a young grandfather? Is the love of a lover on Sunday afternoon the same as the love of the same lover on a dreary Monday morning?) But the point is that if we are going to learn anything about love at all the way *not* to begin is by reinforcing the rigid distinctions between different "kinds" of love. Consider, for example, the distinction between romantic love and friendship (*philia*, as in "Philia-delphia"). Of course there is friendship that stops short of sex, and friendship that stops short of love, but could it be that our notion of friendship is a particularly limp version of what in some societies and often in our own is a particularly powerful bond of affection, difficult to distinguish and often in competition with romantic love? Perhaps the fact that we sometimes choose as "lovers" (that is, sexual partners) people who could never be our friends shows much more about the significance of sex (or lack of it) than it does about the distinction between love and friendship. Indeed, it could be argued that our word "friend," just as much as the word "love," has become cheapened almost to the point of worthlessness. We at least verbally count as "friends" people who more accurately are mere acquaintances, or less. And the idea of living with a friend is usually considered at most a temporary convenience while waiting for something better (namely love) to come along.

It is worth mentioning, without becoming scholarly about it, the classic discussion of friendship to be found in Aristotle's *Nicomachean Ethics*, written in the fourth century B.C. "No one would choose to live without friends," he begins, but what we should add immediately is that the Greeks did not separate sex, love and friendship as we do, and Aristotle's description might serve us as a preliminary entry into romantic love as well. After insisting on the all-importance of friendship-love, Aristotle distinguishes three "objects of love," and three corresponding "kinds" of friendship—love of the useful, the pleasant and the good (VIII.2). He eliminates the love of "lifeless objects" because they cannot give us "mutual love," and then distinguishes:

(1) Friends who are useful. People who can get us what we want. There need be no reciprocal concern for the good of the other, except in so far as this is required for what one wants. A

friend who loans money or grants access to power, for example, would be an example of this kind of "friendship." (Aristotle hesitates to use the word.) But the problem with thus
"using" one another is that the friendship depends wholly on
the changing circumstances and "when the motive is done
away . . . the friendship is dissolved." There is no friendship
except in need, indeed.

(2) Friends who are pleasant. Companions, drinking partners and, one presumes, casual sex partners. A tennis partner
should not be described as someone we "use" to play tennis,
nor a dinner companion described as someone we "use" as
company for dinner. Mutual enjoyment is essential, and such
friendships also tend to begin and end abruptly: "This is why
young people tend to fall in and out of love so quickly, changing even within a single day." But, unlike utility friendship,
friends for pleasure at least enjoy one another, enjoy being together and can with some truth be said to be "friends"—but
not ideal friends.

(3) "Perfect friendship." "The friendship of men who are
good and alike in virtue," who not only wish each other well
and enjoy one another but are a source of mutual inspiration
and virtue. This is the friendship celebrated by the speakers at
Plato's *Symposium,* a kind of love that Aristotle says "should
be infrequent, for such men are rare." Such friendship requires
"time and familiarity," as well as a sense which I will call
"shared identity," not just the friendship of convenience or
pleasure, but something of a "unity," which poets and philosophers have often struggled to describe. But at least it means
this—that there is a sense of shared self, a common good, over
and above just "good for me and good for you too."

Now it is clear that we use the word "lover" with the same
lack of discrimination that Aristotle complains about regarding
friendship, to apply to people who are just "using one another," for sex or social status or security, for a place to call

"home" or a way to keep from being bored on Saturday afternoons. People who enjoy sex together and, perhaps, an occasional movie, drink and dinner are too easily called "lovers," and one claims to be "in love" on the basis of merely a mood, sometimes with candles and flowers, not to mention the moon. But what we should say about love and friendship—leaving the degree of sexuality an open question—is that they are essentially the same, that friendship worthy of the name should have all the characteristics we normally reserve for love, and that "lovers" worthy of the name must be friends as well.

With Aristotle as our guide, we can specify with considerable caution what distinguishes romantic love. First, we should say, as he did not, that romantic love is essentially *sexual*, a form of enthusiasm which is not to be understood as "just sex," and sexuality is not to be understood as heterosexual intercourse. Indeed, there may be (and have often been) overwhelming reasons why romantic love cannot or should not be "consummated," or even acknowledged as such, and this in turn raises the socially horrifying question whether some other "kinds" of love—the love of a mother and her child, the love between a nun and a priest, the roughhouse love between two brothers—might not be considered romantic (but "repressed") as well. It does not follow, of course, that a steamy sexual relationship—even as part of an established couple or marriage —is romantic love. Sex and love are still not the same, even when they cannot be distinguished. Second, romantic love is *reciprocal* love, or what Aristotle calls "mutual"—but again this has to be qualified. So-called "unrequited" love is still romantic love, for actual reciprocity, like sexual fulfillment, is not as such essential to the emotion. It is the desire for reciprocity that is necessary; thus one can romantically love another person, but not a piece of pie or a sports car.[1] Third, let's say in a

---

[1] A recent *Playboy* poll listed "the most important features in an ideal lover." Top honors went to "someone to be totally open and honest with." Next was "someone to feel comfortable with" and then "someone who accepts you as you

preliminary way that romantic love is love for a particular person. Thus we can eliminate the in fact fascinating discussion about the status of my love for my dog as well as the various difficulties involved in a *ménage à trois*. Let's leave it an open question whether one can love more than one particular person at a time, as well as what it means, more precisely, to love a particular person. And fourth, I want to restrict romantic love to Aristotle's third "kind": shared identity rather than mutual pleasure or mere utility. Love is more than companionship. ("If you can't be with the one you love, love the one you're with.") I have already said that I want to leave open all questions of gender, and in what follows I want to make no distinction whatever between hetero- and homosexual romantic love. In fact I want to argue that there is an "equality" requirement that eliminates much of what is (falsely) considered to be one of the most objectionable features of romantic love, namely the idea that males must dominate females, "be the boss"—however more politely or with whatever dubious biological analogues this might be formulated. The equality requirement probably eliminates motherly love from consideration, since there is at least one clear sense in which the love of mother for child and the love of infant for mother are wholly unequal, and it eliminates the love of God, needless to say, which is not, even for the German romantics, romantic love. It also eliminates *agape* as well as Erich Fromm's celebrated notion of "being a loving person," since the love of humanity, however passionate, is neither sexual (presumably), nor reciprocal (perhaps unfortunately), nor personal. Indeed, what is called "Platonic" love is so different from romantic love that it surely

---

are." And, of course, "physically attractive," suspiciously only fourth. What is noteworthy is that my cat fulfills all four criteria; my old bedroom slippers fail only the last of them. The notion of reciprocity—which is not the same as "someone to be open and honest with" much less "feeling comfortable with"— does not enter into the survey at all.

should *not* be called by the same name, much less confused or compared favorably with it.

To say that romantic love is sexual, reciprocal, personal and shared is not to say very much, but even while drawing our boundaries so broadly we can say, without any hesitation, that we are clearly referring to an emotion which is quite specific, which can be described matter-of-factly and without self-congratulation (as Aristotle did *in opposition to* his pious teacher Plato). It is quite obviously a real and tangible passion in our emotional repertoire, not just a myth or an "illusion." "Love" is not just a word, then, but it has been obscured considerably by a variety of images, models and metaphors which are not essentially part of its structure. Granting that we do sometimes have mutual, passionate, sexual (but more than sexual) feelings about another person, the question is, *what more* do we add to this simple set of ingredients to cook up that rich, muddy and sometimes indigestible emotional stew that we call, with considerable confusion, *romantic love?*

# MODELS AND METAPHORS: "THE GAME OF LOVE" 2

*Let me say—why not?—that yellow is the color of love.*
GILBERT SORRENTINO, *Splendide Hotel*, p. 59

We look at love, as we look at life, through a series of metaphors, each with its own language, its own implications, connotations and biases.

For example, if someone says that love is a game, we already know much of what is to follow: relationships will tend to be short-lived. Sincerity will be a strategy for winning and so will flattery and perhaps lying. ("All's fair . . .") The person "played with" is taken seriously only as an opponent, a challenge, valued in particular for his or her tactics and retorts, but quickly dispensable as soon as someone has "won" or "lost." "Playing hard to get" is an optional strategy, and being "easy" is not immoral or foolish so much as playing badly, or not at all.

On the other hand, if someone sees love as "God's gift to humanity," we should expect utter solemnity, mixed with a sense of gratitude, seriousness and self-righteousness that is wholly lacking in the "love is a game" metaphor. Relationships here will tend to be long-lasting, if not "forever," fraught with duties and obligations dictated by a "gift" which, in the usual interpretations, has both divine and secular strings attached.

The "game" metaphor is, perhaps, too frivolous to take seriously. The "gift of God" metaphor, on the other hand, is much too serious to dismiss frivolously. We will discuss it, and the damage it has done, at length in several later chapters. In this chapter what I would like to do is display the variety and richness of the metaphors through which we tend to talk about, and experience, love. Not surprisingly, these love metaphors reflect our interests elsewhere in life—business, health, communications, art, politics and law as well as fun and games and religion. But these are not mere "figures of speech"; they are the self-imposed structures that determine the way we experience love itself. (For this reason, we should express some pretty strong reservations about some of them.)

### Tit for Tat:
### Love as a Fair Exchange

One of the most common love metaphors, now particularly popular in social psychology, is the *economic* metaphor. The idea is that love is an exchange, a sexual partnership, a trade-off of interests and concerns and, particularly, of *approval.* "I make you feel good about yourself and in return you make me feel good about myself." Of course exchange rates vary—some people need more than others—and there is a law of diminishing returns; that is, the same person's approval tends to become less and less valuable as it becomes more familiar. (This law of diminishing returns, which we experience as the gradual fading of romantic love, has been explored by the psychologist Eliot Arenson of the University of California at Santa Cruz. His theory has been aptly named by his students "Arenson's Law of Marital Infidelity.") In some relationships the balance of payments may indeed seem extremely one-sided but the assumption is, in the words of the Harvard sociologist Homans, that both parties must believe they are getting something out of it or they simply wouldn't stay around.

Now this economic model has much to offer, not least the fact that it gives a fairly precise account of the concrete motivation for love, which is left out of more pious accounts that insist that love is simply good in itself and needs no motives. But the problem is that it too easily degenerates into a most unflattering model of mutual buying and selling, which in turn raises the specter that love may indeed be, as some cynics have been saying ever since Marx (Karl) and Engels, a form of covert prostitution, though not necessarily—or even usually— for money. "I will sleep with you and think well of you or at least give you the benefit of the doubt if only you'll tell me good things about myself and pretend to approve of me."

It may be true that we do often evaluate our relationships in this way, in terms of mutual advantage and our own sense of fairness. The question, "What am I getting out of this, anyway?" always makes sense, even if certain traditional views of love and commitment try to pretend that such selfishness is the very antithesis of love. But the traditional views have a point to make too, which is, simply, that such tit-for-tat thinking inevitably undermines a relationship based on love, *not* because love is essentially "selfless" but because the bargain table is not the place to understand mutual affection. Love is not the exchange of affection, any more than sex is merely the exchange of pleasure. What is left out of these accounts is the "we" of love, which is quite different from mere "I and thou." This is not to say that fairness cannot be an issue in love, nor is it true that "all's fair" in love. But while the economic exchange model explains rather clearly some of the motives for love, it tends to ignore the *experience* of love almost altogether, which is that such comparisons and evaluations seem at the time beside the point and come to mind only when love is already breaking down. It is the suspicion, not the fact, that "I'm putting more into this than you are" that signals the end of many relationships, despite the fact that, as business goes, they may have been "a good arrangement."

### The Job of Loving:
### The Work Model

A very different model is the *work* model of love. The Prot-
estant ethic is very much at home in romance. (Rollo May
calls love the Calvinist's proof of emotional salvation.) And so
we find many people who talk about "working out a relationship," "working at it," "working for it" and so on. The fun
may once have been there, of course, but now the real *job* begins, tacking together and patching up, like fixing up an old
house and refusing to move out until the roof caves in. This is,
needless to say, a particularly self-righteous model, if for no
other reason than that it begins on the defensive and requires
considerable motivation just to move on. Personal desires, the
other person's as well as one's own, may be placed behind "the
relationship," which is conceived of as the primary *project*.
Love, according to the work model, gets evaluated above all
on its industriousness, its seriousness, its success in the face of
the most difficult obstacles. Devotees of the work model not infrequently choose the most inept or inappropriate partners,
rather like buying a run-down shack—for the challenge. They
will look with disdain at people who are merely happy together (something like buying a house from a tract builder).
They will look with admiration and awe at a couple who have
survived a dozen years of fights and emotional disfigurements
because "they made it work."

### A Madness Most Discrete:
### The (Melo) Dramatic Model

In contrast to the work model, we can turn with a sense of
recreation to the *dramatic* model of love, love as theater, love
as melodrama. This differs from the game model in that one's
roles are taken *very* seriously, and the notions of winners and
losers, strategy and tactics are replaced by notions of perform-

ance, catharsis, tragedy and theatricality. Roles are all important—keeping within roles, developing them, enriching them.
The dramatic model also tends to play to an audience, real
(whenever possible) or imagined (when necessary). Fights
and reconciliations alike will often be performed in public, and
an evening at home alone may often seem pointless. Some dramatic lovers are prima donnas, referring every line or part
back to themselves, but one can be just as theatrical by being
visibly selfless, or martyred, or mad. Lunt and Fontanne or
Bogart and Bacall might well be models, and lovers will strain
without amusement to perfect for the appropriate occasion
someone else's drawl, insult, posture or sigh. Unfortunately the
dramatic model too easily tends to confuse interpersonal problems with theatrical flaws, to praise and abuse itself in those
mincing terms that are, appropriately, the vocabulary of the
theater critic. (Clive Barnes as Cupid?) The worst that one
could say of such love, therefore, is that it's "boring" or "predictable."

### "Relationships":
### Banality as Metaphor

Blandness can be just as significant as profundity and excitement, and a metaphor may be intentionally noncommittal as
well as precise. Thus we find the word "thing" substituted as a
grammatical stand-in for virtually everything from sexual organs (a young virgin gingerly refers to her first lover's "thing")
to jobs, hang-ups and hobbies (as in "doing your own thing").
Where love is concerned, the most banal of our metaphors, so
pervasive and so banal that it hardly seems like a metaphor, is
the word "relating," or "relationship" itself. There's not much
to say about it, except to ponder in amazement the fact that
we have not yet, in this age of "heavy relationships," come up
with anything better. There is a sense, of course, in which any
two people (or two things) stand in any number of rela-

tionships to one another (being taller than, heavier than, smarter than, more than fifteen feet away from . . . etc.). The word "relations" was once, only a few years ago, a polite and slightly clinical word for sex (still used, as most stilted archaisms tend to be, in law). People "relate" to each other as they "relate a story," perhaps on the idea that what couples do most together is to tell each other the events of the day, a less than exciting conception of love, to be sure. But metaphors can be chosen for their vacuousness just as for their imaginative imagery, and the fact that this metaphor dominates our thinking so much (albeit in the guise of a *meaningful* relationship) points once again to the poverty of not only our vocabulary but our thinking and feeling as well. Anyone who's still looking for a "meaningful relationship" in the 1980s may have a lot to learn about love, or not really care about it at all.

### Love and Electronics:
### The Communication Metaphor

A powerful metaphor with disastrous consequences that was popular a few years ago was a "communication" metaphor, often used in conjunction with a "relating" metaphor, for obvious reasons. Both were involved with the then hip language of media and information theory: "getting through" to each other and "we just can't communicate any more" gave "relationships" the unfortunate appearance of shipwrecked survivors trying to keep in touch over a slightly damaged shortwave radio. The information processing jargon ("input," "feedback," "tuning in" and "turning off") was typically loaded with electronic gadget imagery, and good relationships appropriately were described in terms of their "good vibrations." But, like all metaphors, this one revealed much more than it distorted, namely, an image of isolated transmitters looking for someone to get their messages. It was precisely this milieu that gave birth to Rollo May's *Love and Will*, and his concern that we had rendered love between us impossible. Love was thought to be mainly a matter of self-expression, largely but not exclusively verbal expression. Talk became enormously important to love; problems were talked over, talked through and talked out. The essential moment was the "heavy conversation" and, appropriately, talk about love often took the place of love itself. Confession and "openness" (telling all) became the linchpins of love, even when the messages were largely hostility and resentment. Psychotherapist George Bach wrote a number of successful books, including *The Intimate Enemy* (with Peter Wyden), which made quite clear the fact that it was expression of feelings, not the feelings themselves, that made for a successful relationship. On the communication model, sex too was described as a mode of communication, but more often sex was not so much communicating as the desire to be communicated with. Sex became, in McLuhanesque jargon, a "cool" medium. And, like most modern media, the model put its emphasis on the medium itself (encounter groups, etc.) but there was precious little stress on the *content* of the programming. Not surprisingly, love became an obscure ideal, like television advertisements full of promise of something fabulous yet to come, hinted at but never spoken of as such. In fact the ultimate message was the idea of the medium itself.

### The Ontology of Loneliness:
### Love and Aloneness

In our extremely individualistic society we have come to see isolation and loneliness as akin to "the human condition," instead of as by-products of a certain kind of social arrangement, which puts mobility and the formation of new interpersonal bonds at a premium. This individualistic metaphor, which I call "the ontology of loneliness," is stated succinctly, for example, by Rollo May: "Every person, experiencing as he [sic] does his own solitariness and aloneness, longs for union with another" (*Love and Will*, p. 144). Similarly, Erich Fromm preoccupies himself with "our need to escape the prison of our aloneness," and the radical feminist Shulamith Firestone complains about the same need "to escape from the isolation of our own solitude." Love, then, is a refuge from an otherwise intolerable existence. Our "natural" state is aloneness; our escape from this state, hopefully, is love. "Love," writes the poet Rilke, "is two solitudes reaching out to greet each other."

This is a viewpoint that has been argued by many philosophers under the name of "solipsism" ("the only sure thing is one's own existence") and has been developed by the vulgar philosopher Ayn Rand into an argument for selfishness: "Each of us is born into the world alone, and therefore each of us is justified in pursuing our own selfish interests." But the premise is false and the inference is insidious. Not even Macduff (who was not, strictly speaking, "of woman born") came into the world by himself. And not only in infancy but in adulthood we find ourselves essentially linked to other people, to a language that we call our own, to a culture and, at least legally, to a country as well. We do not have to find or "reach out" to others; they are, in a sense, already *in us*. Alone in the woods of British Columbia, I find myself still thinking of friends, describing what I see as if they were there—and in their language. The idea of the isolated self is an American invention—reinforced perhaps by the artificially isolated circumstances of the psychiatrist's office and our fantasies about gunfighters and mountain men, but this is not true of most of us. And this means that love is not a refuge or an escape either. Our conception of ourselves is always a social self (even if it is an antisocial or rebellious self).

Our language of love often reflects this idea of natural isolation, for example in the "communication" metaphor in which isolated selves try desperately to "get through" to one another. But this is an unnecessarily tragic picture of life and love, and its result is to make love itself seem like something of a cure for a disease, rather than a positive experience which already *presupposes* a rather full social life. Indeed, it is revealing that, quite the contrary of social isolation, romantic love is usually experienced only *within* a rather extensive social nexus. "Sure, I have lots of friends and I like my colleagues at work but, still, I'm lonely and I want to fall in love." But that has nothing to do with loneliness. It rather reflects the tremendous importance we accord to romantic love in our lives, not as a cure for aloneness, but as a positive experience in its own right, which we have, curiously, turned into a need.

### "Made for Each Other": The Metaphysical Model

Standing opposed to the "ontology of loneliness" is an ancient view which takes our *unity*, not our mutual isolation, as the "natural" state of humanity. The classic statement of this view, brilliant in its poetic simplicity, is Aristophanes' speech in the *Symposium*, in which he describes our "natural" state as double creatures, cleft in two by Zeus for our hubris, struggling to be reunited through love. Our own image of two people "being made for each other" is also an example of the metaphysical model, together with the idea that marriages are "made in heaven" and the idea that someone else can be your "better half." The metaphysical model is based not on the idea that love is a refuge from isolated individualism but, quite the opposite, on the idea that love is the realization of bonds that are already formed, even before one meets one's "other half."

The ontology of loneliness treats individuals as atoms, bouncing around the universe alone looking for other atoms, occasionally forming more or less stable molecules. But if we were to pursue the same chemical metaphor into the metaphysical model, it would more nearly resemble what physicists today call "field theory." A magnetic field, for instance, retains all of its electromagnetic properties whether or not there is any material there to make them manifest. So too, an individual is already a network of human relationships and expectations, and these exist whether or not one finds another individual whose radiated forces and properties are complementary. The old expression about love being a matter of "chemical attraction" (from Goethe to Gilbert and Sullivan[1]) is, scientifically, a century out of date; "attraction" is no longer a question of one atom affecting another but the product of two electromagnetic fields, each of which exists prior to and independently of any particular atoms within its range. So too we radiate charm, sexiness, inhibition, intelligence and even repulsiveness, and find a lover who fits in. The problem with this viewpoint, however, is that it leaves no room for the *development* of relationships but rather makes it seem as if, if the love is there at all, it has to be there, and be there in full, from the very beginning.

### Love and Disease:
### The Medical Metaphor

"Love's a malady without a cure," wrote Dryden, and today, our favorite metaphor, from social criticism to social relationships, has become the disease metaphor, images of health and decay, the medicalization of all things human, from the stock market to sex and love. Not surprisingly, a large proportion of our books about love and sex are written by psychiatrists and other doctors. (They used to be written by priests and theologians.) Our society is described in terms of "narcissism" (a clinical term), as an "age of anxiety," and as "decadent" (the negative side of the biological process.) For Rollo May and Erich Fromm, lack of love is the dominant disease of our times. For others, *Love and Addiction* author Stan-

[1] Hey diddle diddle with your middle-
       class kisses.
   It's a chemical reaction, that's all. (Gilbert and Sullivan)

ton Peele, for instance, love is itself a kind of disease, an "addiction," waiting to be cured. Some feminists have seized on the disease metaphor (a disease invented by and carried by men): Ti-Grace Atkinson (in *Amazon Odyssey*) calls love "a pathological condition," and Erica Jong (in *Fear of Flying*) calls it "the search for self-annihilation." But whether love is the disease or love is the cure, what is obvious is that this model turns us all into *patients,* and one might well ask—the professional interests of the A.M.A. aside—whether that is the arena within which we want to talk about love.

### The Art in Loving:
### The Aesthetic Model

Perhaps the oldest view of love, the pivot of Plato's *Symposium*, is an *aesthetic* model: love as the admiration and the contemplation of *beauty.* The emphasis here is on neither relating nor communicating (in fact, unrequited love and even voyeurism are perfectly in order). On this model, it is not particularly expected that the lover will actually *do* much of anything except, perhaps, to get within view of the beloved at every possible opportunity, as one might stand before the fireplace and admire one's favorite painting over the mantel. It is this model that has dominated many of our theories about love, though not, luckily, our actual practices. It is this model that best fits the moaning troubadours in twelfth-century France, composing poetry about the inaccessible beauty of the maiden up there on the tower balcony, visible but untouchable. It is this model that feminists rightly complain about when they accuse men of "putting them up on a pedestal," a charge that too often confuses the idealization that accompanies it with the impersonal distancing that goes along with the pedestal. The objection is not to the fact that it is a pedestal so much as the fact that it is usually a very *tall* pedestal, so that any real contact is pretty much out of the question and the fear of falling is considerable. Or else it is a very *small* pedestal, "and like any small place," writes Gloria Steinem, "a prison."

### Love and Commitment:
### The Contract Model

An old view of love, which dominated much of the eighteenth and nineteenth centuries, was a *contract* model, a specific instance of a more general "social contract" theory that was then believed by most people to be the (implicit) basis of society itself. Contracts in love were exemplified, of course, by the quite explicit and wholly legal contract of marriage, but even then, and especially now, the idea of implicit contracts was taken for granted too. (*Cosmopolitan* magazine last year reran one of its most popular pieces, about "secret" contracts in love, two hundred years too late to be in vogue.) What is crucial to this metaphor, however, is the fact that *emotion* plays very little part in it. One accepts an obligation to obey the terms of the contract (implicit or explicit) whether or not (though hopefully whether) one wants to. The current term for this ever popular emasculation of emotion is *commitment*. In fact there seems to be an almost general agreement among most of the people I talk to that "commitment" is what constitutes love. (The contrast is almost always sexual promiscuity or purely "casual" affairs.) But commitment is precisely what love is *not* (though of course one can and often does make commitments on the basis of the fact that he or she loves someone). A commitment is an obligation sustained *whether or not one has the emotion that originally motivated it*. And the sense of obligation isn't "love."

### Freudian Fallacies:
### The Biological Metaphor

The idea that science itself can be but a metaphor strikes us as odd, but much of what we believe about love, it seems, is based on wholly unliteral biological metaphors. For example, we believe that love is "natural," even an "instinct," and this is supported by a hundred fascinating but ultimately irrelevant arguments about "the facts of life": the fact that some spiders eat their mates, that some birds mate for life, that some sea gulls are lesbians, that some fish can't mate unless the male is clearly superior, that chimpanzees like to gang bang and gorillas have weenies the size of a breakfast sausage, that bats tend to do it upside down and porcupines do it "carefully." But romantic love is by no means "natural"; it is not an instinct but a very particular and peculiar attitude toward sex and pair-bonding that has been carefully cultivated by a small number of modern aristocratic and middle-class societies. Even sex, which would seem to be "natural" if anything is, is no more mere biology than taking the holy wafer at high mass is just eating. It too is defined by our metaphors and the symbolic significance we give to it. It is not a "need," though we have certainly made it into one. Sex is not an instinct, except in that utterly minimal sense that bears virtually no resemblance at all to the extremely sophisticated and emotion-filled set of rituals that we call—with some good reason—"making love." And where sex and love come together is not in the realm of nature either, but in the realm of expression, specific to a culture which specifies its meaning.

There is one particular version of the biological metaphor, however, which has enjoyed such spectacular scientific airplay, ever since Freud at least, that we tend to take it as the literal truth instead of, again, as a metaphor. It is the idea that love begins in—or just out of—the womb, and that our prototype of love—if not our one "true" love—is our own mother.

This would suggest indeed that love is, if not an instinct, common to all human beings. But the argument turns on a number of obvious fallacies, starting from the premise that, because of the extraordinarily slow development of human infants, all of us, from our very birth (and perhaps before), need love. But . . .

(1) This isn't romantic love, in any case, and romantic love is in no way reducible to mere dependency. In fact, despite its "baby" imagery, romantic love presupposes just what infancy lacks: a sense of selfhood and a high degree of mobility and independence. Moreover, the view expresses an obvious male bias and leaves the romantic desires of women something of a mystery (for Freud in particular).

(2) To need love is not to need *to* love. Some people need desperately to be loved but have no inclination whatever to love in return.

(3) Babies need care and comfort, not necessarily love. In fact regular tender care is far more desirable than adoring but erratic attention. Romantic love, of course, thrives on the latter, gets too easily bored with the first.

(4) In few societies is the care of a particular mother expected by either the infant or society, and the idea that one has special affection for one person exclusively is an anthropologically peculiar notion which in fact is disintegrating in our society too. In most societies, increasingly in our own, an infant is cared for by any number of different people, male as well as female, and the idea of a single utterly dominant dependency figure—which so obsessed Freud—is a peculiarity of the Victorian Viennese middle-class ethic, not a universal human characteristic.

(5) It is most implausible that any adult emotion is simply reducible to an infantile need. To identify a radical politi-

cian's moral indignation with infantile rage would be
offensive as well as simply wrong; to think of sexual jealousy as merely an adult extension of a child's possessiveness is not only to misunderstand jealousy but to misunderstand children as well. And even in those relatively
few cases in which the so-called "Oedipal complex" reigns
supreme, it is a mistake to reduce all subsequent affections
to a mere repetition of family dynamics. Some psychologists, Gordon Allport for example, have come to refer to
this rejection of Freudian reductionism as "the autonomy
of motives." No matter how revealing the origins of one's
affections, it is their development and differences that
define them. We think it noteworthy when a man dates a
woman who resembles his mother, not when he does not.
The Oedipal complex is desperately looking for an occasional instance as if to confirm it.

We sometimes plague ourselves with the idea that we are
"hung up" on Oedipal images. In high school I worried about
the fact that the girls I "dated" bore a sometimes striking resemblance to my mother. (They were usually short, bright,
creative and Caucasian.) I had read enough Freud for this to
worry me. Many years later a psychotherapist convinced me,
or I "discovered," that, indeed, I was looking for a woman who
was more like my father, which confused me considerably,
needless to say, but worried me too. But this limited number of
alternatives, always clouded by the threat of "neurosis," turns
out to be nonsense, or worse—it is the Freudian doctrine of
original sin, a new source of unnecessary guilt and just as
much a myth as the original Original Sin. In fact our models
and prototypes of love include not only our parents but
brothers, sisters, teachers in junior high school, first dates, first
loves, graduating-class heroes and heroines, hundreds of movie
stars and magazine pictures as well as a dozen considerations
and pressures that have nothing to do with prototypes at all.
Indeed, even Freud insists that it is not a person's *actual* par-

ent who forms the romantic prototype but rather a phantom, constructed from memory, which may bear little resemblance to any actual person. But if this is so, perhaps one's imagined mother is in fact a variation on one's first girl friend, or a revised version of Myrna Loy. Why do we take the most complex and at times exquisite emotion in most of our lives, and try to reduce it to the first and the simplest?

Or, if the Oedipal theory is right, why didn't Romulus, raised by a she-wolf, rape his dog, instead of the Sabine women? Mere motherhood is not everything, even in ancient mythology.

### "The Flame in My Heart": The Emotion Metaphor

Love is an emotion. But the way we talk about emotions is itself so pervaded by metaphors that one begins to wonder whether there is anything there to actually talk about. We talk about ourselves as if we were Mr. Coffee machines, bubbling over, occasionally overflowing, getting too hot to handle, and bursting from too much pressure. We subscribe in metaphor if not in medicine to the medieval theory that the seat of the emotions is in the heart, and in love it is the heart that pounds, beats, breaks and is bound and occasionally butchered. We describe love in terms of heat, fire, flame—all of which are expressive and poetic but, it is sometimes hard to remember, metaphors all the same. But is love really that sense that one is going to burst? The warm flush that pours through one's body when *he* or *she* walks into the room: is that love? And if so, why do we set so much store by it? It is for this reason, no doubt, that the age-old wisdom about love has made it out to be more than a mere emotion—a gift from God, a visitation from the gods, the wound of Cupid's arrow, the cure for a disease or a disease itself, the economics of interpersonal relations or even "the answer" to all life's problems. But then again, maybe we underestimate our emotions.

What is love? It seems to be almost everything except, perhaps, "never having to say you're sorry." Love is a series of metaphors, which we glorify selectively, picking one out and calling it "true" love, which itself is another metaphor.

Not all metaphors are created equal. Some are profound, some are banal, some increase our self-confidence, others make us feel slimy, defensive or sick. There is no "true" love, for there is no singly true metaphor, but this does not mean that one should not choose carefully. For choosing one's metaphor is, in fact, choosing one's love life as well.

# WHAT I FEEL IN MY HEART    3

Luv dub luv dub[1]

---

[1] Actually I don't feel anything in my heart, since it has no efferent sensory nerves. What I really feel in my chest is the dull thud made by the tricuspid and mitral valves snapping shut just prior to contraction, then the slight change of pressure through the thin skin that covers some of my superficial veins—some considerable time *after* the actual "beat" of the heart. But while I'm so scrupulously paying attention to my pulse, am I indeed paying attention to my love? Or am I rather distracting myself from it? And if I add to the rhythmic contractions of my heart the fact that I'm also slightly short of breath, that my throat feels cramped, my bowels are uncertain and my knees feel queasy, is *that* love? And in the pages that follow, is *that* what you are going to keep accusing me of "leaving out"? Mere *symptoms*?

# LOVE IS AN EMOTION 4

*Love, music, passion, intrigue, heroism,—these are things that make life worth while.*

Love is not a biological drive, not a "need," not a gift from God (much less *is* it God). It is neither natural nor necessary nor necessarily healthy, helpful or human. Neither is it "divine," and it is certainly no "mystery," unless, of course, we refuse even to look at it. Love is an emotion, nothing else.

We have a general view of emotions, however, which explains not only our resistance to thinking, talking and theorizing about love—pretending that it is a mystery and both demeaning and idolizing it at the same time—but also our confused and sometimes tragic attitudes toward emotions in general. One symptom, among many, is the way we criticize emotions in men and belittle them in women. ("Oh, women are so emotional!" he screeched.) Emotions are thought to be inferior, opposed to our "higher" faculties of reasoning, rationalizing and calculating the weekly budget. ("Be reasonable" often means "Don't be emotional.") Emotions, accordingly, are thought to be intrinsically "irrational." ("Don't be emotional" means "Don't cause any trouble.") We are counseled in the "control" of our emotions, as if they were beasts in a fragile cage; we are praised for being "cool" and chastised for "letting ourselves go." We are warned against the dangers of pride, envy and anger, which are catalogued as three of the seven "deadly sins." And in the whole history of Western thought the emotions have been treated as the "lower" parts of the human soul, what we share and inherit from the animals, while it is reason that makes us human, even "a spark of the divine."[1] No wonder, then, that love also finds itself in a problematic conceptual situation, and small surprise that its proponents so often defend it by denying what it really is, an emotion, and turning it into something else.

> "Falling in love" is an inferior state of mind,
> a form of imbecility.
>           ORTEGA Y GASSET, *On Love*

In a book called *The Passions*, a few years ago, I attacked what I called "the myth of the passions," the core of which is this systematic degradation of emotion in favor of the "higher" faculties of reason throughout our culture. But the degradation of emotions is based in turn on a view of emotions which makes it difficult to take them seriously. Quite simply, we have been taught to view our emotions as primitive forces, intrusions in our otherwise orderly, rational lives. We are taught, virtually as a matter of language, that emotions are "feelings," that is, general sensations, the most prominent features of which are a certain sense of innervation, visceral disturbances, including a queasy stomach and a sometimes embarrassing looseness in the bowels and bladder, frequent flushing, blushing, a certain shakiness in the knees, intense irritability and other familiar and generalizable quasi-physiological reactions that we associate with almost every strong emotion, from fear and anger to "falling in love."

Because emotions are so closely associated with these physical feelings and diagnosable on such an obvious physiological basis (the pumping of adrenalin, for example), it is quite reasonably believed that there is little to be said about them and

[1] Goethe, *Faust*. Aristotle, *Ethics*.

even less to *do* about them, except, perhaps, avoid situations
that incite them or take tranquillizers to control them. And because emotions are so clearly bodily (as opposed to cerebral),
it is assumed that they are "instinctual," biologically determined, unlearned and therefore uneducable. Our ways of talking about them show quite clearly that we see our emotions as
*happening to us*, and so we "fall in love," as one would into a
swamp; we are "plagued" by remorse, as if by Alaskan mosqui-
toes, "struck" by jealousy, as if by an Oldsmobile, "crushed"
by shame, like a bug beneath a boot, "paralyzed" by fear, as if
by a stroke, and distracted by guilt, as if by a trombone in the
kitchen. We are "heartbroken," "smitten," "carried away,"
"transported" and "overwhelmed" by emotions. And our vocabulary of romantic love sounds like a surgeon's or a
butcher's: hearts cleft in two, bruised as well as broken,
pounding now and then, grown cold, bursting, aching, torn
and tender. Emotions, as Freud stated so graphically, are part
of the *Id* ("it"), which is opposed to and perennially endan-
gers the tenuous rationality of the poor, noble Ego ("I"). Emotions, for him and most psychotherapists, are typically destructive, dangerous, disruptive. And romantic love, as an emotion,
is surely no exception. Luckily, however, it tends not to last
(except in neurotic "romantics"), and so it can safely be replaced by far safer brands of feelings, nominally "love" too—
habitual conjugal love, which is or can be devoid of the violent
passions of uncertain romance, and emasculated Platonic love,
in which contemplation and quiet faith make love far more
like reason and philosophy (which is also a "love of") than
passion.

Consider, for a moment, the way we talk about anger, as one
representative emotion. We "bottle up" our anger and "let off
steam." Our emotion is "pent up" and when we are ready "to
blow up," we finally "vent our rage." We "dam up aggression"
and "blow our tops." We "feel something bubbling up inside
of us," as if "ready to burst," then we "explode." The image is

*hydraulic*, the human psyche as a boiler system, filled with volatile gas or superheated steam, sometimes contained, always explosive. The metaphors tell us a lot about how we see ourselves, and it is not just the poets who invent them. The most sophisticated psychological theorists, Freud and William James, for example, employ the same images. Freud's terminology of "cathexis" (filling) and "catharsis" (discharge), "repression" (keeping the lid on), "sublimation" (letting it out through a safer viaduct) and "vicissitudes" (alternative viaducts) are all based on the same metaphorical image. And even those many psychologists who openly reject Freud's theories of the mind sometimes fall back to the hydraulic model when discussing emotion. In a debate in the magazine *Psychology Today*, for example, the hot dispute was between those who would "bottle up anger" and the "ventilationists" who encouraged its free release, both of course in the name of mental health. Even "Rational-Emotive therapy," which makes at least some valiant attempt to overcome the traditional hydraulic view by stressing the patient's own responsibility for his or her emotions, ultimately falls back on the hydraulic model of emotions, emotions as "inside" us, beyond our direct control (what we control are our beliefs), still irrational, disruptive and, in excess, unhealthy.

The physiology of the hydraulic model is often medieval, the image of the various "humours" circulating through the body. Though we long ago gave up the physiology, we still hang onto the imagery, and talk without hesitation of "my blood boiling" and "so much bile" or "spleen" or "gall." (Should we resist the temptation to mention "hot under the choler"?) Even the law excuses the most abominable actions if they are carried out "in hot blood." Occasionally the image becomes more centrifugal instead of hydraulic, as in "flying off the handle," but the mechanical model is still in effect, and it is still Isaac Newton who provides our basic emotional models. Even in the ancients, who were less mechanistically inclined, we find the

same kind of picture of anger as an affliction, a kind of
madness, an attack by the "Furies." And in the beginnings of
modern philosophy too, for example, in Descartes and Male-
branche, emotions are identified as "animal spirits," flowing
through our bodies and, typically, causing trouble.

This is not to say, of course, that we can never enjoy these
disturbances. Depending on the cause, these various physiological disruptions can even be interpreted, as they were long
ago, as a kind of divine "possession," such as the rapture of St.
Agatha and, slightly less divine, the common discomforts of an
adolescent in love. But here is where our ambivalence becomes
transparent; in so far as these experiences are deemed profound or significant, they are no longer treated as mere emotions. Religious thinkers have always been hesitant to place
very much confidence in passive emotional trauma, just as
most societies have, quite wisely, known better than to base
the essential structures of marriage and the family on so fleeting and flimsy a foundation as mere "feeling." Love is an instance of the animal in us, not to be dismissed, perhaps, but
not to be taken too seriously either. Romantic love, we still
read in *Cosmopolitan,* is "a matter of chemistry," an image
that has its support even in the writings of the greatest of
poets, in Shakespeare, for instance, and in Goethe, whose novel
*Elective Affinities* (a chemical term of his times) has been
prime reading in Europe for almost two centuries. While anger
is usually viewed as a hot gas, however, love is often compared
to fire itself, "the flame of love" (the lover as "flame" too), fan-
ning and dying embers, and "a fire in the blood." Bad physiology, perhaps, but impressive and telling metaphors, taking us
in for centuries.

We are "passive" regarding our passions; that is the bottom
line of these traditional models. Our emotions happen to us, intrude in our lives, and so they are relegated to the fringes and
interstices of experience: love affairs while on vacation, an occasional bout of anger, a healthy "outlet" at the right time, but

something to be "gotten over" nevertheless. Love is no different in this regard, and it is to save this savored emotion from the degradation due most of our passions (such as those that make the "deadly sins" list) that love is transformed into something else—something impersonal, selfless, abstract and emasculated—"Platonic" love of God or beauty, or that sexless love called *agape* that good people everywhere are supposed to have for everyone, especially the poor, the grotesque and the damned. Romantic love, however, still so tied to the flesh and to passion, still so "out of control" and filled with involuntary (if enjoyable) suffering, is to be tolerated only in small and insignificant amounts. Like a child with a new surfboard, we are permitted to ride the waves of our passions with the understanding that, inevitably, we will come crashing back down on the cold sands of reality. (If God had meant us to soar with our emotions, we read in such philosophers as Aristotle and Kant, he would not have made us so *reasonable.*)

Not only do we say that we "fall in" love, but love "strikes us," often unawares, "from behind," if it does not "slap us in the face." We are wounded by Cupid's arrows—a telling metaphor of love's passivity. Love *poisons* us, drives us "insane." But the theme I want to pursue with love is precisely the opposite. Love is not passive and not something we "suffer." (The very word "passion" literally means "suffering," as in "the passion of Christ.") The passiveness of the passions is indeed a "myth," as I argued a few years ago, but it is not a myth born merely of ignorance. Like most of our false beliefs about ourselves, this one serves a self-interested purpose. How often have you heard someone say (or have you said yourself), "I couldn't help it, I was so . . ."—where the ellipsis names an emotion? "I couldn't control myself, I was in love," or "It wasn't entirely his fault; he lost his temper." The myth of the passions provides us with an *excuse*, a way of denying responsibility (or at least full responsibility) for doing what in fact we want to do *most*. By seeing ourselves as victims, we can remain happily oblivious to those passions which are indeed the main motives in life. But they do not merely happen to us. We *do* our passions. We *are* them. And we have now reached the point where our excuse has turned on us, and it demeans us more than it saves us. We have come to see our emotions in an almost wholly negative light, so that we (ironically) get angry at ourselves for being angry, get embarrassed because we find ourselves embarrassed, become guilty, according to the latest theories, just because we find ourselves feeling guilty. And romantic love is still viewed with suspicion, as being merely "in love with love"; for men, it becomes an excuse to be demanding, foolish, childish; for women, it becomes idealized submissiveness, which, not surprisingly, is encouraged by men.

We do not "fall" into love or, if we do, it is after a lifetime of conscientious activities, not the least of which are our fantasies and constant conversations, ten thousand movies and books, the cultural junk from which we build an emotional nest, ready from the age of twelve to lie or be laid down in it with someone whose fantasies complement our own. And we do not fall "in" love either, for love, like all emotions (even the "withdrawal" emotions) is a reaching *out*, the projection of a structure, a meaning, a way of personally relating to the world. Love is one among the many ways we subjectively organize our experience, see ourselves in certain roles (e.g., the lover) and establish our sense of other people (e.g., as lover too). But to understand love this way, not as something that invades, not as a sometimes enjoyable physiological dysfunction, not as an instinct (nor as necessary and certainly not "natural"), requires an entirely new view of what the emotions, in general, are like. "We are often most ignorant of that which is closest to us," says Nietzsche, and this is certainly true of emotions. And first, we will have to get rid of that almost obvious belief that emotions, in short, are "feelings," for that is where the myth of the passions, the myth of passivity, begins.

# "FEELINGS" 5

*. . . emotions correspond with processes of discharge, the final expression of which is perceived as feeling.*

FREUD

It sounds trivial to say that emotions are feelings, so it would no doubt sound absurd to say that they were *not* feelings. But there are many kinds of "feelings," from Einstein's very sophisticated feeling (intuition) that "gravitation might be explained by way of particle theory" to the not so intricate feeling of cold water running down my thigh. If the sentence "Emotions are feelings" is supposed to mean something like the latter, as William James and sometimes Freud once argued, then emotions are assuredly *not* feelings. It is true that romantic love sometimes includes weeping eyes, a choking throat, loss of appetite, weakness in the limbs, loose bowels and a general sense of excitement that can only tangentially be considered sexual, but it would be absurd to say, as James did, that this set of flulike symptoms *is* the love. Is that the basis of Western romanticism, for which Romeo and Tristan died and kings and queens have yielded thrones? Of course, we might well be suspicious of a lover who never cries, whose physiology remains imperturbable even in crisis and for whom making love is as moving as making breakfast. But feelings are the consequences of love, its physical symptoms at most, and if romantic love is unimaginable without a certain amount of physical discomfort (though even this is highly overrated) this is *due* to the excitement of love, not the other way around. In fact one might say that love is not so much physical as metaphysical discomfort, a revolution in the perspectives through which we see the world.

But surely this leaves something out. At no time do I *feel* love so intensely as those times when I am indeed physiologically distraught, literally choked with emotion. Sometimes, conscientiously, we mutually induce that exquisite sense of sexual desperation, whose purpose is not purely the pleasure of its "release" (as Freud once argued) but the intensification of emotion, building to a never completed crescendo (though the sex, of course, may be completed), which is typically called the "expression" (literally, "pressing out") of love. But again it is not the feeling that *is* the love; rather the feeling *augments* the emotion. (The musical terms are wholly appropriate here; think of the difference between caressing to a Gregorian chant and bouncing away to the Rolling Stones. Can one feel passionate to Muzak or gently touch to punk rock?) Emotions may be supported by (but do not require) the bodily sensations created with or by them, like the musical accompaniment in a Puccini aria, providing a richness and intensity they might not have on their own. But the sensations alone, the "feelings" in this specific sense, are not themselves the emotions.

Where do we get the idea that sensations—"feelings" of a bodily nature—are the essence of emotion? I think the answer comes from a certain limited set of examples—a faulty paradigm of emotions, in which physiological disruptions play an inordinate role. The most common example is this one, taken from William James's still influential essay "What Is an Emotion?" (1884): I'm walking through the woods when from behind a tree appears a gigantic brown bear, and I feel—quite "naturally"—*fear*. What is this fear? It is a visceral disturbance caused by my perception of the bear. It is not just the visceral disturbance, of course, any more than the cause of my emotion is just the bear; it is the *appearance* of the bear, my *perception* of it. The fear itself is my perception of those visceral disturbances in body which in turn cause my "impulse to vigorous action," in this case, an overwhelming urge to run. It all happens so fast, of course, it is difficult to tell what happens first. "Common sense," James tells us, believes that the perception causes the emotion which causes the bodily changes; he says that it is the other way around, that the perception of the bodily changes is the emotion. (Thus, "A woman is sad because she weeps; she does not weep because she is sad.") But this much seems undeniable—that one cannot even imagine fear in such an instance without including an overwhelming physiological feeling in one's image. And from this it is all too easy, whether we agree with James or rather with "common sense," to conclude that the emotion *is* the feeling.

But emotions are not just feelings. It has long been argued by a great many authors in psychology, philosophy and physiology that James's account of emotions as physiological feelings is simply inadequate to account for even the grossest differences between emotions, such as fear and hatred, or love and embarrassment. James's account of the *experience* of the emotion is disastrously incomplete; only part of what we feel, and by far the least significant part, consists of physical symptoms such as flushing, excitement and so on. But we must go further than this and attack not just the details of the "feeling" theory but its very foundations. What James has chosen as an example immediately loads the case toward the feeling view, since in panic it is indeed difficult not to recognize the paralytic flush of adrenalin pumping through one's arteries as the most prominent symptom of the emotion. But to choose this case, or one like it, which is by its very nature based upon an urgent situation and an emergency "gut" reaction, is to choose a paradigm which will guarantee our misunderstanding of an emotion like love. In the case of fear, one does indeed have these feelings, *as well as* the emotion, but one can imagine another kind of fear that, because of its duration, could not possibly be identical with the continuous outpouring of adrenalin, for example, the fear of an employee that he will be fired from his job, for the three months following his boss's announcement that thirty per cent of the staff will soon be let go. The employee may, indeed, have specific moments of panic, but he need not in order to be afraid. His fear is rather the *structure* of his experience, from the time he gets up in the morning until his second martini at night. It is not a sudden intrusion, which so many authors continue to confuse with the essence of emotion itself.

When we turn to love, it is obvious that the emergency paradigm is almost wholly beside the point, except, perhaps, for that first fateful meeting or awkward first date, the evening when one person works up the courage to say "I love you" or an occasional moment by the firelight flushed with wine as well as adrenalin. On these occasions love may indeed involve palpitations for a moment or two, but to confuse these with the emotion itself is to misunderstand the emotion entirely. Indeed, even in panic (which has its place in romantic love too) the emotion is not just a feeling but a complex structure of our experience which the simple "feeling" theory refuses to recognize.

If an emotion isn't a feeling, what is it?

In *The Passions*, I argued at length that emotions must be understood as a much more sophisticated and far more important aspect of our lives than mere feelings, disruptions or even, as in the James-and-the-bear case above, biological survival mechanisms. Quite the opposite of these unlearned, bodily responses, emotions are *activities*, like complex thoughts and fantasies (which were also once believed to be *given* to us, for example, by the gods). We *do* them, and we *learn*, from our culture and our friends, from movies, books and, originally, from our parents, ·*how* to do them. We talk about emotions as "natural," "instinctual," "primitive," but in fact they are cul-

tural, learned and highly educated ways of projecting ourselves into, not just reacting to, our world.

Love, in particular, is a way of living in the world that we
*construct* for ourselves. This is not to say that each of us in-
vents love for him or herself, of course; we imitate our parents,
perhaps, and on successive nights Bogart, Belmondo or Bacall,
Deneuve or Woody Allen, clumsily appropriating lines and
roles that we have learned, the structures of this emotional
world. Occasionally we do invent our own lines, ad-lib the role
so to speak, but only with great difficulty and only *within* the
scenario that we have been learning all of our lives. (When we
speak "from the heart" we are most likely, in fact, to repeat the
most common banalities, the most current platitudes, or the
last thing we happened to read.) *Love is this scenario,* like a
stage setting, in which we act out a role—whether well or ill
defined. It is a scenario *constituted* by us—to use now the
proper philosophical term—literally "set up" (as a *constitution*
"sets up" a government) according to an elaborate but rarely
explicit set of judgments and rules we have been taught by our
culture. Having an emotion thus becomes *the playing of a role*
—for example, in anger—the wronged, in resentment—the martyr, in envy—the deprived, in sadness—the bereaved, and in
love—the lover. Thus William James rightly suggests that "a
woman is sad because she weeps," but not because of her physiology. And Lewis Carroll, in *Alice in Wonderland,* summarizes our theory precisely in his couplet, "'I'll be judge, I'll be
jury,' said cunning old Fury." Our emotions are not feelings of
which we are the victims; they are rather more like theatrical
performances, in which we are both the leading actor and the
director. But then again, we did not write the play, which has
been handed down to us by the whole of our culture.

Theorists have often wondered about the peculiar connection between emotions and their expressions. Charles Darwin,
a hundred years ago, argued the thesis that these expressions
are "natural," and that our tendency to gnash our teeth when

angry, for example, is a vestigial remnant of our once less inhibited urge to *bite* the person who has offended us. Amusing, but what is left out is the incredible finesse and creativity which we add to these evolutionary remnants, if indeed there are any. Edgar Rice Burroughs imagines a people who laugh when unhappy, cry when delighted. This may not be so strange as he thought, but his point is precisely that our expressions are neither necessary nor "natural," but strictly contingent and conventional ("Whenever you feel this, act this way"). But what he leaves out in turn is precisely what Darwin recognized: the functional—if vestigial—connection between emotion and expression. Each of these views is partially correct. There is indeed a connection between an emotion and its expression, but this is not at all some curious linkage between an "inner" feeling and an "external" expression. An emotion is not something "inside of us" that seeks an "outside" expression ("ex-pression" = literally a *forcing out*). An emotion is already "outside"—if this spatial metaphor makes any sense at all—as a projection into the world, the setting of a scenario, the playing of a culturally defined role. It is also, of course, a matter of consciousness—the way we *look* at things—but no emotion is merely this; it is always, in James's phrase, "a tendency to vigorous action" as well, if indeed it is an emotion at all. But "vigorous" is perhaps too energetic a term, for the gentle caress of a lover, for instance, or for the bitter withdrawal of simmering resentment, which, after all, is a form of emotional action too.

Every emotion is a system of judgments, about ourselves and our place in the world (which most often means our relations with other people), through which we cast ourselves a scenario, act out and fantasize a world in which we occupy roles of considerable significance. (Indeed, the function of many emotions, I will argue, is precisely this sense of increased self-importance.) These judgments, scenarios and roles are learned, transmitted by our culture, our language and, more immediately, our family, friends, books and movies. This is not to

deny that there might be easily specifiable "natural" or instinctual or infantile prototypes of these emotional phenomena, but
it is to say that, whatever these prototypes, love like a lover's
first clumsy gestures is wholly taught, refined, interpreted and
encouraged by a particular society. In virtually no case (except, perhaps, for pure panic) are these roles, judgments and
gestures simply "natural"; and to understand romantic love is
not at all to understand anything about human nature, but
rather to understand something about a certain sort of society,
in which blood relations and family ties play an extraordinarily
diminished role and mobility, individuality and chance encounters hold a remarkably dominant position in the determination of "who we are." Indeed, every emotion—love in particular—is a primary mode of judging and acting out precisely
who we are. Emotion, expression and self-identity are learned
as one, first as parody, only later as "natural" (that is, effortless
and accomplished). Lovers are made, not born (but so are
martyrs, revolutionaries, saints and magistrates). To love is to
play the lover. Thus André Gide rightly argued that pretending to love is already to be in love, and wondering whether one
loves is already to love a little less.

Because emotions are composed of judgments which are
learned within a particular culture (or subculture), there is no
reason to expect that all human beings will share the same
emotions. Of course, probably everyone, Davy Crockett ex-
cepted, will feel fear when confronting a large bear in the
woods, but in virtually all other cases, I want to resist the
phrase "human emotion," since this phrase too easily slips into
the *a priori* assumption that there is, in fact, some universal set
of emotions, "human nature," which anyone must have to be
human.[1] Regarding romantic love, in particular, it is important
continuously to remind ourselves how rare this emotion really
is, and how it appears *only* in those societies in which individ-

[1] See my *History and Human Nature* (Harcourt Brace Jovanovich, 1979).

uality is extremely important. And even within such societies, it is worth noting, the roles and rituals and expressions of love are largely dictated by an extremely precise and even explicit set of rules—in Victorian England, for example, as described in Jane Austen's novels. Only Americans presume that they are completely "on their own" when it comes to *making* love, because we have a *choice* of so many roles and expressions. But we too have our restrictions and rituals, though not, in our case, to "control" our emotions so much as to give them some shape, to narrow down a frightening list of possibilities to something more manageable. The process we curiously call "dating" and what we too glibly criticize as "playing games," perhaps even sex itself, are all part of our quasi-institutionalized romantic rituals. A couple never goes to bed alone: they are joined, in a sense, by the whole of their culture and society. And what they "feel," in fact, is their participation in a set of well-established and highly esteemed roles, as "lovers," which have come down to us through generations of stories, novels, movies and communal experience.

The key to romantic love, as an emotion, is the concept of *choice*. Love may sometimes be "spontaneous," but more often than not we talk or think our way into love, and in every case the whole weight of our Western romantic tradition goads us on. But to have an emotion, to be in love, is to enter into a certain kind of world, voluntarily, if sometimes erratically, whimsically or "irrationally." Love is something *done* rather than suffered, not just a feeling but an *art*, as Erich Fromm rightly argued. What seems to be passive and "spontaneous" may be a matter of bad memory. And in a society in which so often love is a relationship between *strangers*, the element of choice—whether fully conscious or not—is inescapable. The fact that we form almost instant and utterly intimate relations with people we have never met before, preferring their company to the continued companionship of our own family and friends, strikes much of the world as a form of lunacy, to say the least. Indeed, what distinguishes romantic love from many other emotions, including other forms of love (motherly, brotherly, etc.), is precisely this emphasis on freedom of choice. Not only do we in some sense choose our emotion (which is true of virtually all emotions) but in love the choice itself—often combined with the contingencies of chance—is its most striking characteristic.

We often talk in terms of the "magic" or the "chemistry" of love, particularly in "love at first sight," when there seem to be no actual *grounds* for affection, only that immediate and most striking "feeling." It is this lack of grounds that leads the radical Freudian sociologist Philip Slater to suggest that "love at first sight," because it obviously can't be based on anything in the present, must be based in the past, in other words, in the Oedipal conflict. This is too quick a conclusion. Indeed, even in a "feeling" view of emotions this is highly implausible: there are other people in one's past in addition to Mom—first loves, grade school teachers, a friend of the family, a dozen movie stars and the girl next door. The tantalizing phenomenon of "love at first sight" is indeed explained in terms of the fact that the person we meet just so obviously fits—or at least seems to fit—the roles we ourselves have been fantasizing for years, but this does not necessarily mean the Oedipal mommy-me-daddy scenario. Nor need it be a single fantasy.

A role is established; it need only be filled. We even say, "I feel as though I've known you for years," and in a sense one has. Fantasy, we all know, plays an enormous role in romantic love but not, as even Webster's Dictionary suggests, as a source of unreality and self-deception. There need be nothing *false* about fantasy. Fantasy is imaginative judgment, projection, expectation, the kind of fantasy that goes into the *direction* of a play, not a distraction from it. It is fantasy that guides the reality of love, even if it *also* leaves lots of room for self-

deception. And it is fantasy, not mystery, that provides the
"magic" of love.

This "magic" is shared by all emotions. Jean-Paul Sartre, in
a small book on emotions published in 1938, called the emotions "magical transformations of the world." And indeed they
are. Every emotion has this ability to transform our world,
"from the inside," to alter through fantasy the way we experience, and so the way we live in, the world. Love, in particular,
may be a sudden but by no means unanticipated transformation of the way we see another person, a change that, at
least initially, requires no change at all—or even acknowledg-
ment—on his or her part. And it is a change that can be main-
tained indefinitely, by continuing "magic." An emotion, like
God's creation of the universe, is a continuous process, not a
"*state*," and the shimmering "magic" of love in particular requires constant attention, like a spell which must be cast continuously, even if it seems—when we do it well—that indeed it
has been cast *on us* instead.

We can now state our strategy with some precision: to say
that love is an emotion is to enable us to look at it with a more
matter-of-fact eye than those who praise it uncritically, but
without falling into cynical reductionism either. Love is nothing more than an emotion, but nothing less either. Many of the
virtues we so readily attribute to love are in fact common to
most emotions, for example, love's celebrated "magic" and its
famous "yearning." Sartre shows how sadness, for example, has
exactly these properties too, how the sad person never seems
sad enough, and how one *chooses* one's sadness as a way of
defining a world. Indeed, the idea that love changes our
whole world around is itself a general property of emotions. "A
depressed man lives in a depressed world," wrote the depressed philosopher Ludwig Wittgenstein. And so indeed
every emotion is a world, a world defined by that emotion and
its judgments. Anger is obsessed with questions of blame and

vengeance. Envy is defined by its sense of inequity. Sadness is voluntarily trapped in the past, while hope is fixated on the future. All emotions are obsessive. All emotions are self-concerned (which is not to say "selfish" or "self-indulgent," though they may be this as well). All emotions seem as if they are unique, and it is just as common to feel that one has never been so angry as it is to believe that one has "never been in love before—at least, not like this." It is not just love that gives life meaning, but emotions in general, and it is not just love—if it is love at all—that "makes the world go round."

But most importantly, rendering love as an emotion and emotions as systems of judgments evaporates the "mystery" that supposedly surrounds love. Indeed, the mystery instead becomes *why* we single out love for special treatment, praising it and distinguishing it from all other emotions, even turning it alone into a metaphysical principle—as if a mere emotion could not possibly deserve such an important place in our lives. But placing love back among its sibling affections also points to the peculiarity of the extreme expectations and demands we apply to just this emotion, for example, the idea that "true" love should last "forever," or for a significant period of time. Imagine saying, "You couldn't have been so angry; you only wanted to kill her for two and a half weeks." Our black and white attitudes toward love ("She loves me, she loves me not") become at least curious in this perspective, and our demand for *total* love becomes absolutely terrifying, because it is so obviously impossible. Our exclusivist view of love—"You can only love one person (at a time)"—is at least thrown into serious question by comparison with other emotions, since exclusivity is clearly not required in order to be "truly" angry at someone, or envious. And the idea that love is a "mystery" is itself partially clarified as we look at the general view of emotions that has been with us virtually since ancient times, for if even such mundane passions as shame and anger have been treated as if they were temporary possessions by devils or furies, why not love too? But neither Cupid nor the sting of his arrows is any longer part of our mythology. Love is not a feeling of which we are the victims but a world of which we are (collectively) the authors. Romantic love is an emotion created and cultivated by a certain kind of society, to serve certain kinds of functions and expectations. Thus the question turns from psychology to sociology: what kind of society? And why romantic love?

# ON THE (ALLEGED) 6
## ORIGINS OF
## ROMANTIC LOVE

*The cultivation of passionate love began in Europe as a re-action to Christianity (and in particular to its doctrine of marriage) by people whose spirit, whether naturally or by inheritance, was still pagan. . . .*

*But this would be mere theory and highly disputable were it not that we are in a position to trace the historical ways and means to the rebirth of Eros. We have already settled on a date. The earliest passionate lovers whose story has reached us are Abélard and Héloïse, who met for the first time in 1118! And it is in the middle of this same century that love was first recognized and encouraged as a passion worth cultivating. Passionate love was then given a name which has since become familiar. It was called* cortezia, *or courtly love.*

DENIS DE ROUGEMONT,
*Love in the Western World*

It is practically a platitude, in scholarly circles, that romantic love began to flower (what other image could be appropriate?) in the twelfth century, mainly in France (where else?) and in particular with a self-styled *avant-garde* kind of popular poet, the *troubadour.* The troubadours did not just fornicate—or not; they *longed* for their women, who, as often as not, were wholly inaccessible, usually married to somebody else and rarely if ever forthcoming with the sexual favors so desperately desired. And when they did grant their

"favors," they took a long, long time about it, even prolonging
the ritual so far as nights lying naked together without a hope
of physical fulfillment. The fact seemed to be, as for adolescents now (and not only adolescents), that the moment of
physical fulfillment was also the end of the poetry and—if it
deserved the title at all—the "affair." As one French proverb
properly put it, the object of desire is not its satisfaction but its
prolongation.

Now, on the one hand, this picture of the troubadours as
paragons and pathetic romantics has its virtues. The discipline
of *devotion*—formerly appropriate only to the Lord and lords—
now becomes favored for a "maiden," usually a young woman,
and on the basis of her beauty alone, above all else. Today, we
find this emphasis on beauty to be dubious, if not offensive,
but at the time, it was something of a discovery. For those of
us who have grown up confronted with *Playboy* and movie
starlets, the very idea of finding a woman primarily beautiful,
instead of *useful*, would seem to be a step backward. But, indeed, it was a first step in treating women as other than property. Of course, there were occasional beauties in history—
Helen of Troy, for example—but the Greek conception of
beauty was concentrated mainly on the male, and when women
were so celebrated it was almost always because they were
goddesses. (The idea that Helen's *face* launched the thousand
ships was coined by Marlowe in the sixteenth century: what
then concerned the Greeks was rather that Paris had stolen
Menelaus' property, a good enough excuse to sack the gold of
Troy.)

Along with the troubadours emerged a very different kind of
character—the chivalric knight, for whom devotion was also a
virtue but chastity not such a necessity—Lancelot and Guinevere, for example. It is with the adoration of the troubadours
and the chivalric ideal of the knight devoted to his lady that
the idea of a woman as the "object" of love becomes of general
significance, and not only "fair maidens" (i.e., white, wealthy

and virginal) but married women as well. (Conveniently, a large number of husbands were off in the Holy Land for the Crusades, through much of the century, though this in fact provided the necessity of chivalry as well as its opportunity.) It is the *forbidden* nature of love that makes it "romantic."

What is most striking about the chivalric ideal, from a historical point of view, is its freedom, bordering on chaos. After a thousand gunfighter and samurai movies, we may well take for granted the idea of the armed free agent, "the knight-errant," roaming the country and devoting himself to whatever tasks he chooses, or to whatever maiden or mistress. But perhaps the key to understanding that whole century is the fact that such figures were quite novel, signifying a breakdown in traditional allegiances, leaving loyalty as well as love open to negotiation and individual choice. And indeed, I shall argue, it is this concept of individual choice, the intelligibility of devoting oneself to an unknown stranger, or someone else's wife, that marks the social-psychological precondition of what we call romantic love.

The new role for women, as objects of love, and the new freedom to choose, together marked the preconditions for love. But the love of the troubadours is almost always argued to introduce a third essential ingredient, whose role in our conception of romantic love is not all that clear. This is the idea of the lovers' *pathos*, desperation, the impossible love, doomed from the start. (Romeo and Juliet, for instance.) One might argue that the romantic sense of *yearning* (or *languor*) appears even in Plato's *Symposium* (in Aristophanes' speech), but the important difference is that Aristophanes' "yearning" continues *through* sexual intercourse. Though not satisfied, the lover is not thereby "doomed," while the "yearning" of the troubadours is based upon non-consummation, deliberate sexual frustration, even fatal desperation, thus leading to the still influential falsehood that the passion of romantic love is derived from

if not wholly based upon frustrated sexuality. And this is true
not only of male adolescents and the Viennese hysterics who
visited young Dr. Freud's medical offices in the 1890s.

One aspect of this pathetic and intentionally desperate love
mythology that was particularly striking and flattering (whatever is made of it now) was the tendency for the troubadours
to keep their ladies *at a distance*, to "put them on a pedestal,"
an image that makes good literal sense when the lady in question was looking down from her tower. The woman became
idealized, excessively so, given the twin confusions of distance
and sexual frustration, to such an extent that the fantasy and
the poetry could bear little if any resemblance to the woman
herself. In fact, *not* knowing the lady, carnally or otherwise,
was wholly intentional, since one of the persistent themes of
the troubadours' poetry is the *happy* fact of that unhappy distance and ignorance, for it is that which makes passion possible. Presumably—though we do not know—this frustration and
ignorance were mutual, and true of the woman as well. Romantic love was not, therefore, between married—even happily
married—couples, but necessarily relegated to the realm of the
forbidden, the illicit, the unattainable. Thus Denis de Rougemont rightly calls the practice of "courtly love" *anti-marriage*
and "pagan." The Camelot story in its modern guise is only
half right; Lancelot and Guinevere were indeed lovers, but
not, in this exalted sense, Guinevere and Arthur. And so too,
our romantic legends abound with the tragedies of Romeo and
Juliet, Tristan and Isolde, and all those other couples, down to
the West Side version by Leonard Bernstein, who long and
perish for a love that is by its very circumstances impossible to
fulfill.

What is most interesting about this picture, however, is what
is left out of it. First, accepting it at face value as *a*—if not *the*
—paradigm of romantic love, it is worth taking a careful look at
the very unromantic nuts-and-bolts alterations in twelfth-century society in general, for romantic love, as we have already

argued several times, can be seen to be the emotional product of a certain kind of society, a society whose origins can be traced to just this time in Western history. But what is also worth pursuing is the idea that the troubadours and their chivalric heroes do *not* in fact represent romantic love at its origins. One must ask, for example, to what extent the Greeks and Romans manifested the characteristics of romantic love, in their everyday behavior as well as in Sappho's poetry and Plato's *Symposium*, a millennium and a half before the troubadours. And, more to the point, we ought to be very critical of the idea, so central to the troubadours, at least, that romantic love is primarily a relationship (if that's the word) at a *distance*. Indeed, would we rather not say that *intimacy* is its essence? Perhaps the scholars' favorite example of romantic love is not that at all, but rather a curious perversion of interpersonal desire—not inappropriate to professors—from whose influence we are still suffering today.

Throughout this book, one of my main aims will be to stress the connection between romantic love and self-identity. Romantic love, in a certain type of society, is the search for and creation of personal identity, through not only one's thoughts and actions (too long the sole focus of philosophical attention, from Socrates to Sartre) but, primarily, through and with other people. We are, excessively, such a society, and in the absence of or in addition to the dozens of other definitive relations in which we take part, romantic love seems to be our obsessively singular source of personal worth, not only for women but, perhaps even more so, for men. But if this is so, then we should expect to find romantic love arise in precisely those epochs and cultures when self-identity is in question, when traditional roles and relationships fail to tell a person "who I am." In other words, we should expect to find the origins—or at least the intensification—of romantic love in the rise of the individual in the "West." And so, I want to argue, we do.

One of the scholarly platitudes of the past few centuries is
that the concept of the individual, along with humanism and
the "dignity of man" in general, came into existence only recently, namely, in the Renaissance, in the fourteenth and
fifteenth centuries. Jacob Burckhardt, who wrote the still
definitive text on that period a hundred years ago, argued in
particular that the rise of the individual, the "discovery of
man," the new sense of *humanitas* and human dignity, the dis-
solution of feudal society and the beginnings of international
commerce on a grand scale, all led to a breakdown of traditional conceptions of identity and social roles, and made not
only possible but necessary the new emphasis on individual
character. But it is now agreed that this process in fact began
several centuries earlier, in the late eleventh and the twelfth
century, not so much as a reaction against the medieval church
as *within* it. (The picture of the Renaissance as a reaction
against the past rather than a development from it was invented by the Renaissance itself, and has continued to be the
favorite stereotype of humanists ever since.) The crucial aspect
of this change, from our point of view, was the attention given
to—one might with some justification even say, the "discovery"
of—*feelings*, or what were then called "affections." And feelings, as I have argued elsewhere,[1] are essential to our conception of ourselves as individual persons. So one might say that
the twelfth century, more or less, was the epoch of the discovery and exploration of *personal character*.[2]

[1] *The Passions* (Doubleday, 1976).

[2] In his classic *De Amore*, for example, Andreas Capellanus suggests three
ways for a young man to "win a virtuous woman"—a fine physique, courageous behavior and a good set of lines (i.e., "elegance of speech"). It is this
last which *De Amore* is designed to teach (the medieval version of "50 Great
Opening Lines and How to Woo a Woman"). But what is important about this
list is that social position and wealth have virtually nothing to do with it, plus
the fact that the idea of "winning" a woman by force of character is one of the
most striking innovations of the period.

Needless to say, I do not mean that no one had "character," that there were no personal characteristics, that people didn't have feelings or that there were no eccentrics—village idiots and the like—before A.D. 1100. But these aspects of a person were considered entirely inessential, even negligible, and self-identity in virtually no sense turned on them. Even St. Augustine, who is usually credited as the foremost psychologist of the whole medieval epoch, spoke hardly at all of "affections," usually of "impulses." His *Confessions* were only circumstantially "personal" and in fact represented him*self* only as a representative of humanity in general. And from Augustine until Anselm, seven centuries later, the general idea was that individuals (a word which to them was strictly a logical category, meaning "not divisible") were but instances of the universal species, "mankind." A person was individual (in-divisible) in so far as each had a *soul,* and individuals could be distinguished by their various social and household[3] *roles,* obligations and loyalties. But character played little part in an individual's identity or distinguishing characteristics. Even *faith,* that singular emotion which has always played such an enormous importance in the Christian conception of individual worth, did not become centrally important as a distinction of *personal* character until, again, the twelfth century, when Peter Abelard, in particular, argued what was then still heresy —that personal feelings such as faith were of paramount importance in a person's relationship to God.

But as important as this new emphasis on feelings—what some have called a "spiritual psychology," others a "clinical theology"—was the renewed emphasis on interpersonal relations, that is, not merely social relations determined by household status and given obligations, but interpersonal feelings,

---

[3] Strictly speaking, it is the household—an economic unit—and not what we call "the family" that is at issue here. Indeed, what we call "the family" and think of as "most natural" was not invented until the seventeenth century.

in particular, feelings of friendship. Colin Morris, for example, in his *Discovery of the Individual: 1050–1200* (Harper & Row, 1973), argues at length that the new "cult of friendship" created an entirely new conception of Christianity, a conception of brotherhood, in which friends on earth became the surest guides to one's chances for salvation. And what distinguished friendship from virtually all other social relations was the fact that it was based on feelings, not obligations; in fact, social roles interfered with and even contradicted friendship, so that, not surprisingly, friendship blossomed best in that one institution where social roles of the usual variety were not to be found: the monastery. And it was in the twelfth century too, not only in the Renaissance, that there was a general turn back to the classics. For the "cult of friendship," the required text became Cicero's essay on friendship, which however "pagan" already included many of the attributes that would soon be incorporated into the new conception of romantic love —for example, the idea that "friendship is forever" and "divine" and that friendship consists mainly in a kind of "union" or "common mind" (*consensio*).

But as friendship was exalted as the "highest" of human virtues, there was no parallel exaltation of romantic love as such. Friendship was taken to be part of the whole Christian tradition (in retrospective interpretation, of course, for there is surprisingly little about it in the *New Testament*). Romantic love, on the other hand, seemed to be entirely new and, needless to say, shocking to traditional sensibilities. Friendship was a religious phenomenon; love remained "profane" and, consequently, clandestine, illicit, even revolutionary. Forbidden love was a dramatic exception (Abelard and Heloise, Tristan and Isolde, etc.), not the general rule. Morris comments, "What the church did for friendship, it signally failed to do for marriage." Sexual experience was deemed to have no religious value, even to the point that, according to one of the teachings of the contemporary Church, "Every ardent lover is an adulterer with his own wife." And so romantic love, which has always been a combination of friendship and sexuality (for the Greeks too, one could argue), became a most uncomfortable concept in the twelfth century, as half of its nature was glorified, the other half condemned. No wonder, then, that the troubadours found themselves split between secular worship (literally, putting their lovers on pedestals) and prohibited sexual desires (pedestals, after all, are safely out of reach). And no wonder too that the emasculated concept of "Platonic love," which is the worshipfulness of romantic love stripped of desire, was invented and first promulgated about this same time by Marsilio Ficino in Italy.

The new emphasis on personal character had its most obvious manifestations in the new self-conceptions of both men and women. Nobles who had formerly been identified more or less completely by their household roles and allegiances found themselves literally "errant" in a society that was coming apart at its feudal seams. Where loyalty had once been a matter of given obligations, it now became a matter of voluntary oath. Where once allegiance had been a matter of social fact, it now became a matter of *devotion*. And warrior-nobles—"knights"—found themselves free agents—individuals, in other words, who could devote themselves and now their oaths as they saw fit. And why not, if they so desired, devote themselves to a lady, not because of political loyalty but out of sheer fascination? The ethics of chivalry, so conceived, became a matter of *distinguishing* oneself, not as a knight "of the realm" but the opposite, as a character, a courageous personality, worthy of love in return. And it is not at all insignificant that this conception of romantic love derived, in its very essence, from the feudal idea of *service*, that is, loyalty and devotion to a master. The master, in this case, was the lady herself, but the origins of romantic love, according to the chivalric tradition, cannot be separated from this conception. (Thus introducing some historical confusion into the male "I'm the boss" role.) The ideas of self-sacrifice and "proving oneself," therefore, are as old as the notion of romantic love itself, and far more important, as far as origins go, than anything like *intimacy*—so central to our own conception, but virtually unknown (and unthinkable) to them.

Romantic love required a dramatic change in the self-conception of women as well. They too were freed ("liberated" would be the term some of my friends would prefer) from an identity that depended wholly on their social roles, that is, their blood and legal ties with men, as daughters, wives and mothers. It is in this period in Christian history that *looks* become of primary importance, that being beautiful now counts for possibly everything, not just as an attractive feature in a daughter or wife (which probably counted very little anyway) but as itself the mark of character, style, personality. Good grooming, as opposed to propriety, came to define the individual woman, and her worth, no longer dependent solely on her social worth, which in turn depended on the social roles and positions of her father, husband or children, now turned on her looks. The premium was placed on youth and beauty, and though some women even then may have condemned this emphasis as unjust, it at least formed a first breach with a society that, hitherto, had left little room for personal initiative or individual advancement. The prototype of the *Playboy* playmate, we might say, was already established eight hundred years ago, and it did not require, as some people have argued recently, Hugh Hefner's slick centerfolds to make youth, beauty and a certain practiced vacuity into a highly esteemed personal virtue. The problem is why we still find it so difficult to move *beyond* this without, like some Platonists, distaining beauty altogether—the opposite error.

But we can go still "deeper" into these "origins" and see that the new emphasis on individual worth and personal identity, and with it the renewed emphasis on personal-emotional relations such as friendship and, with considerable confusion, romantic love, can be explained on the basis of still more general social phenomena, to which we have already referred by such large historical headings as "the breakdown of feudalism" and "the discovery of the individual." Colin Morris provides us with a persuasive picture of a century in the process not so much of "breakdown" as what we refer to in retrospect as "modernization," in particular, the development of commerce and, with it, of cities, and new kinds of loyalty, the centralization of some governments and the resultant "breakup" of others. Consequently, men (mainly) and women found their loyalties divided, their traditional roles in question, not just as individuals (that was the result, not the cause), but as social entities. With the growth of cities and the consequent increase in anonymity, we find the familiar paradox, that personal significance became more important as social significance came more into question. There were choices to be made where there had been none before. A knight could and had to *decide* to whom he would dedicate his talents. A lady had to *decide,* as she could not before, to whom she would bestow her affections. Sometimes she was even able to choose her husband. Merchants could choose their markets and their wares. People could choose their jobs (not a possibility, for example, in Plato's *Republic*). Men could choose their friends. And it is with all this emphasis on *choice* that the individual was "discovered," in fact *created.* (Existentialism in the twelfth century, one might say.) And as persons became more mobile, more malleable, more "free," personality became more of a crucial characteristic, personal feelings became more important, and personal relationships became increasingly all-important. The distinction between public roles and private lives became significant, perhaps for the first time, and love (and to a lesser but still significant extent, friendship) became relegated to the realm of the private. Indeed the separation of the social from the personal, and consequently the public from the private, is part of the very condition in which love is possible.

But is romantic love original to the twelfth century and the more or less poetic moanings of the troubadours? Or should we give more credit to the Greeks? At least some of the most important features of romantic love preceded the troubadours by fifteen centuries, not so much in Plato's *Symposium* (though the languor of love and the appreciation of beauty is to be found there too) but rather in the less effete works of the ancient love poets, the more secular and familiar praises of friendship in Aristotle's *Ethics* and the works of Ovid, Cicero and Sallust in particular. But perhaps more importantly, it is essential to argue against the scholarly tradition that much of the ideal "courtly" love of the troubadours is *not* to be taken as paradigmatic of the tradition they supposedly initiated, particularly the pathetic ideal of love-at-a-distance, such that sexual consummation was tantamount to the destruction, not the expression of love, and reciprocity with one's love was most often a fanciful dream. But we have seen that this perverted attitude is itself the product of a kind of confusion, caused by the diametrically opposed values placed on friendship and love at this time, so that romantic love, as a product of the two, was literally split apart by the twelfth-century emotional ethic. In this sense, the love of the troubadours was as much of an example of *what can go wrong* with romantic love as the dramatic model of its origins. And the Greeks, for whom friendship and sexual passion went, so to speak, hand in hand, become far better paradigms and ideals.

But then again, the lack of intimacy and importance of distance in early romantic love was not peculiar to the schizoid and troubled attitudes of the troubadours. For all of the modern lamenting about the "loss of intimacy in human relationships" (see Chapter 7), there really was very little intimacy, particularly in marriages, until quite recently. (Morris understates the case concerning the late medieval period: "For most, marriage was not an uplifting experience.") The knights who devoted themselves to their ladies were far more concerned with "service" than intimacy, and it is often said that knights and troubadours alike were far less in love with their ladies than they were with their own passions, a charge of "narcissism" which haunts romantic love to this day (e.g., in *The Golden Mirror of Narcissus in Courtly Love,* by the scholar Frederick Goldin, and, in Morris, "the birth of self through love," p. 118). It is true, in an extremely important sense, that both troubadours and knights were, as Morris proclaims, "not encountering others so much as extensively searching for self" (ibid., p. 118), but the charge rings false, not only for the twelfth century but for the twentieth as well.[4] Looking for a self *through* others is by no means tantamount to neglecting or "using" them, although the love-at-a-distance attitudes of chivalry and the courtly poets certainly lend credence to this interpretation. But that is all the more reason why we should, having taken due account of the twelfth-century phenomenon, reject the traditional treatment of it and pinpoint the origins of our own conception of romantic love neither there nor in the philosophical self-congratulation of Plato's Socrates but in the far more ordinary and less divine conception of mere friendship and fulfilled sexual desire, whether in the Greeks or in the forbidden affair between Lancelot and Guinevere, or, better yet, in our own peculiar needs in a society that is quite unlike either fourth-century B.C. Athens or the twelfth century A.D. in France.

> We must beware of the dangers of importing into the 12th century assumptions which are natural to us but would have been entirely foreign to them, for the characteristics of friendship and love, and the language in which they were expressed, differed a great deal from our own experience (Morris, p. 96).

[4] Christopher Lasch, *The Culture of Narcissism* (Norton, 1978).

# THE MYTH OF    7
# PLATONIC LOVE:
# EROS BLOATED
# AND SEX DEMEANED

*Oh Plato! Plato! you have paved the way,*
 *With your confounded fantasies, to more*
*Immoral conduct by the fancied sway*
 *Your system feigns o'er the controlless core*
*Of human hearts, than all the long array*
 *Of poets and romancers:—You're a bore,*
*A charlatan, a coxcomb—* . . .
BYRON, Don Juan, I, 116

O f all of the models of love, one in particular has been around long enough to proclaim absolute domain. Although it is not the same as romantic love—indeed, it often opposes itself to romantic love, as sacred to profane—it remains our richest source of metaphors, hopes and illusions. It is the view of love come down to us from Plato, as developed through Socrates' long-winded speech in the dialogue *Symposium*. It is, in a word, the model of love as an approach to the eternal and the divine, and thus itself divine. It is asexual, having "raised" itself above such "lower" desires as sex and companionship. It is love itself that forms its object, rather than the merely personal attraction of two merely mortal persons. Its goal is wisdom, one's lover becomes a means, and love becomes impersonal, eternity-minded, anti-sensual and wrapped in the metaphors of religion and metaphysics, instead of human relationships.

Plato's *Symposium* is too rarely read (even by students of philosophy), but few writers on love fail to mention and praise it as *the* classic text. Its ideas have filtered down indirectly through Christianity and St. Paul's conception of "Christian love" or *agape* to form what sometimes seems like a permanent bias in the writings of such love pundits as Rollo May, de-emphasizing sex and sensuosity and praising *eros* instead as a "cosmic" and even "daemonic" power. The upshot of all such views of love, whether interesting as metaphysical speculations or not, is that our ordinary emotion of romantic love seems pathetic by contrast, and the penumbra of Platonism encourages us, even forces us, to expect more of our emotion than any emotion could possibly hope to satisfy. Thus this chapter, in my mind crucial if controversial, is necessary to combat the damage, often promoted with the most benign intentions, of the ethereal views of love that still haunt us, twenty-five hundred years later. As well as, we shall see, the bitter cynicism that inevitably follows it.

Love among the Greeks was a perfectly secular, agreeable and tangible passion. No mysteries, no pieties, no cynicism. Plato begins his *Symposium,* for example, with the lament that no one has ever even bothered to sing love's praises; in retrospect, perhaps, that was just as well. And when Aristotle discusses the virtues of friendship, he makes it clear that love and friendship, together, are but one set of virtues among many, including having a good sense of humor, a sense of justice, an adequate income, honor and the ability to handle one's fair share of wine. (Plato makes a point of emphasizing Socrates' extraordinary ability to drink huge quantities as well as to abstain.) Although much has been made of Greek *eros* and the various distinctions derived from the Greek between different "kinds" of love, what is most remarkable is how unified these conceptions were and how integrated with a view of the "good life" (*eudaimonia*) in general. It is for this reason, perhaps, that scholars do not tend to think of romantic love as having a history in Greece. It is not, as it is for us, such a distinctly separate phenomenon, much less to be praised out of all proportion to everything else. Aristotle would have seen the idea that "all you need is love" as some kind of bad joke, and the ability of sexual love to bring about happiness, in isolation from family and friends and social position, would have been utterly incomprehensible to him. And sex, far from being fascinating, a source of continuous frustration and a topic for constant moralizing, was just, as we say, "a fact of life," not worth talking about, taken for granted in a fashion that we, perhaps, might find "promiscuous." This, however, is not at all true, for there was nothing indiscriminate about it. In fact, the *mores* (as opposed to the morals) of sexuality were rather well defined, just far more varied and far less moral than our rather simple-minded and one-dimensional concept of (heterosexual) human nature and "natural law."

Now it is not my point to praise the "natural" life of the pre-Platonic Greeks, an unhealthy exercise in scholarly voyeurism that has been extremely popular in Europe for the past several centuries. (Perhaps it is understandable as a reaction against seventeen hundred years of horror concerning most matters sensuous and "pagan." How many generations never even took a bath in their lives—because it was "pagan.") But it is strange that so many writers have assumed—to our obvious embarrassment—that the Greeks of the fifth century B.C. were so much better at lusty love than we are. Indeed, we have already pointed out that it is something of a cliché among scholars that the Greeks did not enjoy (or suffer) *romantic* love at all, though, as I have also suggested, this may be quite wrong. But the point to begin with, both in presenting Plato and in contrasting him with the mores of his own compatriots, is the enormous difference between us that is not to be measured in time and technology alone. Not least among these differences is the fact that they were not particularly interested in love between men and women.

Greek love was between men and men, with love and sex between men and women a distinctly "vulgar" activity that was strictly a practical concern—having children and keeping the *polis* populated. The love of women even had its own, distinctly inferior *eros*—a separate and "common" god—and was frequently called "lascivious." Paris, for instance, was despised precisely because he had such an unhealthy obsession for Helen, who may have been the romantic ideal for Faust, two millennia later, but for the Greeks was "just a woman." The idea that love was available to everyone would have struck even the democratic Greeks as absurd; it was restricted to male citizens, and mainly the aristocracy (as it would be again in the flowering of romantic love in France in the twelfth and eighteenth centuries). And even within the aristocracy the speakers in Plato's *Symposium* and Aristotle a few years later make it very clear that love is to be restricted to those rare men of virtue (of whom Socrates was the favorite philosophical example) and the most promising of the youths, the young men who would soon be "statesmen" (the highest vocation for anyone, unlike "politicians" in our own democracy). The idea that sex is an expression of love, we should point out, would also have been foreign to them, though the *with whom* (and in what position) of sex was of immense importance to them too. (In early Rome, Julius Caesar was sometimes the butt of sexual innuendoes not because he reputedly slept with everything that moved from the Forum to Britannia, but because he sometimes assumed the passive position, which was considered wholly inappropriate for a man of his rank.) And finally, again but most importantly, what we call "romantic" love, between an older man and a youth, part sexual and part educational, was not to be understood out of the context of everyday life as a whole. It was nothing "divine," nothing earth-shaking, nothing to write a book about.

And then, there is the *Symposium,* that towering classic that is not only the first but the paradigm of all future theories of love. The topic is unusual, as Plato's symposiasts tell us, and even the form of the dialogue is remarkably different from Plato's other works. But what is most important about it is that Plato's view of *eros,* as enunciated by Socrates, is so at odds with everything else we know about Greek culture of the time, so dramatically antithetical to the unpretentious secularity described by Aristotle, and so disastrous in terms of anticipating the bloating and corruption of *eros* to follow.

Now Plato's views and his importance, perhaps, and that of all historical figures, is a matter of fiction but, like all historical fictions, a convenience and, in any case, an already established precedent for all discussions of love. And what we find, or the scholars have found, in Plato, in his *Symposium* but even more in his lesser-known but more pious dialogue *Phaedrus,* is that love is not merely a secular passion between men but a "divine" relation to the Eternal, in which interpersonal feelings play at best a tangential role. Love may begin with the sensual appreciation of someone's beautiful body, but if it deserves the name "love" at all it must quickly be "elevated" to the love of Beauty itself, and thus the love of the Good and the True. And, ultimately, there is no question but that Plato thought that the only "true" lovers would be a band of (all male) philosophers, some young and beautiful as pupils, perhaps, but mainly old and wise enough to see through the merely sensuous and contemplate the Good, the True and the Beautiful together.

Now this is not the place to present a detailed analysis of the *Symposium,* and no doubt my bald description and blatant objections to it appear philistine without that context. One could argue that Plato's own view is not the same as the "Platonic" views of Socrates, or that Plato has been de-sexualized by so many Christian commentators, or that Plato isn't really concerned with "love" at all. But the story (in fact a retelling of a supposed after-dinner discussion at a somewhat drunken party) culminating in Socrates' speech can be summarized in the following way:

Several speakers precede Socrates, who is the last to speak; first is Phaedrus, who praises the practical virtues of love, then Pausanias, who goes on at length about the need to censure the more "vulgar" kind of love, including love between men and women. Aristophanes tells his delightful tale about "the original state of man" as a double creature, cleft in two by Zeus for *hubris* ("as one would split an apple") and ever since yearning to get together with the other half, and Agathon, a young and beautiful poet insists, not surprisingly, that love itself is young and beautiful and a poet. Socrates, old and anything but beautiful, begins his speech by refuting Agathon, thus setting the stage for his own view of *eros* in terms of wisdom, a virtue of age (he was seventy) rejecting the vanity of youth. *Eros,* he argues, too quickly and by way of some extremely dubious arguments, is ultimately aimed not at beautiful people but at Beauty itself, the eternal Idea rather than its merely mortal incarnations. And Beauty, he again argues much too quickly, is also the Good, and the True, and so in a few swift shifts of attention the subject moves from anything we—or Socrates' co-symposiasts—would recognize as "love," to straightforward philosophy, "the love of wisdom."

At this point the dialogue takes a rather remarkable turn: Socrates, who was parodied by Aristophanes and others as a windbag who would never shut up, pretends to yield the floor altogether and speaks instead, through what one might amusingly imagine to be a falsetto voice, as "Diotima," an old wise woman (who may or may not have actually existed). Through her voice, his argument then turns *eros* away from the secular and toward the divine, with the insistence that love is actually the search for immortality. The "vulgar" love between men and women, which has as its almost inevitable result children who will continue one's bloodline, is a "vulgar" and certainly "inferior" form of immortality, compared, for example, with the immortality of Homer—or, it is implied, of Socrates. And so the emphasis shifts further away from sexual relationships and toward the wise man's own search for immortality and wisdom, although Socrates, who had quite a reputation even at his age, insists that it is also his duty to educate the youths of Athens, the beautiful ones of course ("for in deformity he will beget nothing"), which was understood to include certain sexual "perks" as well. ("Alas, we have lost that ethereal sense of education," some of my colleagues cry.)

Then, the very heart of the argument, follows a passage known by scholars as "Diotima's ladder," a step-by-step progression from the "lowest" forms of love—namely, being enamored of beautiful bodies—to the "highest"—namely, philosophy. Having lusted after several beautiful bodies, so the argument goes, one should come to see that they are "essentially all the same." In the context of *Penthouse*, instead of a classic text, this would leave us aghast. But for Socrates, this leads us to the appreciation of beautiful souls instead, ultimately to Beauty as such, and Wisdom. We ordinary romantic folk, of course, are stuck on the lower rungs of the ladder, "clogged with the pollutions of mortality" in Plato's not very flattering words. The dialogue concludes, however, with a dramatically important scene in which Socrates shows himself indifferent to a somewhat heated competition for his favors between young Agathon and the warrior Alcibiades, who crashes the party late in the evening—drunk. The scene shows Socrates himself to be remarkably insensitive, perhaps Plato's way of casting his own doubts on the pretentiousness that has preceded. But in any case the dialogue ends with everyone but Socrates passing out. He goes home, takes a bath and starts his day "as usual," having changed the course of love in the West for another two and a half millennia.

The legacy of the *Symposium* is that ordinary love and friendship are "inferior" to a higher, impersonal love, as well as the more common Greek legacy that love between man and woman is "vulgar" (a legacy that we have not corrected; we have just prohibited the other kinds of relationships between men and men and women and women and rendered them even less legitimate). And to this we can add our distrust of beauty itself, which we consider "superficial" (only "skin deep"), and of intelligence, which we consider pretentious, and of wisdom, which we consider arrogance. And though these are no doubt to be attributed to our Christian and egalitarian heritage rather than to Socrates (who was an unabashed elitist), the etherealization of love to which they contribute is largely his invention. Love, simple sexual and romantic love, is demeaned, while something else, in part a "mystery" with inexplicable linkage to the "divine," is praised in its place.

In the third century A.D. the philosopher Plotinus furthered Plato's bloating of *eros* with a "tractate" of his own, in which he too insisted that the love of beauty itself is "higher" than mere sensual love, and that "universal love," which is no longer of the person but a cosmic principle, is still "higher" than that. Plotinus too treated *eros* as an independent spirit, a god, and thus considered the actual "mental state" only an instance of it, and "not to be confused with the Absolute Love, the Divine Being." In the twelfth century, Plato got his just deserts, when the Italian celibate Ficino coined the term "Platonic love" to refer to that peculiarly sexless and abstract emotion that may be directed *through* a person but ultimately only *to* God. In the *Symposium*, at least, we find an amusing if not always unambiguous mixture of raunchy sensuality and ethereal philosophizing, but in that love named after Plato the first is condemned and the latter becomes Christian theology.

As love is bloated to the level of a religious experience, we
know full well what happens to sex; it is demeaned or condemned, even if, in the restricted circumstances of holy matri-
mony, it can be tolerated, in small amounts, if the pleasure is
not excessive. (More than one early church authority condemned sexual pleasure even in marriage, as a sin as serious as
adultery.) Love, which the Greeks accepted as an everyday
matter, now became elevated to the "divine"; and sex, another
everyday matter, was reduced to the "lower" desires, an animal need, a biological function. But if love was a matter of the
purest of souls and sex was a bodily need, it is hard to see how
the two would ever come together again. And this is true of
not only Christian theologians but our best "humanists" too.
Enlightenment humanism in the eighteenth century included
the battle not only for reason and liberty but for sexual liberation as well; and yet love was still claimed to be a relation of
"souls," which "have no sex." Bertrand Russell, no friend of
Christian sexual morality to be sure, appeals to this abstract
notion of love and a too vulgar notion of sex even when he attacks the Church and its moral restrictions. Rollo May treats
sex as a mere Freudian "tension" but *eros* as cosmically wonderful, thus finding it all but impossible to carry out the aim of
his book, which is "to reunite love (sex) and will." Humanist
psychologist Abraham Maslow opposes sex to love as "lower"
and "higher" needs in his hierarchy, and existentialist philosopher Peter Koestenbaum, in his *Existential Sexuality*, defines
love as a relation of "two consciousnesses," with sexuality a
matter of utter contingency, even if not a need.

We often talk today about love as a "commitment" and sex
as "free," but this again creates an unmanageable and unnecessary tension between the two. Love becomes *serious* and sex
fun. (Or, perhaps, solemn. Russell Baker: "Being solemn is
easy. Being serious is hard. . . . Falling in love, getting married, having children, getting divorced and fighting over who
gets the car and the Wedgwood are all serious. The new sexual

freedom is solemn.") But again, the need to "elevate" love is a *moral* concern; to divorce sex and love is to make love more difficult than it needs to be, and sex much less than it is. And if love is a "commitment" and sex is "free," it is difficult to see what we are going to do with romantic love, which is both sex and love but neither committed nor free.

The Platonic tradition is carried on today not only by Christianity, in which we would expect an emphasis on the soul and the eternal instead of a celebration of physical beauty and sensuosity, but in other quarters, nominally at least opposed to that ethereal viewpoint. In particular, we can find it among the "humanists," of whom Rollo May, Abraham Maslow and Erich Fromm are, with regard to love, the best-known protagonists. *Humanism,* traditionally defined (since the twelfth century) as the respect for humanity, the primacy of people over gods, governments and nature, has become our most prominent religion. In retrospect, Socrates has been declared a humanist. In retrospect, the Church has embraced a partial humanism, and humanism has defined itself as the greatest enemy of the Christian Church, a false charge, considering the number of church doctrines it has taken along with it. And not least of these is the etherealization of love, the de-emphasis of sex, and the priestly status of those who "know" about love, namely, our psychiatrists.

In place of such words as "salvation" (which nonetheless pops up from time to time) we find the metaphors of health and "cure." In the place of the sermon is "understanding" and, most importantly, in place of the "soul" comes a new pretension, "the total human being." Now though these initially look like opposites, with regard to love they turn out to have the same function: to dismiss sex and sensuality and the limited ways in which we are attracted to and relate to each other in favor of an abstraction which is unobtainable, and perhaps unintelligible. And here we see the continuity between the old

Platonic ideal, the traditional Christian conception of love and
contemporary humanism: in every case love is made out to be
something mysterious and extremely difficult if not impossible,
something much "more" than sensuous attachment to a particular person with whom one identifies and enjoys oneself. One
sees it so clearly in Erich Fromm's classic *Art of Loving*, for instance, as he systematically brutalizes all of those forms of love
of which he disapproves—too sexual, too dependent, too independent, too frivolous, too serious—as "pseudo-love," "pathological love" and simply not *love* at all. One finds it too in
Rollo May's *Love and Will*, in which *eros* (continuously con-
trasted with mere sexuality) is praised as virtually everything
Good, True and Beautiful, as "the spirit of life," "excitement,"
"the power which drives men towards God," which "takes
wings from the human imagination and is forever transcend-
ing." *Eros* is power. *Eros* is self-realization, excellence, virtue,
nobility, creativity and, finally, "beauty in the inward soul"
which provides "higher levels of meaning." Thus Rollo May
adopts Plato's ("Diotima's") hierarchy of desires quite explicitly, and one finds it too, with considerably more belligerence,
in British poet David Holbrook's appropriately titled *Sex and
Dehumanization* and in Victor Frankyl's *The Doctor and the
Soul*. One finds it most recently, perhaps, in psychiatrist Sam-
uel Peck's *A Road Less Traveled*. In every case, we are told,
the doctor knows what is Bold, Beautiful and Profound—but
we don't. Unless, of course, we read their books. The message
is in the air, that love is something spectacular and marvelous,
something that changes lives and lifts us "above" the world of
the merely ordinary. And when the initial exhilaration of a
new romance wears off or wearies, we are disappointed and
confusedly come to believe that what is merely ordinary can't,
therefore, be "the real thing."

The humanist's Christian heritage is nowhere more evident
than in the propensity to declare that we are, regarding love,
in the midst of a *crisis*. As if we have lost what we (that is, the

ancient Greeks) once had, perhaps irretrievably. But any past will do, even the much-abused Victorians. They, at least, their sexual hangups aside, had love. In contrast to those often brutal times, however, we find Rollo May and Erich Fromm, for example, bemoaning "modern man's inability to love" and the "disintegration of love in our time." Here is Rollo May:

> The striking thing about love and will in our day is that, whereas in the past they were always held up to us as the *answer* to life's predicaments, they have now themselves become the *problem*. It is always true that love and will become more difficult in a transitional age; and ours is an era of radical transition. . . . The old myths and symbols by which we oriented ourselves are gone, anxiety is rampant; we cling to each other and try to persuade ourselves that what we feel is love. . . . Love has become a problem to itself.
>
> *Love and Will*, pp. 13–15

Of course, every age is a "transitional age," and it is far from clear that any society has believed more firmly that "love is the answer" than our own. In fact, it is doubtful that any society has believed that at all, even including our own, and the "old myths and symbols" are a problem not only because they are *not* "gone" but because we are urged to take them seriously in a way that they never were before. Even Christianity—or especially Christianity—knew how to separate divine but impossible ideals from reasonable human expectations.

Look at Erich Fromm's statement of the same crisis:

> No objective observer of our Western life can doubt that love—brotherly love, motherly love and erotic love—is a relatively rare phenomenon and its place is taken by a number of forms of pseudo-love which are in reality so many forms of the disintegration of love (p. 83).

Historically, one should ask, "compared with what?" With the

mutual devotion of feudal brothers in medieval France, whose
"love" consisted in waiting to poison each other for the family
titles? To the hundreds of generations of mothers who had
children because they couldn't help it or because the farm
needed hands or simply because they were expected to? To the
erotic love of the mythical South Seas—that perennial European sexual fantasy? The sense of crisis and loss of love perpetrated by these authors seems simply false. Indeed, one could
argue without much difficulty—if such matters are measurable
at all—that there is more love in the "modern" world than
there ever has been in the past. Intimacy is, if anything, excessively celebrated in contemporary America. The significance of
brotherhood and the joys of motherhood as well as the passions of romantic love have never been so alive. There is a
problem only in that we expect even more; there is "disintegration" only in the mind of an observer, not objective at all,
who holds up against our comparatively puny passions a heroic
ideal that, ultimately, turns out to be impossible.

There is no "crisis" about love, and love is not a problem.
(Nor is it the answer.) The melodramatic, myth-laden and me-
dicinal picture of love we get from the humanists is, ultimately, a charge of fraud against us—you and me—in Dr. May's
words, "as we try to convince ourselves that what we feel is
love." The new priest has looked into our souls and found them
empty. But as the Word is delivered now in the name of "science" instead of faith, and Rollo May tells us with authority,
for instance, that the most important point in sex is the moment when the male enters the female, that the most enjoyable
moment for the female is when *he* "abandons himself" in orgasm, and when he cruelly abuses women who desire "the
vaunted orgasm, which should resemble a grand mal seizure"
(p. 40), we start to see through the benign face of the therapist
to the puritanical self-righteousness below. If there is a problem about love, it is not, as May argues, "the banalization of
sex and love" but rather its *etherealization*. We have come to

expect *too much* of love, and so have made ourselves vulnerable to these persistent attacks and the fear that we are—whether each of us or all of us together—"incapable of loving." When the fact might be that love is just one among a hundred other emotions, an ordinary emotion which is necessary neither for mental health nor for "self-actualization."

The myth of Platonic love is the self-degrading idea that "true" love is something extraordinary, something religious, spiritual and therefore "above" the merely sexual, much more than mere companionship and shared ideals and identities, much more than fleeting emotions and, indeed—if it's "true"—eternal. Today, perhaps, we tend to be less abstract and more practical; the "higher love" to which we aspire is "the meaningful relationship" rather than Plato's ideal Forms. But the accusation remains the same—why do we insist that love is significant only because it lasts, or because of what it leads "up" to? We say with regret, "It didn't work out," but why assume that we were "working" toward anything in the first place? Why assume that love and relationships are supposed to "go somewhere"? Why not accept love just as it is, an ordinary yet spectacular emotion which Plato, with his eyes on the heavens, never bothered to take the least bit seriously.

# ENTER THE CYNIC  8

*a net*
*work of connections coming down*
*to getting laid or not getting laid and by whom*
SHARON THESEN, *Loose Woman Poem*

gainst the backdrop of bloated Platonic love, cynicism professes a simple diagnosis: love is nothing but lust. Or nothing but an illusion, or a capitalist conspiracy, or a plot to maintain male superiority. Cynicism sees through the arrogant pretensions of Platonism and benign humanism, with a single "whack" knocks *eros* off its classical pedestal and reduces it to something wholly tangible. Sex, usually, or politics. But because its goal is reduction and clarification, rather than intentional obfuscation, cynicism has also succeeded in providing us with some of the best books on love. Embittered feminists, jaded Freudians, sneering Marxists (often some combination of the three) give us hardheaded theses with which we can agree or disagree, which can be tested in the court of our own experience, in place of the ethereal praise of the Platonists and humanists. But at the same time it is not unimportant to see the moral superiority (which Rollo May aptly calls "the new puritanism") that cynicism shares with Platonism. Whereas the latter keeps telling us, "You think you know what true love is, but you don't," the former seems to be telling us, "You think that there's such a thing as true love, but there isn't." In either case we are the ones who are fooled, so we read their books like dutiful children, waiting to be told what to do.

Sigmund Freud was by no means the first but he was the most systematic, most "scientific" and therefore respectable of a long line of cynical but romantic rationalists who saw through the cloud of hearts-and-flowers obscurantism to the primary candidate for the "dirty little secret"—sex. The troubadours, at least, were straightforward about it; romantic love, this momentous "yearning," was fueled by and made possible by the sexual inaccessibility of the (preferably married) "love object." But Freud's contemporary Victorians, with their pathetic verses filled with self-deception, were another matter. They denied sex, and insisted that their frustration was love. And so Freud weaved his intricate but ultimately simple theories—that love is a confusion of frustration and narcissism, that love is inherently irrational, compulsive, childish. He argued that even brotherly and, of course, motherly love were inherently sexual, also a combination of self-love and self-denial—devoid of reason, freedom or self-control. Love is nothing but lust, plus "the ordeal of civility."

The secret was out. The flabby priest was at last defrocked to reveal—Fred the Flasher, in pious disguise. His holy trenchcoat nothing but overalls for frustration. Like the wizard from behind the curtains at Oz, love emerged pathetically, apologetically, all too ready to confess.

And so the cynic has turned to sex itself, with or without love, with his or her own self-righteousness. In *Playboy* magazine, one can still find monthly articles blistering with piety and indignation which document the whole of Western civilization—the Christian part at least—as one long exercise in cruel inhumanity, the denial of poor innocent *eros*. The cynic sees in St. Augustine only a pitiful celibate, his hands in his pockets while his eyes are on the heavens. The cynic snickers at the troubadours, scoffs at old Ficino with his concept of "Platonic love" and, of course, at the Victorians, who, history aside, have continued to be the source of our very unhistorical horror. But the question to be raised against all this is whether there is not indeed something to be said for the "sublimation" and *stylization* of sex, neither of which is the same as frustration. Could it be that the notion of "free sexual expression" presupposes some basic stupidity about the nature of sexuality? And could it be that it is indeed the "yearning"—which is not to say merely sexual longing—rather than the sexual satisfaction, which is the "end" of not only love but sex as well?

The benign face of cynicism can be found in the neo-Freudian view that romantic love, as a product of sexual inhibition and repression, is quickly becoming a thing of the past. In fact, given the theory that love is nothing but sublimated sex, it is not surprising that the pundits are already predicting the death of sex, as well as love, since availability and boredom, it is presumed, go hand in hand. Over ten years ago Marshall McLuhan suggested no less, and more recently *Time* magazine, as infallible mouthpiece of American sensibility, has already run its story, "Love Is Dying" (September 26, 1977). The *Time* article was based on the research of Professor Marian Kinget of Michigan State, herself the most benign of cynics, who concluded that "the very conditions of Romantic love have ceased to exist." These conditions are, of course, the impossibility of sexual fulfillment. "The sting of sex has been removed," she says, and with it "the agony and the ecstasy," and the "longing of romance." These were, we now know, nothing but frustration glorified. ("Take that, Erich Segal," quips *Time*.) If Dante had married Beatrice, we are told, there would have been no *Divine Comedy*. If Goethe had had his chance at Helen (of Troy), we surmise, what then would the world have done for a German *Faust*? If the Brontë sisters were happily in love, would we still have *Jane Eyre* and *Wuthering Heights*? All the longing that made up love, the "oceanic feeling" that Freud referred to with an unusual combination of respect and curiosity, the creative spirit that infused the Renaissance, the romantic poets and the Victorian novelists, must have been nothing but the pumping of blood through the groin via the mind, frustration rendered creative through unhappy genius or, in lesser mortals, made tolerable by the myth of romantic love. If horniness was indeed a virtue, then suffering was the sign of one's sensitivity and humanity. Thus Kinget admits that the end of love will have a "stunting effect on creativity," but this should be balanced by the utilitarian virtue that marriages will now be founded on a more rational basis. Fewer Leonardos but a lower divorce rate by way of compensation.

Beneath this benign position, which culminates in happy households of wisely chosen mates, all the ingredients are available to the more malicious cynic who would like to turn this simple mistaken reduction into an all-out attack on contemporary American life. Suppose that our grandest passion is nothing but impotent self-deception—and perhaps too all our emotions? Suppose that love as such is an illusion artificially created by "civilization," for whatever reasons. Suppose that rare romantic love is in fact nothing but a rarefied distortion of readily available sex. Suppose that love is a form of capitalist prostitution and a form of conspiracy. One finds such a "critique," for example, in the philosophy of Herbert Marcuse. But the point is made most succinctly by Philip Slater, who summarizes the view as well as anyone in his *Pursuit of Loneliness:*

> Romantic love is one scarcity mechanism that deserves special comment. Indeed its *only* [my italics] function and meaning is to transmute that which is plentiful into that which is in short supply. . . . Although romantic love always verges on the ridiculous (we would find it comic if a man died of starvation because he could not obtain any brussels sprouts) Western peoples generally and Ameri-

cans in particular have shown an impressive tendency to take it seriously (ibid).

and

> By the time an American boy or girl reaches maturity, he or she has so much symbolic baggage attached to the sexual impulse that the mere mutual stimulation of two human bodies seems almost meaningless. . . . The setting and interpretation of a sexual act comes to hold more excitement than the act itself (pp. 85–86).

Sex itself is simple; love is a complex illusion. But sex is not at all so simple, and certainly not "meaningless"; against Slater, it is essential that we insist that the meaning of sex is indeed the "interpretation" of its "symbolic" significance. But notice that Slater is opposing May in an interesting way; for him, sex itself is intrinsically meaningful, love is not. In fact, unlike the "natural" pleasures of sex and affection (Slater is careful not to equate sex with just intercourse and orgasm [p. 85]), love is an artificially inflated *commodity*, and it is this economic model that defines his analysis of love: "Why is love made into an artificially scarce commodity . . . pleasures that could be obtained at any time?" (p. 86). But even Freud knew at least that these "pleasures" could *not* be obtained at any time, and not just because of the inhibitions of a "deprived feeling" society (where Slater lays the blame). It is not just in a capitalist society that love must be *earned*, and even mother love (according to most Freudians, including Slater, May and Fromm) is an affection which, perhaps after the first few weeks or months, can be lost or won, though the expectation of motherly affection, to be sure, is easily taken for granted. (Erich Fromm, for example, betrays one common fallacy about parenthood by insisting that mother love is unconditional, father love conditional.) Romantic love, in particular, is not reducible to sex plus economics, for love is not a cause so much as a response to the breakdown of the more "natural" social ties whose loss Slater bemoans: "We make things scarce in order to increase their value, which in turn makes people work harder for them" (p. 86) and "The idea of placing restrictions on sexuality was a stunning cultural invention, more important than the acquisition of fire. In it man found a source of energy which was limitless and unflagging . . ." (p. 84).

It is a classic Freudian motif, the fuels of repressed libido firing up the organism and motivating virtually everything. And by making sex seem so readily available (he assumes that sexual scarcity was a human "invention"; was it?) he easily makes our constant pursuit of it look ludicrous, asking contemptuously, "How did man happen to transform himself into a donkey, pursuing the inaccessible carrot?"

The source of this self-contempt begins with a metaphor, posing as a model, masquerading as hard-headed analysis. It is the economic model, which Freud employed for more medical reasons (he saw the "psychic apparatus" as a quantitative energy system), that Slater and others use just to reduce something we find important to a mere game of supply and demand:

> We can think of this process as a kind of forced savings (indeed, emotional banking was probably the unconscious model for the monetary form). The more we build up an individual's erotic involvement in a restricted relationship the less he will seek pleasure in those forms that are readily available. He will consume little and produce much. Savings will increase, profits will be reinvested . . . (p. 87).

In other words, we tease and manipulate ourselves, a "ridiculous" enterprise made even more embarrassing by quick comparisons (donkeys and carrots, an obsession with brussels sprouts). But love is no commodity, *not* because it can't be quantified (see Chapter 9) but simply because its structure commands a very different interpretation, an interpretation in terms of significance and meaning, not merely exchange rates. This is not to say that love can't be bought and sold, nor even that it is not often a matter of exchange of some kind. But it is not the exchange and its commodity status that is primary or definitive. Perhaps a simple comparison with art and aesthetics will illustrate this point better. Of course art does enter into a "market," in which art works are commodities and value is determined by supply and demand; rarity increases demand and too easy obtainability lowers the price. But virtually no one, one would like to think, would say that the existence of an art work *as art* depends on its market value or its scarcity. Paintings by Vermeer may be particularly valuable because they are so few, but surely their value *as art* is irrelevant to their number. Balinese masks are or were, before their entrance into the international commodity market, easily accessible to every household, which made them no less significant. And the same must be said for sex and love: whether or not they are bought and sold. (We can agree that prostitution is a readily available metaphor for most of our interpersonal transactions—but why use it?) They are not primarily commodities but rather matters of intrinsic cultural significance, which is precisely what Slater the sociological cynic leaves out of account.

The commodity model introduces another consideration, brought out in Slater's comparison with "the man who loved brussels sprouts." Though surely amusing in a grim sort of way, the analogy makes too light of the fact that love (even sex) tends to be highly *selective* for us, not as a matter of cultural conspiracy (to make us work harder) and not simply as a matter of finickiness. Selection of mates is as "natural" as sexual desire itself, and if one thinks sex (much less love) is readily available in the state of nature (as Rousseau used to lustily imagine) one need only watch a small troop of baboons, for example, with one pathetic smallish male trying to sneak a quick entry into a female without being mauled by the alpha male, or a couple of caribou knocking their brains out to decide who gets a chance at the female. Our selection is not "natural," of course, in the sense that it is grossly influenced by our own cultural inventions: *Playboy* bunnies and Hollywood muscle men, witty talk show hosts and self-consciously neurotic "sex symbols." But it is one of the fantasies of the cynic that sex and love are "easily obtainable," so that (everyone else's) difficulty in obtaining them can then be a matter of ridicule. But the simple fact of the matter seems to be that the easy obtainability of even sex is a fantasy (thus Slater, like Freud, takes pains to insist that sexual satisfaction is not necessarily gained through sexual achievement). Sex need not be scarce but it is always selective.

Not even the most vulgar cynic would say, except as a matter of mere theory, that "everyone is just like any other," for this is to misunderstand not only the very essence of love but even sex as well. (One is *not* like any other.) Love is defined, as much as by any other factor, by its particularity. But to confuse this with a "scarcity mechanism," or to deny it in favor of some utopian vision of a world of anonymous (androgynous?) mutually replaceable creatures is not only a complete misunderstanding of love but a degrading depiction of human emotions. It is a form of cynicism that goes back to St. Paul: try to apply love—which by its very nature is highly selective— to everyone equally, and when this universal love turns out to be impossible, condemn *us* for being "incapable of love." The polar opposites of piousness and cynicism begin to look very similar indeed.

"Love . . . Yuck! . . . it's one of those things they've erected . . . A bunch of nonsense . . . What's important is why they did it."
                    MARILYN FRENCH, *The Women's Room*

The reduction of love to sex consists of a serious misunderstanding of both love and sex, but this is not the only source of cynicism. A much more powerful diagnosis is to be found in a certain set of feminist[1] arguments against romantic love, in essence, that romantic love is a *political* invention rather than a matter of economy, a question of power rather than the distribution of a commodity. Love, in short, is a male strategy for "keeping women in their place." It does this by assigning the female an emotional role, a role of submissiveness and dedicated passivity, which is then in turn justified by the tremendous importance of the emotion itself.

Until very recently the majority of writing about love and women was provided by men, who promised that love would make a woman happy, fulfilled and truly a *woman*. In fact men's enthusiasm about love tends to remain largely their own. (A recent study by the social psychologist Kephart revealed that sixty-five per cent of the men insisted they would not marry a person they did not love; seventy-two per cent of the women said they "weren't sure.") When psychiatrists talk about "the need to love," they inevitably end up defending— sometimes explicitly—a mode of behavior which is visibly disadvantageous for a woman, in which "femininity" or romantic attractiveness is in direct conflict with her career (unless her career itself happens to be romantic attractiveness). Thus love, so the argument goes, is a culturally created emotion, not a real need at all. It has been invented by men whose purpose is political superiority, as a way of keeping women isolated and at home, content (or feeling that they should be) with love alone, competitive with one another but out of the competition for social status and power, which is by default left to men alone.

Now, first of all, it is entirely correct to say that love is a culturally created emotion, not a natural need. Second, it cannot be denied that romantic love has indeed been used in precisely

[1] I do not want to give the impression that I think there is a single view of some single group called "the feminists." What concerns me here is a specific argument, which has many variations.

this mollifying way, to console women for their lack of power under the false guise of "what a woman needs to fulfill her." But the question concerning love as such is the question whether love itself is *nothing but* this political strategy, whether love is just a male conception, and whether the romantic roles which have been traditionally carved out for women are in fact essential to romantic love. Furthermore, even while one can agree that there is more than a small amount of flimflam in the intentional obfuscation of the everyday concept of love by male writers from Plato to Rollo May, it does not follow that love itself is an illusion, a "myth," a *man*-made concept which has been purposely obscured in order to hide the abuses it makes possible.

The problem appears most dramatically in a double bind which has been described by a great many women authors, from Virginia Woolf to Marilyn French. One has the intelligence and the political savvy to see through the myth of romantic love, but still carries the desperate feeling that one cannot live without it. Thus Val at the end of *The Women's Room* feels caught between a need she cannot deny and a cynicism she cannot reject. Doris Lessing, no friend of this passion either, catches her characters in the bind between needing love "and all that," on the one hand, and being destroyed by it. Ti-Grace Atkinson calls love "a pathological condition," and Shulamith Firestone, several years ago, argued most systematically that love is a male invention, based on the traditional division between the sexes but now an artificially enforced sense of *need* that no longer has any relationship to real biological needs at all. And yet, through all of her cynicism, she clings to love's ideal, wishfully.

Feminism, unlike cynicism in general, deserves a detailed answer to its charges; what we shall have to show is that the structures of love are not based on the power differences between male and female by way of dominance and submissiveness, and that, more generally, love has a set of defensible structures which are not mere "myth" or illusion. But this, of course, presupposes an over-all theory of love. Then, perhaps, we can show how it is that romantic love and feminism need not be antagonistic but, quite the contrary, mutually support and reinforce one another.

But for now, one point only ought to be made, which is why I want to at least introduce this feminist position under the rubric of "cynicism." The point is that a great many of the women who write about and find themselves in the double bind between needing love and despising love do exactly what their male cynical counterparts have done: accept what can indeed be called the "myth" and illusions of romantic love—derived from Platonism—as the "ideal" of love, and then bemoan the fact that what we actually experience as "love" falls so far short of that ideal. To the illusion comes the disillusionment. Thus one very recent feminist, Jill Tweedie, begins her diatribe against love:

> We die of love and die without it, our hearts beat for it and break for it. Love built the Taj Mahal, wrote the Song of Solomon and cooks a billion meals every day, across the world. Love is the only thing that matters, after all. . . . Or so they say. And in my opinion what they say, give or take an epigram or two, is rubbish. Take off the rose-colored glasses and what does a close examination of the facts reveal to the naked eye? That love, true love, is the rarest of all emotions and one that has been conspicuous by its absence ever since mankind dropped from the trees. . . .[2]

But perhaps one can reject the ideal as an illusion without thereby concluding either that we have failed to achieve it (if it is an illusion) or concluding that love itself is an illusion. Perhaps, indeed, that much more ordinary set of emotions that we

[2] *In the Name of Love* (Pantheon, 1979).

do, sometimes, feel for each other should be appreciated for what they are, and for no more, and as nothing less.

Looking back at the twentieth century, historians, if there are any, will no doubt be impressed by the invention of the airplane, nuclear weapons, the electric guitar and frozen foods; but the great revolution in our lives, wrought by simple technology, more significant even than pocket computers and excursion fares to the Orient, are the parasexual discoveries of the mid-century—effective birth control and penicillin. Already we children of the second half of the century take these utterly for granted and, with them, sex without terror, not "free love" but at least sex free from fear. Gone with a shot or a daily swallow is the biblical vengeance of unwanted pregnancy and venereal wrath. Gone too is "the fallen woman," the ruined life, the shotgun marriage, the Errol Flynn and Charlie Chaplin paternity suits. It is difficult for us to remember—or even imagine—what it once was like, to have sex so inescapably bound up with such threats and hazards, to feel so threatened and inhibited that any amount of sexual frustration was endurable given the risks and alternatives. And we might well understand how in such circumstances love could be confused with sexual frustration, or at least how difficult it might have been to tell them apart. Thus the desperate metaphysics of Platonism—in order to pry them apart. And thus the sneering revelations of cynicism, putting them together once again. But the cynic has been refuted by the times and, along with the cynic, the Platonist. For what is crystal clear is that the so-called "sexual revolution" and the new freedom of sex have not put an end to our sense of romance; on the contrary, they have made it possible, by purifying our motives, by eliminating fear and, as some of the feminists have aptly stated it, "by liberating us from our biology." Love has been freed, not left behind, and despite the predictable desperation of parents, preachers and Platonists, love can at last be seen and appreciated for what it is, distinguished quite clearly from mere lust: an ordinary emotion with a complex structure which plays an extraordinary role in our society. What we now have to do is to understand this emotion, without piety, without cynicism, without moralizing, without metaphors. And so, naturally, we turn to "objective" science for some unemotional understanding. What do the scientists tell us?

# HOW DO I LOVE THEE? LET ME MEASURE SOMETHING 9
## (LOVE AND SOCIAL PSYCHOLOGISTS)

*Like Leporello, learned men keep a list, but the point is what they lack; while Don Juan seduces girls and enjoys himself—Leporello notes down the time, the place and the description of the girl.*

KIERKEGAARD, *Journals* (1834)

Within the last twenty years an academic industry has emerged, the measurement of love. Not surprisingly, it has attracted its detractors, including the Golden Fleece and research-minded William Proxmire, who lambasted the National Science Foundation, fuming, "No one can argue that falling in love is a science. . . . The impact of love . . . is a very subjective, nonquantifiable subject matter. Love is simply a mystery." The senator's lament is echoed by many people today, though without the power to withhold funding, on the grounds that love can't be studied "objectively," that love is "subjective," "ineffable" and a "mystery." That is, there is nothing that can be said about it.

Now that would be surprising if it were true, given the millions of words, many of them insightful, most of them at least

relevant, that have been said about it. To say that love is
"ineffable" or a "mystery" is a dangerous bit of nonsense. But
this leaves open the question whether love can be studied "objectively" and what is meant by "science." Two researchers in
particular, Elaine Walster (University of Wisconsin) and Ellen
Berscheid (University of Minnesota), who have published extensively on the topic, rightly comment:

> It is odd that the notion that attraction, particularly
> such intense forms as romantic love, are simply "non-
> quantifiable" has lingered to the present day. It seems es-
> pecially strange when we consider that each of us, every
> day and in a variety of ways, manages to quantify our at-
> traction to others and measure their attraction for us.
>
> *Interpersonal Attraction*, p. 5

Of course, many of these "ways" are highly untrustworthy—for
example, "I love you more than I've ever loved anyone." But
the point is well taken. The problem is, what to measure? How
does one measure an emotion? And here the layman's com-
plaint begins to develop some teeth. Even if love is not a mystery and not immeasurable, it does not follow that what psychologists measure is love. And though we should applaud the
attempt to deflate the bloated romanticism of the humanists
with some hard-nosed research into what exactly *is* this thing
called "love," we have to be very careful that, in trying to find
something to measure "objectively," we don't measure something else instead, and miss the content of the emotion altogether.

There is nothing wrong with science or "objectivity" in the
realm of emotions; in fact, some of the emotions themselves
(for example, "the love of knowledge") are inseparable from
the goals and structures of scientific, "objective" and even impersonal discipline. But there is more than room for suspicion
when, in the name of this same impersonality, a researcher
(who presumably has been in love) mentions not a word of her
own experience but instead feels compelled by her discipline

to lure a hundred unsuspecting freshmen and sophomores into a superficial setting in which their barely articulate verbal responses to a contrived and in any case shortsighted set of questions are to count as the "data." For instance, a popular professional ploy called "semantic differential" involves an enormously sophisticated statistical technique to measure what students think they mean by the words they frequently abuse; for example, ask them what they mean by "love." But wouldn't we be better served if the theorist—who takes some care in analysis and in any case has to stand by the results—simply tried to say what he or she means by these words? In what other context do we trust undergraduates—*en masse*—to do our research for us?

Meg Greenfield of the Washington *Post* and *Newsweek* recently assaulted "our statistical society." She wrote:

> My theory is that we are the most weighed, counted, measured and analyzed society in the history of civilization; that most of our political fights concern who gets to do the weighing and counting (Keeper of the Data is our Keeper of the Flame), and that as a consequence of this obsession we have begun to talk about ourselves as if we were someone else [*Newsweek*, September 10, 1979].

And, indeed, to analyze love, scientifically or poetically, on the sole basis of *other* people's experience should strike us as odd, to say the least. The problem, in other words, is not the use of science but a certain emasculation of science, an absurd set of restrictions on what can be considered, and considered seriously, and what cannot. Indeed, when the word "science" (*Wissenschaft*) came into common usage, only two centuries ago, it was an explicit appeal to the totality of one's own, carefully analyzed experience; the word "empirical," which today is used to eliminate the observer from the observed, originally meant precisely the appeal to what one did him/herself experience (in the work of philosopher John Locke, for example).

Two thousand years ago Ovid wrote his great observational treatise on love (*De Amore*), something in the style of sociologist Erving Goffman today, sitting on the sidelines, participating on occasion, taking notes. It is now increasingly apparent—in physics as well as psychology—that observer and participant are not separable roles, so the idea of a "participant observer" is no longer suspicious. But then, why not *begin* with the recognition of the psychologist's own familiarity with the subject? (It's bound to sneak in somewhere anyway.)

Ovid observed and participated and offered up what has endured as the classic seduction manual of Western literature, far closer to the nitty gritty of love than Plato's effete and sexless *Symposium*. He observed, for example, that an excellent way to woo a lady was to arouse her at the gladiatorial arena, since the emotion inspired by the various disembowelments and dismemberments below could easily be transformed into emotions of a very different type, a theory-laden bit of observation which has found its way into some of the most modern scientific theories of emotion, to be disemboweled shortly. But it is significant that Ovid has become a perennial starting point for today's social scientists interested in love, not so much for his observational hypothesis, but as an excuse to lament the fact that he was not a disciplined observer; for instance, he conducted no formal surveys (though no doubt he talked quite a bit with his friends). He set up no controlled experiments of his own, in which "controlled" may mean that the normal parameters and conditions of emotion are eliminated and replaced by a wholly artificial set of circumstances in which normal emotional response may be inappropriate.

Ovid was not a scientist.[1] We have no idea what measurement he used for "arousal," except for his own observation that

[1] Zick Rubin, for example, dismisses Ovid because "his recommendation was based on personal observation and experience—or, perhaps what we would call common sense—rather than any underlying scientific principle," *Liking and Loving* (Holt, Rinehart and Winston, 1973).

many if not most of the ladies so suitably aroused did indeed have sex with their arousers. (The modern university measure seems to be "accepting dates"—not quite the same.) But how many, what percentage, what is the likelihood of error in these observations? Could the same experiment have been repeated in Attica, where the gladiatorial events more often included wild animals? And what was the control group? Only those women who were seduced without the inspiration of the arena, and this was, even in Ovid's own experience, a most indefinite and ill-defined group, as were the conditions for their arousal. Ovid, in other words, "never transcended his own limited, personal experience."

A few years ago the social psychologist Robert Zajonc announced to his colleagues that "more than 90% of all social psychological research has been conducted during the last twenty years, and most of it during the last ten," thus dismissing Ovid and a thousand other Goffmans of all ages, simply out of hand.[2] Augustine's candid and sometimes pathetic descriptions of his own "impulses" obviously don't count, nor does Aristotle's remarkably insightful analysis of the social passions in his *Rhetoric* and *Ethics*. Shakespeare just didn't know how to quantify, nor did Elizabeth Browning, who suggested she count the ways, but then didn't. ("Factor analysis" is a relatively new invention.) What is now called social psychology, however, is among the *oldest* of the sciences (depending on how you measure). People have always been fascinated by people, and as a matter of necessity. One has to know at a glance whether the stranger outside your cave really just wants a bite of mastodon or has his eye on your dog or daughter. Mothers have long cultivated the art of sizing up a suitor by the way he stands, walks, looks. It was not just the art of seduction that inspired our ancestors to observe and manipulate the circumstances conducive to emotions of all kinds, but also the

[2] *Social Psychology* (Wadsworth, 1966), p. 3.

need to inspire fear in enemies, loyalty in the troops and faith in the congregation. Zick Rubin is right, perhaps, when he says his psychological colleagues have arrived "late in the party," when much of the work is already done. Indeed, as philosopher Frithjof Bergmann has argued, the problem with the social sciences is the fact that we already know *so much*. And that is all the more reason why a psychologist has to start from experience, not the pose of objectivity and personal indifference. Social psychology is nothing less than the sum total of the whole of our social experience—and the place to start looking for it (but not, by any means, the end of the search) is in our own so-called "personal" experience, which is nothing less in turn than the collective wisdom and foolishness of a generation or an entire culture. And it is here that we can understand how social psychologists do indeed contribute valuable insights and —even more important—new questions to our thinking and feelings about love. But it is a continuity with common sense, not a rejection or suspension of it, that makes this possible.

When an experiment is an extension of a real-life problem that already imposes itself upon us, results tend to be interesting, even fascinating, and hypotheses to explain them much in demand. Eliot Arenson (1969) begins to explain the diminution of love in terms of the increasingly predictable and so less supportive approval of a lover over the years, while the random approval of a complete stranger thereby takes on inordinate attractiveness ("Arenson's Law of Marital Infidelity"). But the findings and the theory wouldn't have much import if we weren't already concerned with the problem of love's fading and wondering how, if possible, to keep it alive. Experimental psychologists Jecker and Dandy (1969) have shown that benefactors come to love those on whom they have *bestowed* favors. (We usually assume that we love because we are bestowed upon.) Think of this next time you consider giving a dozen long-stemmed roses to your lover, not only in order to express your feelings but to intensify them. And this has implications too about the wisdom of turning down a gift, wrongly thinking that your humility will serve you well. Social psychologist Kephart (1961) provides us with a corrective to our romantic wanderlust: "Cherished notions about romantic love notwithstanding, it appears that when all is said and done, the 'one and only' may have a better than 50-50 chance of living within walking distance." This is the same theorist who more recently (1967) provided us with the survey asking students if they would marry someone they didn't love "if they had all the other qualities you desired"; few said yes, perhaps, but far more men than women said no, indicating the truth of what many of the feminists have argued—that romantic love is more a male than a female fantasy and men are more "romantic" than women. Social psychologist Heider (1958) has shown that people in love will believe almost anything to keep a relationship together ("to make the sentiment relationship harmonious with the unit relationship") and a large number of theorists have argued, with contradictory conclusions, the relationships between "falling in love" and self-esteem (Chapters 12, 23). The experiments are varied and sometimes ingenious, but the point to be made is that the above results are revealing only in so far as they continue and utilize our "pre-scientific" conceptions of love. On the other hand, ignoring or suspending those pre-scientific conceptions leads all too easily to results which do indeed earn the public abuse of the Proxmires of the world, such as: (1) people in love tend to think more highly of one another (Thurstone, 1928); (2) people in love tend to sit closer to one another (Byrne, Ervin and Lambreth, 1970); (3) people in love tend to do favors for one another (Bramel, 1969; "If we truly like someone, it pleases us to see him happy and it hurts us to see him suffer"); (4) people in love tend to make more eye contact than people who are not in love (Argyle, 1967; Rubin, 1970). Indeed, Zick Rubin has publicly bemoaned the unsympathetic treatment he has received from the press on his research on love (*Psychology Today*, January

1980). But the question he did not reply to—and the question that a critic from the outside can't help asking—is *why* an experiment measuring the amount of eye contact between lovers should even be necessary. Consider this:

*We were sitting in a small Italian restaurant on Beach Street when it struck me what was wrong. Tonight, all evening in fact, you've been staring at your soup, watching your wine, looking askance at the table next to us. Even when you talk to me, your eyes are on the door, flitting to the waiter to your wine to my eyebrows, then down to the silverware. I even said to you, "I miss your eyes," and you glanced down painfully, gave a little smile, looked at me, and I knew it was over. You looked away; I cried, "Why won't you look at me?" You said, "I am," and there was nothing else to say.*

There is nothing more to understand here, certainly no empirical question mark about its meaning. But here we hit the crux of the problem, which is not merely that such "findings" seek only to confirm the obvious, but rather that they take as an empirical question what is actually part of the essential structure of the phenomenon. The distinction between "empirical" and "essential" is not absolute, perhaps, but in any given domain of inquiry, the topic itself has its limits and its defining characteristics *within* which one asks more or less probing questions about its details. But to think of reciprocal attention and mutual looking as part of the detail of love, instead of its very essence, is to betray a preference for the empirical which looks suspiciously more like an antipathy to theory, an evasion of the hard work of science, which is not measurement but thinking.

One much-maligned symptom of the unnecessary isolation and anti-common-sense attitude of this self-consciously scientific discipline is its vocabulary. Is "companionate love" really "more precise" than "friendship"? Is "dyatic attraction" really less prone to misunderstanding than "How two people feel about each other"? Is "behavioral reinforcement" really easier to measure than "What are you getting out of this anyway"? Is the definition of "love" as "a state of intense absorption in another" any less metaphorical than a well-wrought line from Shakespeare's sonnets? Indeed, is this definition even plausible—as a characterization of what we ordinary folk mean by "love"? And if it is not intended to be that, but only a technical term for a measurable operation performed only by psychologists, why name it "love" at all? Again, the problem is a forced discontinuity with our personal experience and our way of talking about it.

There is, however, a powerful argument to the contrary. It is that our "common sense" conception of love is confused and that anything one says about love is just as likely to be correct as anything else. For example, we all know that "absence makes the heart grow fonder," but isn't "out of sight, out of mind" also true? So much for common sense, so the argument goes, and what we need is a carefully calculated experiment that will prove, once and for all, which of these common-sense platitudes is true and which is false. Indeed, some recent experiments throw fascinating light on this particular question, that is, that the first is true for men, the second more for women. But the place of experiment and the futility of common sense needs further argument, for the problem with these common-sense platitudes is rather that they are wrenched from context, namely, the context which picks out the appropriate guideline when we actually *use* these bits of ancient wisdom (deciding whether or not to accept a job away from home for a while, for example). But of course we can be wrong, and the experiment in question shows us one way we can be wrong. But what the attack on "the obvious" tends to prove is not the singular necessity of an experiment but the all-important role of *context* in developing any psychological knowledge. Psychology, like physics, begins not with a cosmic hypothesis but with a local and specific observation, a query, a question in context. But in psychology, unlike physics, that context is likely to be embarrassingly personal; to remove that personal context, rather than try to refine it, is not then to become "scientific" or "objective" but rather to give up the "data" (the given) with which any hypothesis must begin.

It is the question of context that raises the question I have not yet mentioned at all, namely, what kind of a view of emotions, what conception of love, do such theories tend to presuppose? Because they reject the legitimacy of personal experience, many experimenters thereby restrict themselves to "publicly observable (and measurable) phenomena." This includes physiological changes in the body, circumstantial stimuli, various bits of behavior (including first-person reports from other people) and, perhaps, a complex of biological, environmental, evolutionary and sociological variables.

The dominant model of the emotions in some psychological circles today was propounded by Stanley Schachter of Columbia University nearly twenty years ago. It is worth examining in some detail, because in it the necessity for a more personal and more experience-oriented ("phenomenological") theory of emotions becomes apparent. The theory begins with the often demonstrated defects of an illustrious theory developed simultaneously by William James in America and C. G. Lange in Denmark, just at the turn of the twentieth century. James and Lange argued that an emotion is a visceral reaction or, more accurately, our conscious perception of a visceral reaction. (See Chapter 5.) The problem was, this provided no mechanism whatever to distinguish between the various emotions, many of which have identical physiological components. Furthermore, it is possible to have the appropriate visceral reactions without having any emotion at all—immediately after being startled, for example, or when one has a fever or has been given a shot of adrenalin. So the question is, what makes a physiological reaction an emotion? And what determines what emotion it is?

It is here that Schachter, in a classic paper with Singer in 1962, advances his theory: an emotion has *two* components, both publicly observable (thus he discounts the "feelings" of his subjects in favor of their physiology) and both measurable. First is the physiological reaction itself, which can be measured by the amount of epinephrine or whatever else has been injected into the poor undergraduate subject. Second, as a solution to James's and Lange's deficiencies and as an answer to both of our questions above, there is the *"labeling"* of the emotion. In other words, what the subject *names* it.

Now this does indeed resolve James's deficiency, but only at the cost of an outrageous trivialization of the problem. Love is indeed distinguished from other emotions and mere physiological reactions by its correctly being called "love," but what, we have to ask, makes the label "correct"? Consider this: I am walking through the woods when a bear lumbers out from behind a rock: I see the bear, I have a rush of adrenalin. I have an emotion, presumably fear. The example is James's, and against him, one might ask, "How do you know that you were afraid of the bear? Perhaps you have just fallen in love?" James, to take care of this apparently absurd question, appeals to subsequent behavior, which does indeed make a difference but fits in quite badly with his theory. Schachter, on the other hand, solves the problem by insisting that the label one applies to one's emotion must be "appropriate" to the circumstances. Thus it is the circumstances, no longer what we would call the emotion, that provide the criterion for labeling. Thus we find ourselves in a theoretical dilemma: either our theory of emotions now becomes a semantic theory about the appropriateness of applying certain words in certain circumstances, *whatever I actually feel,* or else we fall back to the Jamesian physiological theory without any adequate way of distinguishing one emotion from another. But in either case what drops out is the emotion itself, the emotional experience. For whether or not the physiological reactions are similar to various emotions, our experience of different emotions is decidedly different. Moreover, as some of Schachter's disciples have repeatedly pointed out,[3] we are often prone to "inappropriately label" our emotions, especially love. But how can a label be "inappropriate" to the emotion if the emotion itself is not the criterion for its own identity? And, indeed, are not our emotions themselves often "inappropriate,"—love again in particular—out of context, out of character? Circumstances surely do not make the difference; it is flatly absurd to suggest that I can only love a person who is standing right in front of me (as a "stimulus") and to expand "circumstance" to include the whole of one's life loses all specificity. Indeed, I sometimes love most precisely when I am in wholly irrelevant circumstances, not at all aroused or otherwise physiologically excited, and indeed, not at all prone to—perhaps even resistant to—the labeling of my emotion as "love."

The various problems in Schachter's model which I have here only suggested can be reduced to the counterclaim that *neither* of the components in his "two-component theory of emotions" is either necessary or sufficient for emotion. The idea that not only romantic love but moral indignation, nagging jealousy, political resentment, religious devotion, morbid grief and Kierkegaardian dread are no more than adrenalin plus a word is so contrary to our emotional experience—so neglectful of our emotional experience—that one can only look for an explanation of its prominence within the parameters of social psychology itself. There is nothing in the "data" or even in Schachter's ingenious experiments that would suggest this emasculated view of emotions, *sans* experience. It is rather the requirement that a "scientific" view of emotions cannot begin

[3] For example, Elaine Walster and Ellen Berscheid, *Interpersonal Attraction* (Addison Wesley, 1969).

with—cannot even include—the description of emotional experience. And so it falsely concludes that the emotion is something else—the physiological cause and accompaniment of the emotion, plus its name in a particular society. Does that mean one could not have an emotion he or she could not name? Or that what we naïvely refer to as "the same emotion" in different linguistic groups (say, English- and French-speaking Québecois) are rather two emotions, perhaps as different as joy and jealousy, which indeed also differ—according to this theory—only according to their names? An emotion is neither a visceral reaction nor a name; it is an experience. And anything else, no matter what theoretical attractiveness it may yield, simply is not an emotion.

The romantic consequences of the Schachter theory have been spelled out laboriously by Elaine Walster and Ellen Berscheid. They have hypothesized, in a wide range of well-known essays and books, that the most widely praised of all of our emotions is nothing more than the label "love," applied (by whom, in what culture and context—and why?) to the physiological feelings of "sexual arousal, companionship and shared enjoyment."[4] The initial plausibility of the James-Schachter-type theories for fear and anger—where a visceral or "gut" reaction is typical of the emotional experience—is not in evidence here. What are the typical physiological feelings of companionship? Or shared enjoyment? Is sexual arousal *love*—if only one chooses to call it that? Indeed, that ploy has temporarily soothed the conscience of many a virgin, but the transparency of the ploy is exactly why we know to distinguish sexual arousal from the emotions which may—or may not—go along with it. Even passionate romantic love need not be characterized in terms of its enduring physiological symptoms, particularly when it goes on for months or years, and we will all

[4] Op. cit.

too readily admit that it is at least possible to love someone for quite some time and never be tempted to "label" it love. Yet indeed, constrained by the limited parameters of their theory, these authors argue this position to its absurd conclusion. Elaine Walster, for example:

> To love passionately a person must first be physically aroused, a condition manifested by palpitations of the heart, nervous tremor, flushing and accelerated breathing.
> Once he is so aroused, all that remains [!!] is for him [sic] to identify this complex of feelings as passionate love, and he will have experienced *authentic* love. [!!!] Even if the initial arousal is the result of an irrelevant experience that usually would produce anger, or even if it is induced in a laboratory by an injection of adrenalin, once the subject has met the person and identified the experience as love, it is love.[5]

"All that remains"!? "Authentic love"!? And "even if [the experience] is irrelevant"!? Has ever a theory produced counter-examples more fatal to itself? Indeed, in another article, Walster has argued that jealousy too is arousal *cum* label, and after some sensitive prefatory remarks proceeds with a similar conclusion—that we could eliminate jealousy if we could just get people to call it something else (sort of like eliminating crime in New York by repealing the criminal code).[6] It is as if the experience of jealousy—like the experience of love—does not count at all. I imagined a scene (The University of Verona, Psychology Department):

[5] From E. Berscheid and E. Walster, "Adrenalin Makes the Heart Grow Fonder," *Psychology Today* (1971, 5 (1) p. 47), though a virtually identical passage can be found in Walster's more professional essay "Passionate Love" in Murstein, ed. *Theories of Attraction and Love* (Springer, 1971). Expletives in brackets are my own.

[6] "Jealousy," in Gordon Clanton and Lynn G. Smith, *Jealousy* (Prentice-Hall, 1969).

ROMEO: But soft! What light through yonder doorway breaks? It is my social psychology 261b professor! O, it is my love! O, that she knew she were!
She speaks.

JULIET: Damn it.

ROMEO: O, speak again, bright angel, for thou art
As glorious to this afternoon
As a winged messenger of Heaven.

JULIET: Romeo? Romeo Montague? Wherefore art thou?

ROMEO: [*To himself*] Shall I hear more, or shall I speak at this?

JULIET: What manner of student art thou, bescreened in the dark of the hallway, so stumblest in on my office hour?

ROMEO: O, I love thee, Professor Capulet!

JULIET: How camest thou hither?

ROMEO: Down the hall, past the chairman's office, led by love, that first did prompt me to inquire.
He lent me counsel, and I lent him eyes.

JULIET: What is love? [*Sighs*]
Love is a smoke raised with the fume of sighs,
Being purged, a fire sparkling in the eyes,
Being vexed, a sea nourished with tears.
And what else?
But just a word, and nought else besides.

ROMEO: 'Tis true, I feel a fire, and my heart
poundeth in my bosom; I am sweating profusely
and I am nervous as a laboratory rat. But 'tis
the circumstances and the uncertainty.
Dost thou love me? I must know, or I'll frown and
be perverse, and most likely flunk thy course.

JULIET: What's in a name? That which we call love,
by any other name would be something else.
Without that label, Love, doff thy name,
For thou art not.

ROMEO: I know not how to tell thee what I feel,

Except by its name, 'tis true.

JULIET: But 'tis hardly appropriate, for thou knowest me not.

ROMEO: I've taken thine every course, and I've loved thee for three semesters.

JULIET: And thou hast been in such a state all the while? Thou must be exhausted.

ROMEO: My present anguish is my fear that thou mayest lower my grade, for surely I am none so wrought elsewhile.

JULIET: Perhaps then thou despiseth me; that would be more appropriate, but the same feeling as well.

ROMEO: Of course it's inappropriate, that's why I feel thus, but it's love. I beseech you, tell me, tell me.

JULIET: Dost thou love me? I know thou wilt say "Ay"
And I will take thee at thy word,
For that would be but a self-fulfilling prophecy,
Since thou art obviously aroused.

ROMEO: O wilt thou leave me so unsatisfied?

JULIET: What satisfaction canst thou have from me, this afternoon?

ROMEO: The exchange of thy love's faithful vow for mine.

JULIET: Indeed I am blushing.

ROMEO: Then call it love, before thou calmeth down.

JULIET: I have no joy in this contact,
It is too rash, too unadvised, too sudden
And inappropriate.
Next time, let's meet for dinner, with flowers and candles.

ROMEO: Swear by the blessed moon that thou will.

JULIET: Indeed, I feel a madness most indiscreet,
A choking gall and persevering sweet.
I'll not swear by the moon, so inconstant,
like my visceral disturbances,
Hark, I hear a noise within.

ROMEO: 'Tis thy belly churning, I heard it myself from here.

JULIET: But how do I know that it's thou, Romeo?

ROMEO: It matters not, by thine own theory. But label it "love," and all is well.

JULIET: Three little words, dear Romeo, and it will be a good night indeed.
If the bent of thy love be honorable,
Send me the words tomorrow.

ROMEO: I will not fail. 'Tis twenty year till then, but do bring some epinephrine to once again assure thy blush.

JULIET: Yet I could kill you with so much passion. But good day, good Romeo, parting while blushing is such sweet sorrow That I shall say good day till it be morrow.

[*Exit*]

ROMEO: Hence will I to my chemistry professor's close cell,
His help to crave and my good fortune to tell.
And to keep myself aroused till tomorrow.

[*Exit*]

Tolstoy once said, what is undoubtedly untrue, that all happy families are the same, but every unhappy family is different. But when it came to understanding human relationships, whether the tragically unhappy marriage of Anna K. or the banal bliss of Pierre and Natasha, he knew that the studies he presented in such artful detail were both faithful to the experience of millions of readers too. No survey of separated couples in the Ukraine would ever add up to the essential insights of *Anna Karenina,* and no Pavlovian experiment with the undergraduates at Moscow U. could display the structures and complexities of love so well as the simple character of Natasha. The idea that a "controlled" experiment with 123 strangers is more revealing and more "objective" than the description of one's own experience is a view that has nothing to do with science or objectivity; it was by projecting the daily experience of gravity to the Heavens, not by ignoring it, that Isaac Newton succeeded, where centuries of science had failed, in seeing the continuity between the two. And when we study emotions—they are *our* emotions after all—what we are looking for are the common structures of experience which are to be found only through the thoughtful examination of our experience. For *that* is the emotion, not its physiological accompaniment, not what we happen to call it, and not the mere circumstances of its evocation. To quote Meg Greenfield once again, "It is a very insecure society that won't credit its own experience." Or, more scathingly, Margaret Atwood writes,

> I approach this love
> like a biologist
> putting on my rubber
> gloves and white lab coat.
>
> . . .
>
> You asked for love.
> I gave you only descriptions.
> MARGARET ATWOOD, *Power Politics*
> (New York: Harper & Row, 1973)

# WHAT DO I WANT WHEN I WANT YOU? AN INTRODUCTION TO (TWO) METAPHYSICS

## 10

*The intense yearning which each has towards the other does not appear to be the desire of intercourse, but of something else which the soul desires and cannot tell, and of which she has only a dark and doubtful presentiment.*

Aristophanes in PLATO, *Symposium*

What do I want when I want you? There is a familiar adolescent, primarily male experience—no doubt some Freudians feel it too—which provides the most misleading answer to this seemingly simple question. The experience consists, first of all, in a ravenous desire, usually but not always explicitly sexual and obsessive, which is frustrated for one reason or another and whose result is a sense of urgency bordering on insanity. The troubadours did it to themselves; teenagers in the 1950s had it imposed upon them. (It may now be an experience whose frequency is on the wane.) Anyway, some horny Romeo exclaims his passion as nothing less than undying love, thus effectively overcoming the resistance of his rightly suspicious but much-flattered Juliet. She yields, perhaps because of her naïve belief that an emotion so intense could not possibly be other than what it seems to be.

We know the sad end of this little story. Perhaps immediately, in any case soon, our Romeo becomes indifferent, even cruel. Perhaps he is still possessive, but now out of pride rather than affection. He wonders what he was so excited about; she concludes that he never really wanted anything but "a good lay," as she puts it, with intentional crudity (and a bit of flattery for herself). The impression is often indelible on women, but seemingly even more so on some theorists about love. It is as if the "intense yearning" of love were nothing more than sexual desire, whipped to a frenzy, the love itself an illusion and the yearning wholly satisfied by sexual consummation. It is a shoddy view of love, and a pathetic one. Aristophanes, in any case, was not so easily fooled. He knew that the yearning of love was for something much more, and that the answer to the question, "What do I want when I want you?" was far from obvious.

Of course Aristophanes knew what many "Platonic" theorists later denied, that one does indeed want intercourse, but *also* something more. As soon as we try to characterize this "something more," however, we find ourselves too easily removed from concrete sexual desire and off into the abstract realm of metaphysics, for what one wants, as Aristophanes argued so dramatically, is nothing less than an ontological miracle, the eternal reunion with one's other "original" half, the re-creation of a "natural" whole. But it would be a mistake of profound proportions—though indeed it is the dominant tendency of the whole history of Western philosophy—to think that such "yearning," or desire in general, *must* be aiming at some such final and presumably eternal goal, some state of *Being* or an absolute "union." This was Plato's idea, and one finds it again in Plotinus and the medieval philosophers and in Spinoza and even in Freud and Jean-Paul Sartre. And if this seems so, we should not be surprised to hear that the ultimate love is the love of God (or the desire to *be* God), for where else would we find absolute identity, unity and eternity, if not with Him?

But the cost of this metaphysical vision is that the emotion it-self, and the merely fleeting time one actually spends with a lover, is dismissed as insignificant, and love is said to be "true" only in so far as it *lasts,* indeed forever, as if duration, and not the passion itself, were the ultimate test.

But there is another answer to the question, "What do I want when I want you?" besides mere sex and the absolute. That answer is, "To want you." What I want when I want you is to want you—thus we are introduced to an entirely different metaphysics, in which states and eternity and even satisfaction are no more than illusions, and in which desire is not a tempo-rary deficiency seeking to be fulfilled but is itself the end of life, its very essence, and of love too. Fulfillment is just another step to further desire.

In one of the few great books of philosophy to deal with the passions at length, David Hume distinguished, in his *Treatise on Human Nature,* between the *calm* and the *violent* passions. He thought these were *types* of emotions (for example, love was a violent passion, but the love of justice a calm passion)— whereas I would argue that virtually all emotions can take ei-ther form. Love, in particular, can be either calm or violent, and one of the most frequent debates in the history of the sub-ject, between Aristophanes and Socrates, for example, is which of the two is more "true." A calm passion is no less a passion, however, and a violent passion, no matter how out of propor-tion, is not thereby "false." But we can see in Hume's distinc-tion something more than a recognition of the various inten-sities and durabilities of the emotions; it is also the key to two very different visions of the cosmos, in which all talk of love inevitably participates. My purpose in this chapter is to make these clear, as well as to indicate my own metaphysical bias.

Ever since ancient times, before the first philosophers were crawling over the craggy peaks of Asia Minor, our dominant view of the world, the cosmos and ourselves, has been a wishful, *static* metaphysics, built upon the concept of *reality*, which boils down quickly to a series of tautologies, such as "Everything is what it is," and "Truth never perishes" (Seneca). However traumatically the world changes and our bodies and societies change, degenerating, finally dying, reality remains, eternally. In fact, reality was *defined* as that which does not change. Plato was the final step in a long line of thinkers who insisted that the *real* world was unchanging and eternal, a world of "Being," while changes, traumas and death were, ultimately, mere appearances. Before Plato, the philosopher Parmenides argued that reality was unknowable but nevertheless only reality, to state the obvious tautology, is real. After Plato, Christianity, imported from the Orient as much as derived from the Greeks, theologized this same metaphysics in an Eternal God and, by equating God and love, made love "real" too, but only by making it no longer a transient feeling but an eternal state. (Nietzsche: "Christianity is Platonism for the masses.")

The fear of growing old and ugly, losing one's fleeting beauty, even the fear of death, could be overcome by the knowledge that what was eternally beautiful, the invisible soul, would live forever. There was a political pay-off, too, since all souls, as opposed to minds and bodies, could be considered equal. The soul has no determinable characteristics; so too, this bloodless abstraction allowed the invention of the modern concept of "humanity," as if we were all, "deep down," metaphysically the same—whatever our culture, race or character. And so love too could be in all of us—as part of our "human nature"—whether or not we were willing to recognize that eternal verity in ourselves.

This soothing image of an unchanging reality came to define Western philosophy and religion. It continues into modern times. In chemistry, for example, the bases of nearly all theories up until this century were the various "conservation" laws, which say, in effect, that something—matter, energy, some basic particles—can be neither created nor destroyed. Something must be constant. The ancient assumption is that the "natural" state of things is equilibrium, "harmony." In Newtonian physics, an object tends to stay at rest unless pushed; it tends to move at a constant speed unless forced to slow down. It is a lazy universe. Even in Einstein, the *laws* are eternal, if nothing else is. And in high school biology we all learned the basic principle of *homeostasis*—namely, the tendency of organisms to stay in the "same state." If one is thirsty, one drinks some water; if hungry, one eats; if horny, one screws; if lonely, one loves. Freud picks up this image (he was, after all, a physician) and retains it throughout his career. He calls it his "constancy principle," and it says, in effect, that the "psychic apparatus," as he calls it, "divests itself of energy," tending to a state of rest. Excess energy, or *cathexis*, is experienced as pain, and release of energy, *catharsis*, is experienced as pleasure, and all the vicissitudes of psychoanalytic theory are descriptions of the "economics" of this apparatus, which ultimately wants to sleep. In 1927, Freud discovered the "death principle," in which the organism achieved its ultimate state of rest; this is a familiar feeling when one is very tired, perhaps, but a dubious foundation for a theory of human life.

We are afraid of death, afraid of aging, afraid of change, afraid of losing what we have. So we imagine a universe without change, an underlying state of *being*, devoid of life, perhaps, but also devoid of death and decay. Love, as an ideal, is the ultimate, eternal, harmonious state.

A recent and particularly impressive version of this cosmology has appeared in Gregory Bateson's *Mind and Nature* (Dutton, 1979), which, on the one hand, continues Bateson's well-known career as iconoclast eccentric regent at the University of California and on the other hand serves as a bridge between biology and moral philosophy. An idealist at heart, *the idea* holds center stage for him as it does for Plato. "Na-

ture thinks," he insists, and the question is, How? The answer
is cybernetics, a system of context-bound feedback and response systems, nature as fundamentally *conservative*, interrupted by aberrations and turbulence, striving to set itself back
into balance again. Like most ecologists, Bateson puts all of his
stress on this "balance," giving service to challenge and upheaval, but always putting his bets on the urge to a "steady
state." Even evolution is a search for a steadier state.

We like to think in these terms—balance, states, security, evolution, growth, peace and predictability. We praise people for
being "cool," for having an "even temperament," we encourage permanent relationships, predictable behavior, simple desires, calm passions and being "reasonable." Ideal love is love
without ripples or squalls, life without dangers, love that endures as a steady state. Plato set the tone—the ideal life is the
life of contemplation, a minimum of desires, peace of mind,
"wisdom," Nirvana. Living beyond anxiety, vanity, wrinkles
and trauma.

On this model, desire is a kind of disruption. Creativity is a
danger, or an attempted solution to a self out of equilibrium.
Emotions are superfluous, even if unavoidable, destructive interruptions of our otherwise "natural" and "rational" (orderly)
state of being. Sex, like food, drink and sleep, is a *need*, a lack,
an *excess* of libido, a *deficit* of love. (Sex *versus* ego, Freud
thought: perhaps sex *as* ego—in either case, a need, a
deficiency, a lack.) Satisfaction is a return to equilibrium, and
all is well—that is, a state of well-*being*—until desire and emotion come again. (The passive imagery is essential.) Sex is
transient tension, and romantic love, accordingly, gets clas-
sified with lust as a disruption, enjoyable, perhaps, leading
to important things sometimes, but in itself wholly intolerable,
a mere indulgence, "infatuation." We hate the thought that we
will be wanted "only skin deep," so we pride ourselves on an
invention, "deep inside," the *real* self, a soul, that won't wrin-
kle or wear out, eternally lovable. We shift the beauty that ex-

cites to something more secure, something abstract, and therefore indestructible.

Now we don't live this way, of course. Even those who sincerely believe in eternal souls and eternal love and an eternal God find themselves worrying about their fading beauty, fighting with their supposedly eternal partners, getting divorced and finding a new eternal partner, treating sex as something more than a transient need and life as more than mere vanity, despite the warnings of the eternal Church. But it is an image that we carry around with us, a tacit measurement that we use continuously. We might not believe that love is "forever," but we do say, of a glorious fling that lasted three months, "It didn't work out." What were we supposed to be working *for?* Why measure the success of a relationship by how long it lasts? (Consider, for example, someone who considered himself *really* angry only when he was angry for years.) We want a good thing to last, of course, but why build endurance into our conception of the emotion itself? Indeed, perhaps love thrives on change, occasionally even frenzy. It is revitalized, not merely punctuated, by insecurities and uncertainties. And even when love lasts a lifetime, is it ever the case that it is to be conceived as a *state*, rather than a continuous *consuming* of life and love itself?

Since and even before the ancient Greeks, too, there is a second metaphysical picture. It is most often mentioned in conjunction with the philosopher Heraclitus, a contemporary of Parmenides and also an influence on Plato. It was Heraclitus who supposedly said that you can't step in the same river twice, which led some of his critics to accuse him unfairly of bathing only once in his life. Heraclitus chose as his favorite element the vibrant dancing of fire, never at rest, consuming itself, disappearing altogether. For Heraclitus, permanence was the illusion, change or "flux" the reality. (He also believed in

an underlying order, or *Logos,* but that is not particularly
relevant here.) *States* are mere appearances, objects seem at
rest only between moves. Security is a human delusion, and
life is gluttony, power, *dissipation.* Even within the bounds of
physics and chemistry, Nobel laureate Ilya Prigogine has developed a complex theory of "dissipative structures," organ-
ized complexes that emerge from chaos, temporary exceptions
to entropy, structures that are based on change rather than
steady states. It is an idea that has its most belligerent spokes-
man in the German philosopher Friedrich Nietzsche. Life is
not a state but frenzy; desire is its substance, emotion and passion its meaning. Transient order emerges from chaos and consumes itself before coming to rest. "From desire I rush to satisfaction," writes the poet Goethe, "but from satisfaction I leap
to desire." *Dis*satisfaction is the meaning of life; satisfaction is
death. (Thus the absence of desire is quite rightly noted, by
Buddhists and by Freud, to be ontologically akin to death.)

It is sometimes said that life is a process or progress, a metaphysical view that has been argued by Hegel and Whitehead,
for example, in reaction against the more static Platonic model.
Reality is history, says Hegel, in effect, but one look at history
and we know that it is chaos, and any contemporary sopho-
more will tell you that every step in life is a step toward death
and disintegration as well. The very idea of process, or
progress, or "growth" (the modern favorite) presupposes an
underlying pattern that is static, a direction, an order, and, not
surprisingly, most "process philosophers" merge their theory
with a theodicy, with God as the underlying and again eternal
pattern (Hegel, Whitehead and Hartshorne, for example).
Thus the image of eternity reappears, with the search for security, rationality and a guaranteed order. And when we talk
about love in terms of a couple "growing" together, or an individual's "human potential," the same picture, of a pattern
which is predictable and to be "worked out," is evident.

One of our favorite metaphors, when talking about love or at least new love, is Heraclitus' "flame" imagery. Love *burns*. Love *consumes*. Fire is heat and transience; it is never the same from moment to moment. And the "hot" passions of sex are not by any means a desire for mere release, nor mere satisfaction; they are frenzied *dis*satisfaction, not just the build-up of desire for catharsis but the urge to continue, the build-up of desire for its own sake, catharsis as a respite, not the end-state. Nothing, not even chaos, can last forever, but why do we insist on limiting such metaphors to only brief or troubled love? Why not love as such?

Between the specious moment, always disappearing, and eternity, which is incomprehensible, there is a more human kind of time, defined by *engagement*, by desire and its projection, time defined by enthusiasm rather than time measured by watching the clock. ("Do you realize we've been here for over five hours?") It is oblivious to time; and it is wholly absorbed *in* time. "A moment feels like eternity." But what does this mean except that those too static concepts of steady-state time have broken down, collapsed indifferently into their opposites, become utterly meaningless and irrelevant to us.

In life and in love, "eternity" is an empty word, a philosopher's fantasy, a daydream for the desperately dissatisfied. It is no part of experience but rather, in its lack of content, the desire for an end to experience, an end to passion, which is inescapably caught up in time. Love is not a state, but a set of erratic movements. True love is not "forever," but rather perpetually out of equilibrium, slightly off balance, oblivious to questions of eternity, however desperately it seeks to continue. It can last indefinitely, but not forever. It looks forward, but only to the concrete future, the next moment, the next time we're together, a trip in the future, perhaps even parenthood or old age together—but always in the form of the specific, never the abstractions of mere endurance. Love can be calm, of course, but it is every instant aware of its own contingency; it thrives on violence and change, even though it may not wel-

come them. It can be confident, but it is the confidence of a
race-car driver, with that fateful sense of skilled but tentative
control that feels itself skimming along the track as if over
solid ice. It is that sense of movement, fraught with dangers,
and here even Aristophanes transcends his own story, for he
too sees that there is never a return to one's "original state"—
which is only a fiction—but always the perpetual effort, the
struggle, the "desperate yearning" that never ceases.

Can such love continue? That, of course, is the crucial question. But the point is not to confuse the desire that it will continue with the Platonic wish for eternity, and not to confuse
the confidence that comes with continued love for the calm
taken-for-granted security that comes with comfortable and
accustomed indifference, which often goes under the same
name. On the other hand, it is equally essential not to confuse
the repetitive newness of several affairs for the rekindling of
passion either, for if love is a *becoming*, however erratic and
without direction, then it cannot be mere repetition and the
uncertainty of random encounters.

I have an old and very dear friend. She leaps from one impossible love to another, each more desperate than the last. "I
can't live this way," she complains every time, but she loves it.
She's radiant. She works hard. She suffers. She walks with an
arrogant confidence. She is—but certainly don't tell her so—
happy. She is thriving, living. But in between, which seems
like forever, she's bitter, cynical, lonely, *bored*. God forbid she
should live "happily ever after." She would be miserable.

Now this second metaphysics isn't "real" either; it is hard to
imagine what it would be like to live constantly "on the edge"
without some fiber of security to hold us together. Today, both
Romeo and Juliet probably have nine-to-five jobs and careers
to pursue. Even the most "romantic" relationships have to face
those thousands of small decisions—which restaurant, "your

place or mine"—and all of those emergencies that emerge with time—the car won't start, a sudden bout of nausea, losing the contraceptives, a friend who calls in need in the middle of the night. Eventually, these do threaten love, which thrives not only on a reckless irresponsibility but also the absence of external distractions. But if *we* are responsible and involved in the world at large, it does not follow that our love is, and if *we* tend still to be caught up in the Platonic imagery of states and eternity, our love is not, for within that small world *a deux*, we know that it is the contingency of love, the fact that it has no guarantees, that defines what we want so much to continue.

What does it mean to be in love? Or, for that matter, to "fall in love"? "To be" seems to be a state, "to fall" appears to be suffering a movement, unexpected, out of control, even unwelcome. But if both of these images seem too simple and too extreme to capture the everyday vicissitudes of mutual affection, they nonetheless lie behind much of our thinking and our wishing, structuring our desires and forming our passions. It is for this reason that love inspires not only so much bad poetry, but bad metaphysics too, which nevertheless is necessary, as part of the emotion as well as its expression. Because what I want when I want you is a matter far from obvious, and what it is to love you, accordingly, is far from obvious too, no matter how simple it seems at times.

# PART II:
## *Love: A Theory*

# WHAT LOVE IS:
# THE LOVEWORLD

*All customs and traditions, all our way of life, everything to do with home and order, has crumbled into dust in the general upheaval and reorganization of society. The whole human way of life has been destroyed and ruined. All that's left is the naked human soul stripped to the last shred, for which nothing has changed because it was always cold and shivering and reaching out to its nearest neighbor, as cold and lonely as itself. You and I are like Adam and Eve, the first two people on earth who at the beginning of the world had nothing to cover themselves with—and now at the end of it we are just as naked and homeless.*

BORIS PASTERNAK, *Dr. Zhivago*

The question, What is love? is neither a request for a confession nor an excuse to start moralizing. It is not an invitation to amuse us with some *bon mot* ("Love is the key that opens up the doors of happiness") or to impress us with an author's sensitivity. And love is much more than a "feeling." When a novelist wants us to appreciate his character's emotions, he does not just describe sweaty palms and a moment of panic; he instead describes *a world*, the world as it is experienced—in anger, or in envy, or in love. Theorizing about emotion, too, is like describing an exotic world. It is a kind of conceptual anthropology—identifying a peculiar list of characters—heroes, villains, knaves or lovers—understanding a special set of rules and roles—rituals, fantasies, myths, slogans and fears. But these are not merely empirical observations on

the fate of a feeling; none of this will make any sense.to anyone who has not participated also. Love can be understood
only "from the inside," as a language can be understood only
by someone who speaks it, as a world can be known only by
someone who has—even if vicariously—*lived* in it.

To analyze an emotion by looking at the world it defines
allows us to cut through the inarticulateness of mere "feelings"
and do away once and for all with the idea that emotions in
general and love in particular are "ineffable" or beyond description. This might make some sense if describing an emotion were describing something "inside of us." It is not easy,
for example, to describe how one feels when nauseous; even
describing something so specific as a migraine headache falls
back on clumsy metaphors ("as if my head's in a vise," "as if
someone were driving a nail through my skull"). But once we
see that every emotion defines a world for itself, we can then
describe in some detail what that world involves, with its
many variations, describe its dimensions and its dynamics. The
world defined by love—or what we shall call the *loveworld*—is
a world woven around a single relationship, with all else
pushed to the periphery. To understand love is to understand
the specifics of this relationship and the world woven around
it.

Love has been so misunderstood both because so often it has
been taken to be *other*-worldly rather than one world of emotion among others, and because it has sometimes been taken to
be a "mere emotion"—just a feeling and not a world at all. Because of this, perhaps it would be best to illustrate the theory
that every emotion is a world by beginning with a less problematic emotion, namely, *anger*. Anger too defines its world. It is a
world in which one defines oneself in the role of "the
offended" and defines someone else (or perhaps a group or an
institution) as "the offender." The world of anger is very much
a courtroom world, a world filled with blame and emotional
litigation. It is a world in which everyone else tends to become

a co-defendant, a friend of the court, a witness or at least part of the courtroom audience. (But when you're *very* angry, there are no innocent bystanders.) We have already once quoted Lewis Carroll from *Alice in Wonderland:* " 'I'll be judge, I'll be jury,' said cunning old Fury." It is a world in which one does indeed define oneself as judge and jury, complete with a grim righteousness, with "justice"—one's own vengeance—as the only legitimate concern. It is a *magical* world, which can change a lackadaisical unfocused morning into a piercing, all-consuming day, an orgy of vindictive self-righteousness and excitement. At the slightest provocation it can change an awkward and defensive situation into an aggressive confrontation. To describe the world of anger is therefore to describe its fantasies, for example, the urge to kill, though rarely is this taken seriously or to its logical conclusion. It has its illusions too, for instance, the tendency to exaggerate the importance of some petty grievance to the level of cosmic injustice; in anger we sometimes talk as if "man's inhumanity to man" is perfectly manifested in some minor sleight at the office yesterday. It is a world with a certain fragility; a single laugh can explode the whole pretense of angry self-righteousness. And it is a world with a purpose—for when do we feel more self-righteous than in anger? Getting angry in an otherwise awkward situation may be a way of saving face or providing a quick ego boost; "having a bad temper" may be not so much a "character trait" as an emotional strategy, a way of *using* emotion as a means of controlling other people. To describe anger, in other words, is to describe the way the world is structured—and why—by a person who is angry.

The world of love—the loveworld—can be similarly described as a theatrical scenario, not as a courtroom but rather as "courtly," a romantic drama defined by its sense of elegance (badly interpreted as "spiritual"), in which we also take up a certain role—"the lover"—and cast another person into a complementary role—"the beloved." But where anger casts two antagonistic characters, romantic love sets up an ideal of unity, absolute complementarity and total mutual support and affection. It is the *rest* of the world that may be the antagonist. Boris Pasternak describes the loveworld beautifully—the world as Adam and Eve, naked, surrounded by chaos.

It is a world we know well, of course—the world of *Casablanca, Romeo and Juliet* and a thousand stories and novels. It is a world in which we narrow our vision and our cares to that single duality, all else becoming trifles, obstacles or interruptions. It is a magical world, in which an ordinary evening is transformed into the turning point of a lifetime, the metamorphosis of one's self into a curious kind of double being. It may seem like a sense of "discovery"; in fact it is a step in a long search, a process of creation. It has its fantasies and also its illusions: the fantasy of flying off together to some deserted island, the illusion that it will last forever. And as the music swells up and over, the sense of clichéd grandeur makes it quite clear what this emotion is all about—a "heightened" sense of one's own emotional significance, a fragile glorification of one's world by the contraction of everything to just one singsong glorious feeling which, at least for a moment, maybe indeed for a lifetime, dismisses the complex impersonality of the world and scorns it with a simple caress.

Like every emotional world, the loveworld has its essential rules and rituals, its basic structures and internal dynamics. Some of these rules and structures are so obvious that it is embarrassing to have to spell them out, for example, the fact that the loveworld (typically) includes two people, instead of only one (as in shame) or three (as in jealousy) or indeed an entire class of people (as in national mourning or revolutionary resentment). Or the fact that the loveworld involves extremely "positive" feelings about the person loved, perhaps even the uncritical evaluation that he or she is "the most wonderful person in the world." Or the fact that the loveworld is held together by the mutual desire to be together (to touch, be touched, to caress and make love) no less essentially than the world of Newton and Einstein is held together by the forces of electromagnetism and gravity. Such features are so obvious to us that we fail to think of them as the structures of love; we take them for granted and, when asked to talk about love, consider them not even worth mentioning. Having thus ignored the obvious, love becomes a mystery. But other seemingly equally "obvious" features of love may not be part of the structure of the loveworld at all—for example, the comforting equation between love and trust. Here, indeed, there is some room for "mystery" in love, not the emotion itself but its essential lack of predictability, the fascination with the unknown and the attraction that comes not with trust but with vulnerability, sometimes even suspicion and doubt. Similarly, we presume as in a cliché that romantic love presupposes respect ("How can you say that you love me when you don't even respect me?"). But it may be too that the nature of romantic love renders respect irrelevant, so that even when respect begins as a prerequisite for romantic attraction it gets booted out of the loveworld just as assuredly as a pair of fine leather shoes gets doffed as we get into bed. But each of these features has to be examined in turn, for the problem with talking about love is not that there is a mystery to be cleared up or that so much seems so obvious but rather that we take what we are told so uncritically, conflate the loveworld with everything that is good, true and desirable, confuse the structures of love with the conditions for security and happiness, assume without thinking that because suspicion is so painful trust must be essential to love, assume as a matter of wishful thinking that the same person who is in love with us must, if our lives are to be unified, respect us for what we do as well. So, at the risk of being extremely pedantic, I want to take these "obvious" and some not so obvious features of love and look at them one by one, here and in the chapters to follow, just to see what is, and what is not, the nature of the loveworld, its "object," its dimensions, its supposed "mystery" and "magic" and the ways it works for us. For those who want straightforward romantic praise, instead of somewhat tedious analytical prose, however, I am afraid the speculations that follow may seem excessive.

### The "Object" of Love

Talking about the loveworld is not only a way to avoid the hopeless conception of love as a feeling; it is also a way of rejecting an insidious view of love—and emotions in general— which many philosophers have come to accept as "obvious," particularly in this century. The view simply stated, is that love is an attitude *toward* someone, a feeling directed *at* a person, instead of a shared world. The view is often disguised by a piece of professional jargon—an impressive word, "intentionality." It is said that emotions are "intentional," which is a way of saying that they are "about" something. What an emotion is "about" is called its "intentional object" or, simply, its "object." Thus shame is an emotion which is "about" oneself, while anger is "about" someone else. The language comes from the medieval scholastics, by way of an Austrian philosopher named Franz Brentano, one of whose students in Vienna was the young Sigmund Freud. Thus Freud talks all the time about the "object" of love, not without some discomfort, for though the conception fits his general theories perfectly, he nonetheless sensed correctly that some considerable conceptual damage was being done to the emotion thereby.

The idea—though not the terminology—of "intentionality" and "intentional objects" was introduced into British philosophy by the Scottish philosopher David Hume. He analyzed a number of emotions in terms of the "objects" with which they were "naturally associated," for example pride and humility, which both took as their "objects" oneself, and hatred and love, which both took as their objects another person. But we can already see what is going to be so wrong with this familiar type of analysis. First of all, all such talk about "objects" leaves out the crucial fact that, in love at least, it is the other as a "subject" that is essential. To be in love (even unrequited) is to be looked *at*, not just to look. Thus it is the eyes, not the body (nor the soul), that present the so-called "beloved," not as object but as subject, not first as beautiful or lovable but always as (potentially) lov*ing*. It's the eyes that have it, nothing else.

One supposedly looks "into" the lover's eyes; I never could. One no more looks into them than at them, for what one sees is always their looking back at you. The eyes, only the eyes, are the organs of love. I could imagine her as pure phantom, as tall or rotund, but not without those eyes, looking at me. Or not looking. Every lover, I would suppose, has beautiful eyes, for it is only the eyes that look back at you, that refuse to allow even the most beautiful lover to become a mere "object" of love, thus refuting with a glance some of the greatest philosophers in history.

Love is not just an attitude directed toward another person; it is an emotion which, at least hopefully, is *shared with* him or her. Sometimes it is said that the very word "object" is "dehumanizing," but this is probably too strong. (In treating Einstein as "the object of study" in physics class, for instance, are we thereby "dehumanizing" him?) But what is true is that such "object"-talk, in Freud in particular, too easily underscores our tendency to think of love as admiration, need or desire-at-a-distance, like the troubadours' pathetic versifying in the direction of their inaccessible ladies in the tower (or Stendhal swooning and bursting and hardly containing himself as his lovely Italian countess strolls into the ballroom). Sometimes, perhaps, and in some emotions, "object"-talk makes perfectly good sense; sadness at the loss of one's high school class ring, or the love of one's favorite first edition. But any account of love that begins with the idea of an "object" of love is probably going to miss the main point of the emotion, namely, that it is not an emotion "about" another person so much as, in our terms, a world we share.

This suggests in turn an even more serious problem in the "object" analysis of emotion, love in particular. When Hume picks out the "object" of love, he quite naturally chooses the person one is in love *with*. But this already leaves out half of the picture. An equally essential component of the loveworld is *oneself*. Love is not just an emotion directed toward another person—like Cupid looking for someone to shoot with his arrows. We are not in love *at*, but rather *with*, another person. I am not just the person who *has* the emotion; I am also part of it. The same is true of anger; when I am angry, I am not just the person with the emotion, I am also one of its crucial ingredients. Thus the talk about "intentionality" and the "object" of love leads us to look at only half of the emotional scenario, which will inevitably result in our hopelessly misunderstanding it.

The most obvious misunderstanding is this: the Christian view of love is not alone in teaching us that love is essentially *selfless*. Proponents of romantic love have argued that too. The idea is that love is thoroughly "about" another person, so that any degree of self-love is incompatible with, or at least a detraction from, "true," that is, selfless love. But this is not only not true; it is impossible. There is no emotion without self-involvement, and no love that is not also "about" oneself. The other side is just as confused, however; La Rochefoucauld, for example, insists that "all love is self-love." But to be self-involved is not yet to be selfish, nor does self-involvement in any way exclude a total concern for the other person as well. The practical consequence of this confusion, in turn, is the readiness with which we can be made to feel guilty at the slightest suggestion that our love is not "pure" but turns on "selfish" motives, and it renders unaskable what is in fact a most intelligible question—namely, "What am I getting out of this?"—to which the answer may well be, "Not enough to make it worth while." But then, love is not just what one "gets out of it" either.

Talking about love as a world with two people avoids these problems and misunderstandings. But there is one last set of complications which has been much discussed in the "object" way of talking which deserves special mention. The idea that the "object" of my love is another person suggests too easily that love is "about" a person *simpliciter*, the whole person, nothing but and nothing less than the whole person. This is simply untrue. I love *you*, indeed, but I love you only in so far as you fit into the loveworld. That may be for any number of reasons—because I think you're beautiful, because you love me too, because I admire you in your career, because we cook fine meals together. The list might well seem endless, but it never is. I might love you for just one reason, or I might love you for a hundred and fifty reasons. But those reasons (I might always discover more) circumscribe your place in the loveworld. The person I love is, consequently, not simply *you*, the whole person, but rather you circumscribed by that set of reasons. I might say, in a moment of enthusiasm, "I love everything about you," but that's just myopia, or poor editing. Sometimes I'm surprised. I find a new virtue, that I've never seen before. But sometimes I'm disappointed too. Sometimes I manufacture new and imagined virtues, as Stendhal suggests in his theory of "crystallization"—the "discovery" of ever new virtues in one's lover. But love is never unqualified acceptance of a lover, "no matter what," however much one would like to be loved, if not to love, without qualification. But this raises sticky questions about the vicissitudes of love, not least the nature of these reasons and the possibility that, if I love you "for reasons," might I not love someone else, just as much as or instead of you, for precisely those same reasons? Or is it possible that one might not know *whom* one loves, if it is true, for example, as every teenager soon learns, that one can love "on the rebound," transferring the frustrated love of one lover immedi-

ately onto another, who becomes something of a sparring partner to keep us in shape for the more important bout to come,
holding a role in a loveworld in which he or she has no real
place. The identity of the "beloved," in other words, is by no
means so obvious as the "object of love"-talk would make it
seem. It is even possible that the "beloved," as Plato argued in
a more pious way, is nothing more than a set of ideal properties, indifferent indeed to the particular person who at any
given instant happens to exemplify them.

To make matters even more complicated, we might point
out that similar questions arise regarding one's own identity in
the loveworld. I do not love "with all my heart and all my
soul," but rather (if we want to talk about hearts and souls at
all) only with half a heart—but not half-heartedly—and with a
fraction of a soul. I love you in so far as I am a lover, but I am
only rarely *just* a lover. No matter how much I'm in love, I do
not live just in the loveworld. You may be the essence of the
loveworld, but you don't fit into my career or, for that matter,
into the world I enter when I watch Japanese movies. I love
you when I feel romantic, perhaps too when I'm just relaxed,
but when I'm frustrated about my work, or absorbed in a lawsuit, the self that is so involved is not the same self that loves
you. It's not that *I* don't love you, or that I love you any less;
it's just that the loveworld isn't my only world, or yours either,
even if we agree that it is, for us, the best of our possible
worlds. To say that love is a world of two people, therefore, is
not at all to say something simple, much less "obvious."

### The Dimensions of the Loveworld

If an emotion is a world or, in part, a way of "seeing" the
world, then certain visual metaphors become particularly useful. I call them "scope" and "focus"[1] and the camera analogy is

[1] *The Passions,* Chapter 10.

particularly apt. Scope, quite simply, is the *size* of an emotional world. Some emotions, such as cosmic dread and depression, take in the whole of the universe; others, like petty anger and embarrassment, restrict their scope to a single event or incident. Focus, on the other hand, refers to what is attended to and clearly defined, what is rendered essential *within* that world. Even an emotion whose scope is cosmic—certain kinds of resentment, for example—may have an extremely narrow and sharp focus, sometimes seizing upon a single incident as a representation of the whole. Sometimes broad scope may combine with a virtual absence of focus, in joy, for instance. Albert Camus liked to dwell on the cosmic emotions; Jean-Paul Sartre loved the detail of the petty, the narrow, the obsessive. (But then, it was Camus who was wounded by small offenses, Sartre who took on the universe.)

Now love is often talked about as a cosmic emotion; lovers are said to love everything, and they sometimes stare at the stars. But though indeed lovers have their cosmic pretensions, and may at times demonstrate a particularly tolerant mood toward the "outside" world, the scope of love is in fact famously small, limited to a strictly private world of two people only. ("I only have eyes for you," for example.) In so far as the rest of the world is included, it is merely as a stage, perhaps as an audience to our impenetrable and even belligerent privacy. Sometimes the "outside world" simply serves as an enemy—the feud of the Montagues and the Capulets threatening the loveworld of their rebellious son and daughter—which makes love all the more "romantic," because forbidden. Thus it is rightly said that love is *amoral*, all but indifferent to the problems of the world and the larger issues of morality and community. And it is wrongly, even foolishly said that love is itself the spirit of community and even the glue that holds people together. Quite the contrary, romantic love has such small scope that it cannot even *see* the larger community (which is why political radicals are more often *against* it). So much for the "love should rule the world" of Mozart's *Magic Flute*, Plato's *Symposium* (Phaedrus' speech), St. Paul, and G. W. F. Hegel in his youthful works. In love, even three is a "crowd." Indeed, love thrives on rebellion and the rejection of community expectations and mores (Romeo and Juliet, Tristan and Isolde, Paris and Helen, Faust and Gretchen, Tom Jones and Sophie—just to name a few).

Only in a society with an enormously powerful ideology of the individual, in which the "alienation" of the individual from the larger society is not only tolerated but even encouraged and celebrated, can the phenomenon of romantic love be conceivable. Romantic love is not only distinct from, it is opposed to, *agape*, the "love of humanity," and one's "proper place" in society. It is, quite literally, "a little world of its own." The scope of the loveworld, in a word, is microscopic. It is a rejection of the world at large, and privacy is its domain. It is worth noting, with that in mind, that romantic love is just beginning to blossom in mainland China, not coincidentally among the same generation of former "red guards" who are also responsible for the sudden and sometimes alarming rise in "anti-social behavior" in the larger Chinese cities.[2]

The *focus* of love in the loveworld too tends to be extremely narrow, restricted not only to a single person but, as I have argued in a preliminary way, wholly concerned with certain aspects of a person—his or her beauty, or intelligence, or those activities we enjoy together, sex and conversation, presumably, foremost among them. The scope of love always includes the two of us, but the focus of love is indeed mainly concerned with the other person, "the beloved," and thus includes much of what the "intentionality" theorists have described in their talk about the "beloved" as an "object." For example, the "beloved" is always viewed from a certain perspective, defined by the emotion itself, in which virtues are exaggerated and faults

[2] Jay Mathews, reporting in the Washington *Post*, December, 1979.

are ignored or minimized. The intentionality theorists are also fond of pointing out that the "object" of one's love might not even exist (one can still be in love with a lover who has died, for example). Indeed, the actual person might be very different from the lover's conception (thus the many tales of the killer or prostitute who finds at least brief happiness in the eyes of an unknowing and unsuspecting lover), and indeed the alleged lover might be someone else altogether (thus Shakespeare's and Oscar Wilde's delight in mistaken identities). But the point to be pursued is that the focus of love is always something less than "the whole person" and, indeed, often includes features that are more fantasy than intimate knowledge, more wishful thinking than acute perception. But this does not mean, as it is sometimes said to mean, that love is essentially an illusion, any more than photographs, because they are able to distort and exaggerate, pick out and edit out, beautify the ordinary or dramatize the trivial, ought to be dismissed as illusory. Biased, yes; false, no. Focus is a part of seeing, which is not more true the less there is of it, or any less true because it can be so extreme.

### Beyond the Mystery:
### On the Outside Looking In

My friend Christopher, who is a very fine poet, once pointed to a flower on the table in front of us. It was slowly opening up its petals before our slightly drunken eyes, and he called it a "mystery." I could not disagree with him. Not because I did not know about turgor and transpiration and absorption and all of the other hydraulic processes which we were forced to learn about in high school biology, but because to provide an explanation for the "mystery," in those poetic circumstances, would have been simply gauche.

What seems like a mystery may be only a refusal to listen to

—or the inappropriateness of—an explanation. What is said to
be "magic" may only be an unwillingness to step outside the
puzzle and see what is behind the curtain or up someone's
sleeve. The wonder of the loveworld—without detracting from
it—might well be accounted for by taking a step back, by looking in from the outside, and by seeing where this particular
world fits in with all of the others.

Inside the loveworld, poetry reigns. Mawkish metaphors are
perfectly appropriate, but explanations are not. In any particular case, it is easy enough to "explain" the attraction between
two people—her resemblance to the woman who dumped him
last year, his being just the opposite of the husband who gave
her such a hard time. It is easy enough to explain what she
gives to him, and he to her, but these explanations are simply
out of place within the loveworld itself. Thus (as in all anthropological excursions) we find ourselves in a curious position: as
outside observers of the rules and rituals, we are in a position
to explain them, to understand why they should be as they are
and not some other way. But as participants in the loveworld,
we have to accept these rules and rituals as they are, without
question and without explanation. There is no other way to understand, except by understanding that, on the inside, one systematically refuses to understand. Thus the "mystery."

The explanation of love, in general, the account of its importance in our culture, is easy enough—from the outside. We
have already discussed it in some detail. Romantic love is an
emotion that provides a powerful bond between two people,
possibly strangers, on the basis of a single readily available
shared and complementary set of attributes which we sometimes lump together with the simplistic name "sex." One can
ask, from the outside, why we do not form our primary relationships on the basis of something else, something more indicative of our interests in life or our general living patterns, perhaps the people we work with or those who share the same
dining habits, read the same books, or enjoy playing the same

sports. Perhaps we could, and sometimes we do. But the fact is that sex has been chosen just because it is most commonly shared and at the same time most private. It varies only slightly from person to person, thus providing a universal vehicle for intimacy which can be (almost always) assumed to be ready and waiting from the outset in anyone whatsoever. From the inside, our meeting was "fate"; from the outside, it was mere chance or convenience, one possible encounter, perhaps out of thousands.

To say that sex is "natural" is to say, ultimately, just that everyone has it—or ought to. But this in turn can be explained when we understand the function of romantic love in the culture as a whole, as a means of very quickly establishing extremely strong interpersonal bonds among people who have left their more "natural" ties in family and the community they grew up in and gone off to "find themselves." In a strange city, a new job or a different university romantic love can provide for us what no other emotion can so well provide: instant intimacy, even where there is no one whom one has ever met before. It is thus, in a society that recognizes so few other interpersonal bonds as significant, that we give romantic love such exaggerated importance. Every emotion may provide some meaning to life, but it is romantic love that provides the specific meaning we need the most: the "meaningful relationship," that sense of belonging, in a world that has made belonging an achievement rather than a presupposition.

This is the explanation for the importance of romantic love, but inside the explanation is the "mystery" of the loveworld. Inside of love we narrow our view to the tiny world of the two of us, and instead of looking at the loveworld as part of the larger culture, indeed as one of its primary institutions, we pretend that we are in love *despite* its wishes, against its intentions, an act of rebellion instead of *the* all-American and favorite European ritual. But this too has its explanation; in a society that so prizes individuality and rebelliousness, it is

extremely important that social institutions, including education, the press and teenage gangs, have the appearance—at
least to themselves—of anti-establishment attitudes. And love,
most of all, proves its role in the larger world it chooses to ignore by manifesting in a particularly belligerent if usually
harmless manner its own sense of absolute autonomy and
amoral social indifference.

It would be a mistake, however, to describe and explain the
loveworld just as a deficit, a gap, a need to be filled in our
larger social world. The loveworld is not just compensation for
families lost and communities uprooted, the desperate search
on a rather frivolous sensuous basis for replacements for intimacy that have become no longer possible. The emotion of the
loveworld, first of all, is a far more powerful form of intimacy,
for most of us, than the intimacies we left behind. It more than
fills the gap and has virtues of its own. Participation in the loveworld provides us with a sense of self-esteem and grandeur, so
obvious both in the emotion and in the music that sometimes
accompanies it, which cannot be reduced to mere sexual intimacy, much less in lieu of a once playful relationship with a
brother or a sister as children. Grandeur and self-esteem are
motives in their own right, not mere "compensations." Finally,
the seeming indeterminacy of the loveworld is itself wholly a
part of the ideology of our culture in general. Romantic love is
*freedom*. It is the freedom *from* determination by our families,
from arranged marriages and fixed community roles, but it is
also freedom *to* form our ties as we choose, for reasons that
need be nobody's business but our own. What rules exist for
love are there to be flaunted: the prince falls in love with the
commoner, and he gives up the throne rather than give up his
emotional autonomy. Free emotional choice reigns over pre-
established social status. The Baptist boy from Texas falls in
love with a Vietnamese girl, much to the horror of his parents,
and the woman who has been groomed all her life to make a
match in society turns around and falls in love with a cowboy.

It looks like caprice, emotional anarchy; but this is the rule of the loveworld. The lack of rules is itself the rule, or so it seems.

The hero and heroine of the loveworld make a choice and stick with it. At least for a while. The odder the choice and the greater the obstacles, the more heroic they are. Thus Romeo and Juliet. And Tristan, Lancelot, Isolde and Guinevere. It is the inappropriateness of their love, and their willingness to fight all odds because of it, that make them our romantic heroes. But to see the tragedy of these romantic heroes as the *ideal* of the loveworld is also to miss the point, for what makes them heroes is precisely the fact that their choices stretch the limits of the loveworld. They are heroes, ultimately, in the name of freedom. But the tragic *results* of their excessive freedom, their impossible demands and, consequently, the inevitable collapse of their increasingly desperate love, are not the ideal but rather the limit of the loveworld, its outer boundary. Even freedom has its limits.[3]

Love is not merely a need, and the loveworld is not just compensation for social deprivation. Romantic love provides us with our most powerful form of intimacy, a fact only partly explained by the gap in relationships encouraged by our society, which is not at all explained by the thrills of sex alone. Romantic love provides a sense of self-worth and an aura of grandeur that must be understood in its own terms, as an emotional strategy for enriching our world. Most of all, romantic love has to be understood as an emotion that thrives on *freedom,* as an emotion built around mobility and choice, as a lack of determinacy that we sometimes choose to ignore by pretending that love is primarily a matter of fate. But the power and grandeur of love and the loveworld lie precisely in the fact that, however "lucky" in love we might happen to be, it is our freedom and our ability to choose that make this emotion so enormously important to us.

[3] Thus feminist Uta West rightly writes, "Romeo and Juliet, Antony and Cleopatra,—what did they have to do with 'meaningful relationships'?"

Still looking in from the outside, however, this indeterminacy of love has one more consequence of some significance
in understanding the "mystery." Most emotions, anger for instance, have a single scenario. One can describe the structures
of anger pretty much all at once, and anger is fully anger even
if it only lasts for an instant. Love, however, is more of a process than a single scenario; its progress is not merely a plot but
rather a complex and conflict-ridden process called a "dialectic." This means that love takes some time. (This does not
mean "forever.") Love is a development, a matter of mutual
creation. What is created, however, is love. It is sometimes
said, often by theorists who are not themselves either creative
or in love, that love and creativity go hand in hand, supporting
this dubious thesis with a dozen well-chosen anecdotes about
painters and poets and their passions. But the truth of the matter seems rather to be that love, though indeed creative,
spends most of its energies creating itself, whether or not it
also inspires further energy for creating anything else. As creativity, however, love tends to be less predictable, as well as
more complex in its vicissitudes, than most other emotions.
And from the inside, indeed, this indeterminacy may well
seem to be a "mystery."

### What Love's About: Self

What love is about—the poles of the loveworld and the goal
of its development—is the creation of self. But this does not
mean that love is just about oneself, any more than love is just
about another. For the self that is created through love is a
*shared* self, a self that is conceived and developed together. It
is not only the loveworld that is indeterminate but, as part and
parcel of our largely indeterminate culture, our selves are always under-determined too. Jean-Paul Sartre states this as a
paradox, that we are always more than we are. Our selves are
formed in the cradle of the family, soon to be confused by the

welter of different roles into which we are thrown with play-
mates, peers and even the most rudimentary social rituals and
responsibilities. And all along we find ourselves redefining ourselves in terms of other people, people with whom we identify,
those whom we admire, those we despise as well as all of those
more or less anonymous faces and voices that surround us
every day—smiling, abusing, criticizing, congratulating and ca-
joling. And in that confusion of roles and rituals which in
our society (not all others) tends to be without an anchor,
without an "essence" according to which we could say, once
and for all, "I am x," we look for a context that is small enough,
manageable enough, yet powerful enough, for us to define ourselves, our "real" selves—we think wishfully—and what could
be smaller or more manageable than the tiniest possible interpersonal world, namely, a world of only two people. And so, in
love, we define ourselves and define each other, building on
but sometimes fighting against the multitude of identities that
are already established, starting with but not always ending
with the images, fantasies and roles which drew us together in
the first place, made us seem so compatible, even "meant for
each other." Romantic love is part of our search for selfhood,
and the power of the emotion, our sense of tragedy when it
fails as well as its overall importance in our culture, turns
largely on the fact that it comes to provide what is most crucial
to us—even more than survival and the so-called "necessities"
of life—namely, our selves.

All emotions are self-involved. (In *The Passions,* I even
define emotional judgments in terms of this self-involvement.)
In love, what is so peculiar is that the self that is created in the
development of the emotion is a shared self, an *ego à deux,*
whereas in most emotions the self is set up in opposition to or
in isolation from other people. In romantic love, as opposed
to motherly or brotherly love, for example, the self is also
created virtually anew, as if "from scratch," no matter how
many influences may be behind it and no matter how thor-

oughly this might be explained by someone outside that tiny yet seemingly all-inclusive loveworld. To understand romantic love, therefore, is to understand this peculiar creation of a shared self, and to explain the importance of this one emotion in our world is to explain, most of all, its singular success in promoting our sense of ourselves and the meaningfulness not of a mere "relationship" but of life itself.

Most if not all emotions have as a motive the enhancement of self, or what I call *the maximization of self-esteem*. Thus in describing the world of anger, even in a brief paragraph at the beginning of this chapter, I commented that anger is a spectacularly *self-righteous* emotion. Through anger, we feel good about ourselves, morally superior, even in (especially in) circumstances which would otherwise feel extremely awkward. Someone insults me; I feel embarrassed; but with a single swoop of will I turn the tables, even if only in my own mind: I get angry, and my embarrassment turns to indignation; his insult becomes a crime and I am all judge and jury, ready to do him in. Thus a bad temper may well be a strategy for continuously manipulating other people and putting them on the defensive—a trick often learned in childhood temper tantrums. Anger is one of our favorite ways of making ourselves feel superior, providing ourselves with an air of potency, maximizing our self-esteem. And we do the same, in different ways and through different scenarios, in the different worlds of jealousy, resentment, scorn and envy, even—as Freud saw so clearly—in guilt and depression.

But of all the emotional strategies for self-enhancement, none succeeds so well as love. For one thing, the inevitable opposition in anger invites a counterattack of equal self-righteousness, and competitive emotions make it highly likely that one of us, at least, will lose. But in love two selves mutually reinforce one another, rather than compete with one another, and so the self-enhancement of love, insulated from the outside by indifference, mutually supported in a reciprocal way on the inside, tends to be an extremely powerful and relatively durable emotional strategy.

Love is grand; but built into the loveworld itself is this sense of grandeur. There are, from the inside, no petty passions. We construct the world around ourselves so that our passions seem to be "everything," at least for the moment. (The problem comes when we come to believe from the outside too that "love is everything" and "the answer to all of our troubles."⟩ But love has a special sense of grandeur, in part because of the insulated mutual congratulation built into the loveworld. (After all, it is hard to celebrate by yourself.) But the sense of elegance and grandeur is also built into the very scenario of love—as self-righteousness is built into the world of anger. Much of this, of course, is sheer fantasy, but the fantasy of grandeur is just as essential to love as the sense of justice is to anger, and in no sense does that make these emotions "false." Fantasy must be carefully distinguished from illusions. Fantasies need not be false; illusions are. Fantasies, shall we say, are enthusiastic embellishments of the truth, exaggerations or celebrations but, in any case, not self-deceptions. And it is through fantasy—making comparisons with Bogart and Bacall, sunning in the tradition of the great lovers of history, treating ourselves to a rare evening at the Plaza and dining with an extravagance that we never have before, making love to Gregorian chants instead of the top-40 radio station or drinking together our first bottle of Dom Perignon (1955), punctuated by our own clumsy love talk (which sounds like pure poetry at the time)—that we create this sense of grandeur. It is not that the emotion itself is grand; the loveworld is grand. It is part of its structure, and to play the lover *is*, in part, to follow this long tradition. There is, even in a society without an energy crisis, no romantic loveworld without a few candles.

### Love and Autonomy:
### The "Dialectic" of Togetherness

So what is love? It is, in a phrase, an emotion through which we create for ourselves a little world—the loveworld, in which we play the roles of lovers and, quite literally, create our selves as well. Thus love is not, as so many of the great poets and philosophers have taken it to be, any degree of admiration or worship, not appreciation or even desire for beauty, much less, as Erich Fromm was fond of arguing, an "orientation of character" whose "object" is a secondary consideration. Even so-called "unrequited" love is shared love and shared identity, if only from one side and thereby woefully incomplete. Of course, occasionally an imagined identity may be far preferable to the actuality, but even when this is the case unrequited love represents at most a hint toward a process and not the process as such. Unrequited love is still love, but love in the sense that a sprout from an acorn is already an oak, no more, however beautiful.

In love we transform ourselves and one another, but the key to this emotion is the understanding that the transformation of selves is not merely reciprocal, a swap of favors like "I'll cook you dinner if you'll wash the car." The self transformed in love is a shared self, and therefore by its very nature at odds with, even contradictory to, the individual autonomous selves that each of us had before. Sometimes our new shared self may be a transformation of a self that I (perhaps we) shared before. Possibly all love is to some extent the transposition of seemingly "natural" bonds which have somehow been abandoned or destroyed, and therefore the less than novel transformation of a self that has always been shared, in one way or another. But the bonds of love are always, to some extent, "unnatural," and our shared identity is always, in some way, uncomfortable. Aristophanes' delightful allegory about the double creatures cleft in two and seeking their other halves is charming but false. Love is never so neat and tidy, antigen and antibody forming the perfect fit. The Christian concept of a couple sanctified as a "union" before God is reassuring, as if one thereby receives some special guarantee, an outside bond of sorts, which will keep two otherwise aimless souls together. But the warranty doesn't apply. What is so special about romantic love, and what makes it so peculiar to our and similar societies, is the fact that it is entirely based on the idea of individuality and freedom, and this means, first of all, that the presupposition of love is a strong sense of individual identity and autonomy which exactly contradicts the ideal of "union" and "yearning to be one" that some of our literature has celebrated so one-sidedly. And, second, the freedom that is built into the loveworld includes not just the freedom to come together but the freedom to go as well. Thus love and the loveworld are always in a state of tension, always changing, dynamic, tenuous and explosive.

Love is a *dialectic*, which means that the bond of love is not just shared identity—which is an *impossible* goal—but the taut line of opposed desires between the ideal of an eternal merger of souls and our cultivated urge to prove ourselves as free and autonomous individuals. No matter how much we're *in* love, there is always a large and non-negligible part of ourselves which is not defined by the loveworld, nor do we want it to be. To understand love is to understand this tension, this dialectic between individuality and the shared ideal. To think that love is to be found only at the ends of the spectrum—in that first enthusiastic "discovery" of a shared togetherness or at the end of the road, after a lifetime together—is to miss the loveworld almost entirely, for it is neither an initial flush of feeling nor the retrospective congratulations of old age but a struggle for unity and identity. And it is this struggle—neither the ideal of togetherness nor the contrary demand for individual autonomy and identity—that defines the dynamics of that convulsive and tenuous world we call romantic love.

# SELF, LOVE AND SELF-LOVE 12

"I wanted to go out with him into the world, to announce us
as a unity. We love each other, we are together. Not for the
sake of showing off, but out of, well, joy. I mean, it's as though
you have a new identity; you're Mira and you're Mira and Ben.
You want the world to recognize both. . . . But then of course
you—well women, anyway—lose the other one, the private one.
Men don't seem to, quite as much. I don't know why."
MARILYN FRENCH, *The Women's Room*, p. 471

A ll love is self-love," wrote La Rochefoucauld.
Well, no, but love is essentially about oneself.
What makes this familiar proverb unacceptable is the
inevitable implication that love is *just* self-love, to the exclusion
of the other person, the person purportedly loved. And this of
course is nonsense. What makes love love is the *kind* of self
that is loved, and that is a *shared self*, a self defined with, in
and through a particular other person.

All emotions are about oneself, in the sense that they involve
casting oneself into a role, in a specific emotional world. Sometimes that role may be secondary, or even infinitesimal, as in
Iago's envy or Kierkegaard's humble but passionate religious
faith, respectively. But whereas most emotions define the self
in juxtaposition or opposition to other people (for example, the
antagonism of anger, the hostility of resentment), love involves
a mutual, as well as reciprocal, definition of selves. As I boost

my image of you I boost my image of myself, through your eyes, and vice versa. In fact a somewhat Laingian if not overly "knotty" characterization of the dynamics of love, which might be found even in the dialectical vicissitudes of a first date, might look something like this: I feel good about myself because I'm with you. And part of the reason I feel good about myself because I'm with you is because you obviously feel good about me, in part because you feel good about yourself when you're with me. And that's no doubt in part because you see that I feel good about myself and good about you when I see that you feel good about yourself and good about me when I'm with you. And so on. But this should not be interpreted merely as mutual "feedback" of approval and admiration so much as the dialectical development of something quite different, the alteration of self through this process and the creation of a new conception of self in which the most crucial single determinant is the other person and his or her virtues and opinions, including those that I merely imagine or fantasize as well as those which he or she fantasizes and shares with me.

Even in this simple sketch, it should be clear why the process of love tends to be so explosive, makes us feel so vulnerable, and fills us with such joy and terror. Romantic love, even after a long and earnest search for love, involves nothing less than a change of self, and suddenly we find ourselves precariously dependent upon one another, exhilarated by our discovery but inevitably terrified as well. It is an inherently unstable situation, halfway between two identities, and we are no longer assured of either. We see what we would become, and we have our doubts. We look back at what we were, if only by way of contrast, and the differences overwhelm us, even if the only difference is the source of the identity itself.

The exhilaration of love is to be found in this sense of discovery and creation, and in love's tensions and insecurities too. Those who see love simply as a "union" misdescribe the emotion and lead us to expect a lifetime of calm satisfaction punctuated by joy and sometimes tragedy. In fact love is a struggle, albeit sometimes a delightful and always essential struggle, for mutual self-identity and a sense of independence at the same time. Lovers' battles are not gaps in love but part of its process, and indeed, love may be strongest between individuals who are themselves most vehemently individualistic and autonomous, in whom the struggle rages most violently. Conversely, love may be weakest in those who think they "need" it most, just because, so willing to "give themselves" to love, they may well have little self to give in the first place.

The idea that love is a shared self requires the rejection of a number of ideas that are far too impotent to characterize this often powerful emotion. For example, it is quite often said that love requires *compromise,* and of course living together or doing almost anything with another person does require compromises of all kinds. But in so far as one makes a compromise, one still holds one's self *in opposition* to another self, and this then is less than love. You can compromise with someone you love, but love itself isn't a compromise.

It is often said that to love is to give in to another person's needs, indeed, to make them more important than one's own. But to love is rather to take the other's desires and needs *as* one's own. This is much more than a merely grammatical point. It is a redefinition of the self itself, as a shared self, as a self in which my personal desires no longer command a distinctive voice. (Of course a shared self, like an individual self, might be inconsistent or schizoid.)

It is said that lovers want to be together, which is true, of course, but we should rather say that lovers want to *be* together, with that peculiar emphasis that has meaning only in metaphysical matters. For at least part of the answer to that strange question "What do you want when you want someone?" is "To become essential to that someone, to be everything for him," as Jean-Paul Sartre rightly puts it, indeed to *be* him, or her, a single unity without further thought of the possibility of separation or the conflict that could divide us. Even if, as we have argued, to be is only to *become,* and never in fact to *be* at all.

### Shared Selves

This creation of a shared self is sometimes described in an overly mystical manner, as if common sense cannot fathom the synthesis of a single identity out of two atomistic and autonomous human beings. The assumption here is one of the metaphors we discussed in Chapter 2, which I called "the ontology of loneliness"—the idea that each of us is born into the world alone, an atom floating around in a hostile social universe, looking for companionship and protection. Given such a view of the self as an isolated monad, the concept of shared identity is indeed strange. But in fact there is nothing mystical about shared selfhood, self-identity conceived through identification with another person, or group, or institution. Being on a team with "team spirit," for example, is a sharing of one's self, at least for a few hours, perhaps for the season. One identifies with a dozen or so others *as* a member of such-and-such a team, in which the peculiarities of one's character are submerged or ignored altogether in favor of a group identity (as winners, losers, having a good defense or the worst coach in the league). Mutual recognition is the paradigm, but not necessary. (A "fan" of the team, for example, may, unbeknownst to the team, wholly identify with it.) But this simple example also underscores a very different point about shared selves—namely, that, although individual identity may become of minimal significance, this does not mean that individual differences are submerged. One's *position* on the team, for example, now becomes the most important single feature about oneself, which is, on the one hand, still an identification wholly in terms of the team, but nonetheless an identity that may be had by just one person.

In much the same way, in love one may come to identify oneself wholly in terms of the relationship, but it does not follow that individual roles and differences are submerged, or that opposing or conflicting roles might not be just as essential to the love as shared interests and agreed-upon opinions. Much of what women rightly fear as "loss of identity" in a relationship is not so much the fact that one does indeed take on a new identity as the fact that women, in particular, are often forced to *conform to* their male lovers. They are encouraged not to form a shared new identity but rather to become mere reflections, to accept roles that are strictly subservient, to accept as their own *his* old identity. But forming a shared identity is no more self-sacrifice than it is compromise or "giving in"; it is coming to accept a view of one's individual self as defined in and through the other person. This does not mean that one person becomes like the other, but rather that they define their differences—as well as their significant similarities—together.

### Creating Your Self (Through Love)

> "I don't make the rules."
> "Sure you do, we all do."
> GARSON KANIN and RUTH GORDON,
> *Adam's Rib*

What we call "self" is a creation, the creation of a certain kind of culture and, ultimately, a concoction made up out of grammar. We refer to ourselves as a matter of syntactic necessity and come to suppose that we must be referring to some specific and concrete entity, our selves. Furthermore, we distinguish between our selves as we appear and our selves as we "really are," thus pushing the self below the surface into the depths, protecting it from too easy first impressions but also rendering it mysterious and inaccessible. Thus our entire psychological literature has grown up around the "depth" metaphor, the assumption that our "real selves" are down there below the surface: the immutable soul, the good intention, "depth of character" and, with a Freudian Jekyll and Hyde twist, the world of suppressed desires and wishes. A character like Jean-Jacques Rousseau could defend in his *Confessions* the goodness of his "inner soul" despite the fact that everything about him was mean-spirited, selfish and paranoid. Thus we too have the idea that our "real selves" are not necessarily, or even likely to be, what most people might believe us to be.

There are cultures with no conception of "self" in our sense at all. The German philosopher Hegel, in the early nineteenth century, insisted that the only real self is the One Self (which he called "Spirit") shared by all of us. In most cultures, what we call the self is a well-prescribed set of social roles and expectations, determined to a large extent from the circumstances of birth (boy or girl, first or second, where and when, social status, wealth, health) and fully determined by young adulthood—or what we call adolescence. In our culture, however, the most important single observation on selfhood in general—over and above our belief in a "real self" below the surface and hidden from public view—is the *indeterminacy* of self, the fact that not only is the self not fully determined by the time one is a young adult, when the question of self-identity is commonly most painful, but that it is *never* fully formed, always an open question and always open to change. Perhaps the most dramatic single example of that open-endedness is to be found in the standard Christian-Faustian story of the moment-before-death conversion, the salvation-transformation of self or "soul" even after a lifetime of sin and wrongdoing. But the idea of indeterminacy of self permeates our view of ourselves in a thousand less dramatic moments, in everything from our notion of "will power" to our conception of romantic love as the emotion "that will change your life." Without our

belief in the indeterminacy of the self, there would be no such
emotion as romantic love. But without our enthusiasm for romantic love, our conception of self would not be the same
either.

What determines the self? This is one of the perennial dis-
putes among philosophers and psychoanalysts, but certain ingredients are obvious: the simple facts about us (age, race, social status, skills, family) and the way we learn to think about
ourselves. The two are often at odds, however, as the existentialists have pointed out so dramatically, since the way we
think of ourselves in this society typically includes the denial,
rejection or intention to overcome at least some of those seemingly "given" facts about our selves. I may be Jewish, but I
hide that fact. I may be crippled, but I refuse to be treated any
differently from anyone else. I may be a coward, but I intend
to become a hero. We could argue about how effective such
thinking and resolutions can be, but that is not our concern
here. What is our concern, however, is the way in which romantic love fits so dramatically into this picture, for whether or
not we can, as individuals, easily resolve to change our selves,
it is clear that, with the support of a single other person, even
against the whole of society and with all of the facts against us,
such changes seem to be commonplace.

What is sometimes left out of the existentialist argument
about the importance of self-determination—the determination
of self even in the face of facts to the contrary—is a full appreciation of the extent to which our conceptions of self—and thus
the self itself—are formed in and with other people, through
interpersonal discourse and intercourse, in mutual roles and
expectations. For Martin Heidegger, the German existentialist, for example, the self is originally formed through
identification with the anonymous "they" of society in general,
but his whole early philosophy is worked around the suggestion that this self is "inauthentic," and that the true or "authentic" self must be asserted by breaking away from this

"they-self" and becoming truly "one's own." But what is missing in this pseudo-heroic picture of the individual against the whole mass of society is the importance of those small and specific interactions through which we define our selves which are not merely infusions of society (the "they") as a whole but very particular and very much voluntary inter-actions between friends, family and lovers, as well as colleagues and acquaintances. For our purposes here, we need not worry about the general determination of self by society (or what most of my eighteen-year-old students call "being conditioned" or "brainwashed") or about the extent to which change of self through self-manipulation ("pulling your own strings") is possible. But much of the determination of self—a process which is never completed—is to be located in our specific interpersonal relationships, not just what I think of myself but what *you* think of me, and what I think of the way you think of me, and what you think of the way I think of you, and so on.

Romantic love, as an emotion of shared self, must be under-stood in just these terms, as shared determination of self. And in a society that presents us daily with a dozen different deter-minations of self, many of them unflattering if not embarrass-ing, most of them beyond our control, romantic love becomes our way of choosing the self that we want, through mutual agreement with a single person who shares our most treasured self-images, which we can then define as "my real self," even against the consensus of all the facts and the opinions of all the world, as well as against our own uncertainties. ("If only I could get just one person to believe me, just one.")

Thus convicted felons and dastardly types can be defended by their wives or husbands or lovers with the plea, "If you only knew how he/she really is"—and we tend to believe them. And when we find it hard to believe that this so-called "real self" could be so different from all appearances, even then we are willing to give love the benefit of the doubt. "I don't know

what she sees in him," is our skeptical way of acknowledging
that the real self may be so hidden from view that no one but a
lover has ever been able to see its virtues.


### Roles

Jackie refused to greet relatives on inauguration day, preferring the entire nation on TV rather than her family. To
the nation, she was the first lady, to the Bouviers, just
Jackie. To please both roles required an impossible shift of
emotional gear.

> KITTY KELLEY, *Jackie Oh!*, p. 117

Being a lover—in other words, loving—is playing certain
kinds of roles, not just for others but (primarily) for oneself.
We sometimes think of the lover as a very narrowly defined,
primarily male role, played by a special type of character
(Don Juan or Flaubert's Rudolphe) and inimitable by virtually
everyone else. But in fact playing the lover is not a single role
but an extremely diverse set of *complementary* roles—that is,
roles that one can never play by one's self but always with a
partner (or several partners, though one doesn't have to be a
Don Juan to be a "lover"). Playing the lover is a role that is
open to virtually anyone (like being a coward, a "bastard" or a
cheapskate). Anyone who is in love plays the lover, whether
well or badly, and to understand what it is to love is largely to
understand what it is to play this certain kind of role—or
rather, certain kinds of complementary roles.

We sometimes think of roles as merely superficial, external
impositions and impersonal slots that people fill despite themselves, in which the real self doesn't count at all. But though
this may be true of bureaucrats (whose public role is defined
by their impersonality and anonymity) it is not true of most
roles—our roles as poets, bullies or saints, for example, or, most
importantly, as lovers. We think of ourselves as *playing* a role,

as if playing a game; but roles need not be frivolous or merely entertaining. They may be deadly serious. And roles need not be superficial; some of our roles define our selves, even our "real" selves. Sometimes we protest that we are "only playing a role." But just as often we may be playing the role of the person who is only playing a role, a role which in fact is central to self-determination and our self-image. This ploy is of no small importance in romantic love, where the dualism of selfhood allows easy shift of blame (as in any team effort in which individual efforts and errors are not easily discernible). But people choose their lovers as they choose themselves (since they choose the one through the other), and so one can choose a self even while complaining about it bitterly and blaming it on the other person, or on love itself. A person chooses to be a martyr and picks a lover who is certain to be oppressive, and then complains, self-righteously and full of self-pity, about the oppression. A person seeks an excuse to avoid responsibility, or to escape the tensions of a flagging career, or to flee the uncertainties of single life, and chooses a lover accordingly, then complains about it. In such cases one defines one's self both by playing the role and at the same time playing the role of just playing the role. But the self is not the face behind the various masks we wear; it is the wearing of the masks. And it is in love, we like to think, that the "real self" is to be defined. Thus some of our masks and roles—the ones we play in love—have been made into trump cards, the way we "really are," regardless of the strength or the suits of the others. To reject these roles as unreal is almost always to stop loving as well.

The roles that are played in love are distinguished by the fact that they are *personal* roles and essentially *private* (even in a melodramatic couple that enjoys playing out their affairs in public). Only in certain societies, however, are personal or private roles even possible, or, at least, distinguishable from public or social roles, and it is perhaps only in our peculiar culture that we insist on defining one's "real self" in terms of only

personal and not public roles. Romantic love has utterly nothing to do with, and no concern for, social roles, a fact which is
obvious in our literature, as princes fall in love with showgirls
and empresses take as lovers their gardeners or mad monks
from Siberia. Indeed, it is the separation of personal from public roles that makes romantic love even conceivable, and it is
for this reason that the love among the ancient Greeks is sometimes denied to be romantic—since the distinction between the
private self and the public self would have been incomprehensible to them—and it is for this reason too that the origins of romantic love are often located in the twelfth century
in Europe, when this distinction first began to enter the social
world.

Romantic love is strictly personal in that its roles are defined entirely in face-to-face confrontation, with a particular
person (occasionally, persons). The fulfillment or failure of
these romantic roles lies entirely within the domain and judgment of the persons involved, *and no one else*. Public or social
roles, on the other hand, are entirely defined in their fulfillment or failure by "objective" standards, which means
that what any particular individual thinks about them is of no
relevance whatsoever. To fill the role of "the most powerful
man in America" means to satisfy the entirely objective standards of power, no matter what delusions of importance one
might have oneself and share with a small circle of friends. But
to be "a wonderful lover," within the context of a particular
sexual relationship, requires satisfying only one person, in addition to oneself, of course.

The question of satisfaction, however, has to do with
fulfillment and failure, not with the definition of the roles
themselves. Indeed, it would be hard to think of a role, or the
general conditions for its fulfillment, which was not learned
from society at large—from movies, stories and the examples of
others. And of course it is possible at any time for public
measurements to intrude and destroy what is a perfectly satis-

factory set of personal roles, for example, when the sexologists repeatedly tell couples what they *ought* to do and enjoy, when psychiatrists in popular magazines portray a single standard of "true" love without any concern for personal differences, or when feminists impose the "objective" criterion of an "equal" relationship, which may make no concessions whatever to the personal feelings—whatever their origins—of the men and women who are so engaged. But the distinction between personal and public roles is, for us, all-important. Indeed we cannot imagine our lives or our conceptions of ourselves, much the phenomenon of romantic love, without it.

### Personal Roles

The Danish philosopher Kierkegaard commented that it must always appear absurd to a third party, when two awkward lovers play the parts of love. But of course this is just the point; such personal roles as the role of the lover are not intended for anyone else. Indeed, the public role of the lover—the Valentino image, for instance—is quite rightly suspected of indicating the very opposite of love. A couple kissing and cooing or making love are playing a part only for themselves, and questions about how "well" they do it, from some outside point of view, are completely irrelevant. To love is to play the lovers, just for one another, not only in gestures of tenderness and sexual excitement, but in a thousand other roles and mutual activities as well, which together define the shared self that emerges in love.

A simple example of a personal role which has no obvious connection with sex or love but yet is one of love's common products is this: every couple I know includes one person who is "the sloppy one" and the other as "the neat one." In fact, they might both be terrible slobs, or terribly neat, by any reasonable "objective" standards. There may have been no difference in their habits whatsoever before they started living

together, and in another relationship they may have had just
the opposite roles. But somehow, early on, the difference is
defined, the roles are cast, and each person plays into them,
the sloppy person even taking some pride in sloppiness, the
neat one taking pleasure in his or her remarkable toleration—or
enjoying the continuous opportunity for criticism. And indeed
one *is* sloppy, the other neat, and it does not matter at all what
anyone outside of the relationship might think. What we call
intimacy is built out of such seemingly unromantic, even
conflicting roles.

Talking baby talk (which babies rarely do, and then in imi-
tation of adults) is the playing of intimacy roles; so is doing
what in public (or if overseen or heard) would be making a
fool of oneself. The powerful executive goo-goos his or her
lover, but quite the contrary of foolishness, the person who refuses to indulge in such play in private is more likely to be considered an emotional coward than a fool. The viability of such
childish roles is often in contrast to the power one has in the
public world; a successful man or woman might feel wholly
free to regress to infancy in love, while a man or woman unsure of his or her status may be much more hesitant to play the
same role. Couples fighting are as often as not playing roles,
rather than trying to settle a point. Mindless conversations are
badly understood as a pathetic exchange of information; they
are role-playing too. The couples in which one person is responsible and the other not, in which one person is mechanically gifted, the other incompetent, the one socially adventurous, the other shy, may all be, like the sloppy-and-neat
couple, playing roles, in which neither the real differences between them—or their similarities—make any difference.

It is a popular question among adolescents and some college
professors: "Do we tend to fall in love with people like—or
unlike—ourselves?" On the one side, we envision "Joe Fratrat"
and "Mary Sorority," dressed like two beans in a pot in their
matching red Izod shirts and Calvin Klein jeans; on the other,

Lady Chatterley and her lover, as opposite as one can imagine. But the question, like most simpleminded questions about love, fails to appreciate the complexity of the emotion in the too-familiar attempt to reduce it all to a simple one-dimensional model—in this case, the attraction and repulsion of likes and opposites. But love depends on both differences and similarities, mutually defined; love is itself the creation of similarities and differences, for that is how we define our selves. Indeed, to confuse the shared identity of love with mere similarity is a guaranteed way not to love at all.

"I had a date with my clone, but it didn't work out."
—*True Confessions* (May, 2081)

# WHY DO I LOVE YOU? 13

KIP: *Mrs. Bonner, I love you. I love lots of girls and women and ladies and so on—but you're the only one I know why I love. And you know why?*

AMANDA: *What?*

KIP: *Because you live right across the hall. You are mighty attractive in every single way, Mrs. Bonner—but I would probably love anybody just so long as they lived across the hall. It's so convenient! Is there anything worse than that awful taking girls home and that long trip back alone?*

GARSON KANIN and RUTH GORDON, *Adam's Rib*

Why do I love you? What is it about you—your eyes, your hair, your smile? No, that can't be it. The fact that you make me happy? The way we have fun together? Sex together? Oh, I don't know—I just love you, that's all. I love *all* of you, nothing less.

But that's not true. Do you love all of me? The fact that I'm always five minutes late to everything? What about my athlete's foot? (After twenty-nine years, it certainly deserves to be considered a part of me.) You've always said that you'd leave in an instant if I were ever to strike you, and you'd certainly stop loving me too. It's not true that you love all of me, and it's not true that you love me "no matter what." Suppose I were to turn into a frog. Not a handsome prince turned into a frog, and not me temporarily a frog, but just a frog, and a frog forever. Would you still love me? Of course not. Granted you might give me a certain priority over the other frogs, at least for a while. And you might not eat frogs' legs again. But soon I'd be just one of the frogs to you, and there isn't much question about whether you'd still love me.

Now perhaps it's an accident of grammar, but the person you love is *me*, referred to by a simple pronoun, a single name. But this leaves entirely open the question of what or whom it is that you love. I love *you*, you know, but I don't love all of you either. Your jogging leaves me cold, and your addiction to okra repulses me. I don't love you "no matter what," much less "forever." I wouldn't love you if you turned into a frog. Indeed, I probably wouldn't love you if you got irreversibly fat. I don't love everything about you. In fact, most of the facts about you are a matter of indifference to me, not ways or reasons I love you at all. Of course, there is a sense in which I *accept* everything about you, including all the things that annoy me, the habits we fight about, the flaws I'd rather ignore, but that's a matter of ontological necessity, not love. It just happens that the things I don't like and don't care about are attached to the same person whom I do love and care about.

Does this mean that I don't love *you*? It does not. It only means that I love you—as you love me—*for reasons*. Some of these may never be stated as such. Some of them are "superficial." Some of them are sufficiently complex that it is unlikely we could ever state them. But nevertheless they are the reasons I love you, and the reasons you love me, and they define the conditions and the limits of our love.

### Love and Beauty

He kept telling her she had a "terrific body," one of several things she despised him for.

TOM WOLFE, "The Independent Woman" (*Esquire* 1979)

One of the reasons I love you is that I think you are beautiful. It is not the only reason I love you, I hasten to add, but it is, I think, one of the most important. Does this mean that I would not be in love with you if you weren't so beautiful? Possibly. Perhaps probably. Of course I love you for many other reasons too. But then again, it would depend on just how much less beautiful you had become. (You couldn't turn into a frog, for example.) But my saying this jars our sensibilities. Love is not supposed to be conditional, and, in particular, it is not supposed to be conditional on such a temporary advantage as beauty. Why not?

Beauty, we are told, is only skin deep. It is "superficial," which is why it is not supposed to be a valid reason for loving someone. But of course it is a reason, and in the history of love almost everyone from Plato to the present has recognized the essential linkage between love and personal beauty, albeit often in the spiritualized version of "a beautiful soul." But the only picture we have of the human soul, wrote the philosopher Ludwig Wittgenstein, is the human body, and even Socrates argued, not without ulterior motives, that those who deserved the best education were also those who displayed the most beautiful bodies. (Not exactly the principle espoused by the National Education Association in this country.) Like it or not, we always end up coming back to the body, including, of course, the face. So what is the objection, to be found in Plato, then in St. Paul and so on in a hundred generations of "spiritual leaders," to beauty, albeit "superficial," as a reason for love—indeed, even as *the* reason for love?

The objection begins with a fear, first of all, among those who lack beauty and attractiveness that they will be less lovable and less loved. In the absence of other reasons, they are right. There has always been, and always will be, resentment of the beautiful, and the wishful ideal that love will see "deeper" than that. But the fear infects those who are unquestionably beautiful as well. "What will happen when I lose my beauty?" It is a reasonable question, and the answer, again in the absence of other, more durable reasons, is that one will no doubt lose one's love as well. But the objection to beauty as the reason for loving goes "deeper" than fear, indeed involves the "depth" metaphor itself which is so much a part of our psychology. Beautiful people do not want to be loved because they are beautiful. We have this sense that beauty is not a legitimate reason for love; it is too ephemeral, too "superficial." We imagine that beneath that obvious façade there must lie some deep reason for loving a person, namely, the soul, to which all of the trappings of beauty as well as intelligence, success, power and fame are mere vanities. Or, in more modern and less theological language, it is the "real" person, the "whole human being" that one comes to love, not for any single reason, much less a reason so impersonal and "superficial" as beauty.

The metaphysical move is simple, almost so quick as to be indiscernible, from the quite reasonable claim that one should not or cannot love a person simply for the reason that he or she is beautiful, to the metaphysically vacuous claims that one loves the inner soul or the total person. The idea that one loves a soul, "no matter what" the more superficial changes and blemishes, or loves "the total person," in which any particular reason is submerged in the whole, is the same familiar Platonic strategy of denying ourselves and pretending, instead, that in love, at least, we are safe from the ravages of time and the world. But it is not just beauty that is so dismissed as a reason for love; *all* reasons are rejected as irrelevant. It is not just the fear of losing that initial attractiveness which made one loved in the first place; it is an avoidance of being compared or evaluated in any way as if, in love, stupidity and lack of consideration, slovenliness and lazy self-indulgence all will be tolerated without question. We imagine love is eternal because we don't want to recognize that it is always conditional; we reject beauty as a reason for loving someone because beauty is so obviously but a temporary condition, and so a striking representative of all conditions. But the fact is, quite simply, I

love you because you are beautiful—if for a thousand other
reasons too—and to deny that or hide it under the metaphysical confusion of "a beautiful soul" is just not to understand what our love is all about. I love you for reasons, and
though those reasons may change and new ones will no doubt
emerge, those reasons set the conditions of love and its limits.

The objection to "reasons for" loving is in fact aimed against
certain kinds of reasons, those that are, because most tangible,
also the easiest to identify. The idea that a person might be
loved "for money" horrifies us even more than love for beauty.
The idea that a reason for loving someone might be mere convenience horrifies us even more than that. Loving someone for
his or her intelligence seems not to be so despicable, but here
perhaps we should object, "Why not?" Is intelligence any less
superficial than beauty? Any more definitive of "the real person"? Are the public poses in the *New York Review of Books*
any less calculated, any less obscene, than the poses in *Playboy*? What about loving a person for his sense of humor? Or
her tough-minded way of asking questions? Or his skill at
whipping up a batch of Chinese dumplings? Or her ability to
fix the T.V. set? Why should these not be reasons for loving?
They often are. But once one adds up the possibly large (but
by no means infinite) number of such equally "superficial"
reasons, need there be anything left over or left out for which
we have to introduce the idea of the soul or "the total person"?
Indeed, to insist upon either notion (the minimal self or the
total self) is to obscure and ultimately to deny precisely what
reasons one has for loving, and, as always, to make love itself—
as well as love's demise—a "mystery."

### Love for Reasons

Money can't buy love, but it improves your bargaining position.

LAURENCE J. PETER

What can count as a reason for loving someone? Could the fact that you were born on December 2 be a reason for loving you? Certainly those who write the astrology columns believe that it is. Could the fact that you are the third richest woman in America be a reason for loving you? Most people would say no, but they would probably point out too that it is a fact one should not let stand in one's way. Is your fame, your glamor, your success a reason for loving you? Well, at least it is obvious that these might well be reasons for being attracted to you in the first place, and it would be strange, to say the least, if they then were to drop out of the picture as if, once we are together, I love only your soul.

Loving a person for reasons, speaking phenomenologically, is to see that person from a certain perspective, within a certain kind of context. One might fall in love with a stranger in Rome whom one would not think of entertaining at home, and lovers who have lived together too long in the daily tedium of everyday rituals find that the passion they used to enjoy together is quickly rekindled as soon as they go on vacation or re-create the conditions of their original courtship. An exemplary if overly amusing case of a change in perspective is that of the male gynecologist who falls in love with one of his patients. There is an obvious sense in which he sees his lover in quite a different perspective from the way he saw his patient, although on rare occasions he may revert back to the former way. So too one rarely loves one's lover all the time; rather, love is an emotion which is more or less confined to certain situations, perhaps spilling over in expression or habit to a dozen other situations as well, but nevertheless quite distinct from

them. While we're balancing the checkbook, one of us looks up
and interrupts this compulsively practical activity by saying,
"I love you." But balancing the checkbook together is not
(usually) a reason for loving. Neither are living together, having children and making love necessarily reasons for loving,
but needless to say they are usually very good if not overwhelming reasons for loving, and the fact that one loves, in its
turn, may be a good reason for any of them.

It is hard (but not impossible) to imagine a circumstance in
which a reason for loving a person would be the fact that he or
she weighs exactly fifty kilograms, about the same as a very
large sack of potatoes. (What would it mean to say, "I love the
way you accelerate when you fall?") To describe a person as a
biological organism, as a doctor does in diagnosis, is hardly a
perspective in which love finds its reasons. ("I love the way
the blood flows through your capillaries.") And this is true no
matter what part of the body is being described, as long as it is
mere biology. The way a penis or clitoris works might indeed
be fascinating, and the fact that it works may indeed be a
precondition if not a reason for some relationships. But it is
hardly a standard example of a reason for love—which is not to
deny that love has its biological preconditions.

Where the question of reasons becomes most difficult is that
arena which is, on the one hand, typically public, social and
even impersonal but nevertheless provides the most common
reasons for one person's attraction to another. But attraction is
not yet love, and reasons for attraction are not necessarily
reasons for love. One might be initially attracted to a person
because he or she is one of the great young violinists of the
age. Or because he or she is particularly "attractive," that is,
beautiful. Or because he or she is remarkably wealthy. When
are they reasons for loving and when are they not?

Let us take the most difficult example—loving a person for
his or her money. And to make it a more difficult, but purer
case, let us even say that he or she is loved *just* for the money—

that is, if the money is lost, so for certain will be the love (allowing for a short period of courtesy of perhaps a week or so). But even this leaves open an essentially ambiguous set of alternatives. It is one thing to love *the money* (which means that, if one could take the money and run, one would do so). It is something else again to love the person because-of-the-money. Suppose a woman loves a man because-he-has-money. She has no desire for the money alone (perhaps she would not know what to do with it). She enjoys spending the money, but mainly *with him;* indeed, it is the one thing they like best doing together. We have postulated that she has no other reasons for loving him, but we should probably suppose, without rendering her a particularly disagreeable if not unbelievable character, that she finds him at least tolerable if not likable, perhaps even charming, attractive and pleasant to be with. But it is the money that draws them together, the money that keeps them together—the money that provides the network of shared activities and identity that constitutes their love. Is this possible? Can love be based on so "vulgar" a reason? Why not? The fact that he has money is no longer merely a matter of social impersonal fact but has been made very personal, now in the sense that it is the vehicle that they share, the way in which they value one another, the way in which they define themselves. And indeed, if this is not a love that we would bear ourselves, why do we insist on condemning it in others as a matter of moral principle, instead of personal taste?

We can add even more to the illustration by supposing that the man quite rightly sees himself as a person with no particularly lovable features; he is physically unattractive, intellectually clumsy, not particularly fun to be with except while shopping; he has no sense of humor to speak of and little of what can be called "style" except what money can buy. And so he identifies with his having money. It is not just the way she sees him; it is the way he sees himself, whether or not he would prefer to have other virtues as well. The fact is, he does not, and he knows it. And the reason he worked so hard for his money, he would be the first to admit, was in order to provide himself with a reason to be loved. And he did. And she loves him for precisely that reason. It is not for his soul, much less "the total person." It is not, the economy being as it is, "forever." But why should we say that it is not love, or that they have no reason for love? So long as those reasons are part of the person, defined in tandem with a lover who shares and mutually helps to define that identity, they are reasons for love. Just as much as, and not so different from, such respectable reasons as "being a good husband."

We play a dangerous game with such reasons. We depict the man or woman who is loved for money as the inevitable victim, as if to assure ourselves that love for us is something much better. We go out of our way to make our love deities as superficial, as one-dimensional and as unhappy as could possibly be believed, as if to assure us all that true love and happiness are best reserved for us modest folk, "for ourselves" and nothing less. Indeed, the conclusion of some of our myths—though rarely stated as such—is that true love is more likely to be found in the poorest and plainest, and for no "reasons" at all.

Suppose a male fetishist loves a woman because she has beautiful feet. (They met, of course, while he was working as a salesman in a shoe store.) Does he love her? That is, does he love *her*? Well, in this case, presumably, he does not have the option of running off with her feet. Nevertheless, we can make the distinction between his merely loving the feet and loving them because they are *her* feet, which means loving her. And this is true even if he *only* loves her for her feet. A truncated example of love, perhaps, but love all the same. If the example seems farfetched and a bit too perverse, I am sure the reader can with the same logic imagine several more standard parts of the body which serve as physical reasons for love. (Recent studies indicate that this is more true of men, who are "turned on" by particular parts of a woman, whereas women tend to be less physical in their reasons. This does not mean that women love "more" than men, however, but only that, as a flawed generalization, they love for different reasons.)

Why introduce a foot fetishist and a gold-digger in a discussion of love? My aim here is not to defend the equal validity of all reasons, much less to celebrate these curiously truncated, fetishistic and one-dimensional cases of love. What I do want to say is that love can still be love for whatever the reasons, and whether a reason is a *good* reason depends and ought to depend not so much on general moralizing as on shared interpersonal identities. If a person prides him- or herself on being beautiful, and perhaps nothing else, then that of course is a good reason for love; if a person truly believes that beauty is vanity and that self-identity lies in loftier characteristics, then his or her being beautiful is a very bad reason for love. Unfortunately, we are not usually so straightforward. A woman who is not particularly beautiful rejects beauty as a valid reason for love out of resentment and envy, but still wishes she were beautiful; someone falls in love with her because he thinks she is beautiful, and the result is, we all know, a confusion of identities. Intelligence is supposed to be a much better reason for loving someone, but again, whether this counts as a *good* reason or not will depend not only on whether it is true that the person is intelligent, but on how that intelligence fits into the overall scheme of shared self-identifications.

In unrequited love, however, one can love a person for any reason whatsoever, unrestrained by considerations of reciprocity and actually shared identities. Thus it is that unrequited love may well for a while provide fantasies and imagined satisfactions hard to find in the rough-and-tumble exchange of real relationships. But this is also to say that the less one feels constrained by the other person's self-identity and the freer one feels to indulge in his or her own reasons and

remain indifferent to the lover, the less this deserves to be
called love. No matter what the reasons. Because, ultimately,
the reasons for love are of a very different kind—not facts
about the person but aspects of the relationship itself.


### The Reasons for Love

Beauty, fame, wealth, breasts, glamor, feet, even convenience can be reasons for love, as well as a hundred even more
trivial and unremarkable advantages, comforts and petty virtues. Nevertheless, it is an exceptional instance of love which is
no more than this, for not only are there a great many different
reasons why most of us love, there are also different kinds of
reasons. In addition to the above, there are also reasons that
have more to do with a person's *personality*—the very word
shows them to be pre-eminently personal. Indeed, even if one
loves for beauty or wealth or whatever, it is difficult to imagine
love that does not also have as its reasons a sense of humor,
that certain playfulness, the hunger for affection, delight in
giving, kindness, charm, a sense of honesty, generosity,
toughness, meekness, a sense of strength, insecurity, self-
sufficiency, childishness, zaniness, efficiency, brutality, hostility. All of these can be and often are (in different people and
in various proportions) reasons for love. But the point to be
made, again and again, is that almost all of these personality
traits are not simply given but *defined within* the relationship.
One person's humor is another's bad taste; what is playful in
one relationship is teasing or hostile in another; what one man
finds honest another considers indiscreet, and what one woman
considers affection another finds weak and offensive. Thus the
reasons for love that make up the complex network of most
relationships are personal not just in the sense that they are
part of one's "personality" but more importantly in that they
are largely defined within the relationship itself. Indeed, some
of the most important and compelling reasons for love may be

aspects of character which are not generally considered part of a personality at all. A man who is universally considered to be brutal may find one woman who considers him, and makes him, gentle. A woman who is considered meek may find one man who thinks her, and makes her, aggressive.

But this set of reasons leads us to another set, even more important but even more difficult to articulate as reasons. They are the complex reciprocal roles and reflections on roles that we call *intimacy*. One might say that intimacy is itself a reason for love (if not also that intimacy *is* love, which is false) except that intimacy is rather a network of reasons and roles, shared attitudes and activities, ways of "fitting" together that, because they are entirely reciprocal and evident only when we're together, may escape our attention as reasons altogether. Indeed, reasons generally become apparent to us *as reasons* only when we back up a step or two and look at them from a distance. Thus, after several years together, I may in one sense forget how beautiful you are, which does not mean that I do not still *see* you *as* beautiful, or that your beauty isn't still a dominant reason for my loving you, but I have ceased to realize—what once was so obvious to me—that your beauty is a reason for my loving you. Lovers after a long time together may even become embarrassed by the very virtues that originally formed (perhaps still do) their reasons for loving—a woman is mortified by her husband's raucous sense of humor, a man is angered by his wife's assertiveness. And even something so seemingly tangible as money may, after a time, be forgotten as a reason and merely taken for granted. But in this most complex and important set of reasons, whose very nature is such that we can't take a step back and look at them, we can see why the most important reasons for love are those which are least rarely evident. And this in turn leads to the facile fallacy of supposing that, for want of anything else to say, what one loves is "the total person" or "something deep inside," when in fact these reasons, like all the others, are strictly superficial.

Intimate roles may be frivolous, so evident in baby babble and other infantile behavior that would be unthinkable in public. They are often sexual, thus leading to the common identification of intimacy and sex as such ("being intimate with" is a polite way of saying "having intercourse"). Intimate roles are by their very nature rare, if not exclusive; when intimate behavior is made public and common it may cease to be intimate and cease to be a reason for loving as well. A person who talks baby talk in public (a popular comedian, for example) loses that role as a vehicle for mutual intimacy, and sexual promiscuity, whatever else one might think about it, renders sex, too, unavailable for intimacy. (Thus prostitutes tend to reserve for their lovers at least one sexual activity which they refuse to their clients.) Beauty and wealth, we can now say, are usually not considered reasons for love because they are essentially public and therefore not matters of possible intimacy. But this goes too far, since, as I have argued, beauty and wealth can be *made* private and even exclusive—for example, in countries where women cover their bodies and faces in public; for couples who hide their wealth or have their special ways of enjoying it together. And despite our obsession with intimacy it is not true that intimacy provides the only reasons for loving (nor is intimacy necessarily loving; hatred can be intimate too).

Roles become reasons for loving when they participate in the formation of a shared self. Whether a particular activity contributes to shared selfhood and thus provides such a reason depends on the activity and on the relationship. For some couples, sexuality is a block to intimacy rather than its vehicle or expression; for some people, balancing the family checkbook might well be one of those intimate activities through which they define themselves. It is not always clear whether one loves because a role is shared or when a role is shared because one loves, but this seems to me to be not particularly important. Whether sex is "fabulous" because we are in love or whether fabulous sex is one of the reasons we are in love is not a worry worth worrying about. Indeed, to worry too much about the reasons one loves is itself an obstacle to love and, eventually, perhaps a reason for *not* loving. As André Gide once observed, "Even to wonder whether one loves is already to love a little less." That is not true, but the opposite may well be: we have so long been told that love is "without reasons" and even "beyond reason," that to specify reasons is already to love less, that we realize to our horror that our love has its limits, and then suspect, wrongly, tragically, that perhaps our love is not "true" at all. But why should love be love without limits, when we are limited ourselves?

# "THE MOST WONDERFUL PERSON IN THE WORLD" 14
## (FANTASIES VERSUS ILLUSIONS)

*I've always loved you, she said, and when you love someone, you love the whole person, just as he or she is, and not as you would like them to be.*

TOLSTOY, *Anna Karenina*

Among the various reasons why we love someone, some are subtle, submerged, barely visible, perhaps unspeakable or shameful besides. But others are outrageous, extravagant, overwhelming; for nothing is more obvious about love than its enthusiasm. And enthusiasm tends to exaggerate, effuse superlatives, turning minor virtues into cosmic icons and ordinary charms into utterly unique and unimaginable blessings. Thus the person we first found attractive suddenly becomes fantastically beautiful, and the person we once thought was "nice" now becomes "the most wonderful person in the world." This is the process that Stendhal called "crystallization," the *creation* of sparkling "perfections" in our lover at every opportunity. Thus lovers discredit themselves, prove that love has an overactive imagination if it is not exactly "blind," which leads too easily to the cynical conclusion that love itself is an illusion, nothing but a peculiar form of madness which we continue to worship only for the flattering reason that, sometimes, we ourselves are the recipients of this extravagant praise.

Some reasons for loving someone seem to us to be bad reasons, and some reasons are quite unreasonable, or else simply false. A reason might be bad if, for example, it is a reason that offends the other person; a nun's beauty might still be a good reason to admire or appreciate her aesthetically, for instance, but not for loving her, since such a "reason" will not contribute (but more likely make impossible) the shared selfhood of love. A reason might be unreasonable if it includes expectations which a person cannot possibly—or in any event is highly unlikely to—fulfill. Loving a person for his or her "potential" usually carries this danger; so does loving someone because he or she "will make me happy for the rest of my life (even though I've been depressed for most of it so far)." A reason might simply be false: if I love you because you've told me that you're the illegitimate daughter of Jean-Paul Sartre, and I find out that that's not true, that's the end of my love—not because you have lied to me, but because my reason for loving you has disappeared. But besides these obvious ways in which reasons can go wrong, there are much more interesting exceptions to these ways, which turn out to be the very heart of love.

One of the reasons I love you is because I believe that you are the most beautiful woman in the world. As a matter of objective fact—if there can be such a thing—this is false, or at least provincial, since there are canons of beauty which you do not even approximate, much less perfectly fulfill. Does this make my reason a bad reason? Does it make my love for you, in part based on that reason, a mere illusion? Does the fact that I overlook your flat feet, or split ends, or chipped tooth, mean that love is a deception, or that I'm fooling myself? Does the very real possibility that someday I might look at you and no longer think you are beautiful mean that my love for you *now* is illusory? Could it be that I don't love *you* at all but simply some beautiful fantasy that I (unfairly) expect you to live up to?

The above questions, set as charges and accusations, have

been put forth in a powerfully convincing way by a number of
recent women writers, most notably Marilyn French in *The
Women's Room*. The entire novel, from our perspective, might
be seen as a treatise on the illusions of love. In one of the most
quoted scenes, the heroine Val goes on at length in mock
awesome tones about the virility, charms and brilliance of a
new lover, in great detail about the magnificence of his arms,
his eyes, his wit, his sex. Then, "suddenly, one day, the unthinkable happens." He says something stupid, and then again;
and then you see "he farts in bed, he's skinny, fat, flabby . . .
and doesn't understand Henry James at all." The logic is simple, and devastating: love leads us to have all sorts of illusions
and fantasies about our lovers which, inevitably, come crashing down in dis-illusion-ment and disappointment.

One answer to this set of accusations is to reply that one can
also love a person *as is*, not as you would like him or her to be,
not as you imagine him or her, not as ideal but just as "Joe" or
"Sally," rather than Apollo or Aphrodite incarnate. But this flat
and initially plausible if hardly exciting answer leaves out one
of the most crucial ingredients of love—*fantasy*. It is simply
false to say that we love—or can love—a person simply on the
basis of "the facts." We select from those facts, and we idealize
some of them. We share daydreams and hopes and plans, and
without them love would be unimaginable. Fantasy, not music,
is the food of love. Furthermore, this "realistic" response asks
us to do the impossible in another sense; it requires us to be
matter-of-fact in an emotion (like most emotions) whose whole
essence is wrapped up in enthusiasm. It's as if we were told,
"It's okay to have an emotion but don't get emotional about
it." The idea of loving a person *as is* is a bit of wishful thinking,
an attempt to reduce this most volatile of emotions to flat perceptions, without the chance of disappointment.

A different answer to the charge that love is an illusion is the
pious answer—that whatever fantasies or illusions might provide the reasons for love, the fact that one loves, for whatever

reasons, is all that counts. The idea, which we have already rejected, is that the reasons themselves don't really matter, that what one loves, if one "truly" loves at all, is the whole person, or the "soul." But reasons matter; the reasons define the nature and the limits of love. So if the reasons indeed are illusions, love will be an illusion too.

To love is to fantasize, to idealize, to see someone as "the most wonderful person in the world," perhaps the most beautiful, the most charming, and so on. This is not to say, however, that the lover is "all perfections," as Stendhal sometimes argues; the most wonderful person in the world might nonetheless have smelly feet, be incapable of carrying a tune and clumsy in certain social situations. Being in love does allow us to appreciate features of a person that might otherwise go unnoticed or unappreciated. Being in love also allows us to tolerate features that would otherwise be intolerable, and benignly ignore features that might otherwise be repulsive. And indeed one can still positively dislike features of a person one nonetheless loves, all of which is simply to say, in effect, that it is surely not true that lovers fail to recognize the faults in each other, that they are indiscriminately enthusiastic about everything. If anything, lovers are more critical, since, ultimately, it is one's *own* identity that is at stake. But this still leaves that core of reasons which are, indeed, unreasonably exaggerated and seem to be, undeniably, illusions. I might be realistic about your smelly feet, but I still think you're the most wonderful person in the world.

### Fantasies (versus Illusions)

But love—don't we all talk a great deal of nonsense about it? What does one mean? I believe I care for you more genuinely than nine men out of ten care for the woman they're in love with. It's only a story one makes up in one's mind about another person, and one knows all the time it

isn't true. Of course one knows; why, one's always taking
care not to destroy the illusion. One takes care not to see
them too often, or to be alone with them for too long together. It's a pleasant illusion, but if you're thinking of the
risks of marriage, it seems to me that the risk of marrying
a person you're in love with is something colossal.

VIRGINIA WOOLF, *Night and Day*

Love is not an illusion, but my argument against this now familiar charge does not deny that love sometimes involves illusions and does not at all deny the essential importance of fantasy in love. The argument turns instead on a distinction, often
blurred over in this flurry of accusations, between fantasies
and illusions, which are not the same. Not all fantasies involve
falsehoods, and even among those that do, not all fantasies are
explosive. Fantasies are indeed essential to love, but illusion
and disillusionment are not.

The most common form of fantasy is simple daydreaming. I
imagine our walking along the beach together. I relish the
thought of making love to you this evening. I think of something amusing to say to you when you get home. I try to picture what we will do in Philadelphia this summer. But there is
nothing illusory about the future, despite the fact that—certain
metaphysical paradoxes aside—it does not exist, at least not
yet. Sharing an identity (or, for that matter, simply having
an identity) involves such daydreaming, planning and imagining, and whether or not dreams come true, indeed, whether or
not they are even plausible, is not always important. Of course,
if one's little plans and daydreams *always* end in nothing, not
only love but one's whole attachment to reality might well be
put in question. But even when a great many of our fantasies
are unreal, it may be the fantasies themselves, especially when
shared, that form the structure of our identity. Indeed, poets
have argued that it is collective myths and fantasies—rather
than anything "real"—that give whole cultures, as well as indi-

viduals, their identities. One can at least imagine a couple at home, Percy and Mary Shelley in their seaside retreat, perhaps, dreaming of a life together when in fact their life together is their dreaming. The truth of daydreams isn't important—only their shared significance. This sense of fantasy is quite distinct, obviously, from the pornographic daydreams that currently enrich our list of pseudo-scientific best sellers.

A second form of fantasy is *idealization*, the representation of one's lover as *ideal*, "perfect," the very embodiment of perfection. It is a mistake to think that idealization necessarily requires distortion, or exaggeration, or deluding oneself into thinking that something is what it is not. In fact, idealization is exactly the opposite, accepting something and celebrating it *for itself*, without distortion or even comparison. And yet idealization often looks like comparison, since it is typically expressed in comparative or superlative form: "the most wonderful," "the most beautiful" and "the best. . . ." But this is one of those times when the language of love—the expletives of enthusiasm—is not to be taken literally. Idealization is a *refusal* to compare. As a lover, I love your nose. Is it a "perfect" nose? "The best"? I haven't the faintest idea what that would mean. I might seek out a set of criteria or standards according to which your nose is indeed measurably perfect, but I would choose the criteria, needless to say, wholly on the condition that your nose fit exactly. Which is to say, the measurement, and the implicit comparison, are beside the point. And yet I say, as if to confuse myself, that it's the most beautiful nose in the world. That sounds like a comparison, but it is instead a way of *blocking* all comparison (as when we say, of a work of art, that it's "*in*valuable"). You ask, teasing but also quite serious, "But what about so-and-so the movie star's nose?" And I dismiss your question, with a bit of annoyance. You have missed the point, which is, "I love your nose."

Anyway, to get away from any suspicion of pronasal fetishism, let me make the point in a more abstract way: the ide-

alizations of love are appreciations, not distortions or comparisons. In the nature of the case, there is nothing that can be
false or erroneous about them, unless for instance one once too
often admires a lover's coiffure and it turns out to be a wig, or
extravagantly praises one's lover's poetic talent only to find out
his verses have been plagiarisms. One can, of course, always
change one's idealizations, now see as common what once
seemed ideal, or now see as vulgar what once seemed generous
or extravagant. Indeed, forcing real comparisons is an effective way of doing this. (One way of falling *out* of love is to
compare one's [ex]lover in a systematically unflattering way—
not only the faults but what one thought to be ideal as well.)
But this is not at all a matter of *disillusionment*—the cracking
of illusions. One has not deceived oneself or believed any falsehood. To see certain features as ideal is simply to be enthusiastic about them, whether as a reason for love or as a consequence. In love, we tend to idealize as much as possible. Out
of love, we do not. But to infer from the fact that one later
"sees through" one's former idealizations to the conclusion that
the earlier idealizations (and perhaps the love too) were illusions is a self-defeating travesty of logic.

These are two kinds of fantasies that are clearly harmless,
central to love, not prone to falsehood or illusions, and therefore not liable to disillusionment. But there are also fantasies
which are by their very nature false and impossible, which
nonetheless may play a crucial role in the shared experiences
of love. Bored to tears at an office meeting, I imagine in
magnificent detail the most physiologically unworkable and
practically implausible sexual fantasy, which I'd like to try
out right after this damned meeting is over. It's wonderful and
later I tell you about it, you laugh, and add some twists and
details I hadn't yet thought of myself. Indeed, the next day
you are caught in an equally horrid office meeting and repli-
cate a similar fantasy, and tell me about it, and this physically
impossible fantasy life becomes part of our private world, a

recurrent activity which allows both of us to feel extremely intimate even when we are very much separated. I can easily imagine, and I say to you, that I'd like to spend all day tomorrow making love to you a hundred times and, the exactitude of the number aside, this is a perfectly reasonable fantasy, provided, of course, I do not try to literally put it in action. I can fantasize about our life in the fourteenth century while we read *A Distant Mirror* together. I can fantasize you as Dido to my Aeneas, your Dulcinea to my Don Quixote, and the impossibility of my fantasies can hardly be viewed as illusions, much less as exemplary of the illusoriness of love. Even impossible fantasies can be distinguished from illusions and can provide a tangible structure for love.

Indeed, real-life, non-imaginary fantasies that are demonstrably false may not be illusory either. Consider this important example: two remarkably ugly people are sitting in front of you at the airport, billing and cooing and obviously very much in love. One's first feeling is akin to disgust, with a second feeling, akin to superiority, following rapidly on its heels. Then a third feeling, also quickly, of guilt and shame, that one should be so unsympathetic. But then there may well be a sense of empathetic delight, rendered up in some clumsy bromide such as "I guess there's someone in this world for everyone," or "There's no disputing a person's tastes." But now, what about the *truth* of their fantasy, which is (one hears them say) that they are both beautiful? In the name of The Truth, should one approach them and invite them to re-examine their partners a bit more objectively, so as not to be fooled into making such clearly erroneous claims? Or is it rather the case that "truth," as we self-righteously call it in such cases, is not of significance at all? Indeed, this is what we mean when we say that emotions are irreducibly *subjective*, not so much that they are false (though they may be) as that what other people think just doesn't matter. And it is in this all-important sense that—no matter what our media-hype single-type image of public beauty may be—*all* lovers are beautiful.[1]

Here, with the notion of subjectivity, we come to the heart of fantasy, which is not, as we preliminarily suggested, just a projection beyond reality but something more besides, a world *over and above* reality, a "sur-reality" which has its own rules and its own "truth" ("subjective truth," the Danish philosopher Kierkegaard called it). This is what distinguishes our fantasies from illusions, not just the negative fact that they are not dangerously false but the positive point that they are beyond objectivity and truth as well. They are simply a matter of the agreement of the participants, and immune to contradiction from anyone else. Two objectively ugly people may stay in love for years; two "gorgeous" movie stars may be repulsed by each other in weeks. This is not to say, of course, that what we believe and what we feel cannot be affected by others; no lover is immune, no matter how fanatic the love, to the constant reminders of friends and associates that his *femme fatale* is actually a less animated version of Miss Piggy, or that her Prince Charming has the personality of a veal chop. But more likely than not, the friends and associates will be sacrificed before the love will be, for it is not self-deception that leads us to protect our fantasies but the very real choice between public agreement and private enthusiasm, and in a society that provides too little public enthusiasm and too bland public fantasies, private fantasies limited perhaps only to the two of us, are bound to be preferable and to be protected even at considerable cost.

This notion of subjectivity, the more or less private creation of a mutually agreeable and irrefutable truth, lies at the basis of our concept of personal roles as well. In love we make our fantasies come true, not necessarily for the world at large, but at least with one other person, and sometimes that is sufficient.

[1] Assuming, that is, that beauty is relevant as a reason for love, in any particular relationship.

A timid man wants to feel dominating and so he finds a woman, who might well be a much stronger person than he is, objectively, who allows him to play that role with her. ("You're a real tiger," she purred, as she helped him into the bedroom.) To feel that one is a giving person, one need only find one person to give to. To feel frivolous (not merely ridiculous), one needs to find only one person to appreciate one's silliness. Sexual prowess can be proven with a single person—in fact, *preferably* with a single person, thus eliminating the possibility of comparison. Indeed, what often goes under the name of "looking for love" is more specifically a sought-after role looking for a partner, and/or a private audience.

The separation of the personal and the public is not, however, always so clear—even in our society (which is one of the few that so emphasizes this distinction). Many emotions include a sense of the public view (shame, for example), and even love, which systematically excludes the larger world, is subject to its opinions. The roles and fantasies according to which one chooses a lover are themselves determined in large part by the culture at large, and the plausibility of a relationship, one's probable success in maintaining the roles and fantasies of love, depends a lot more than we would like to think—in the initial arrogance of love—on the uninformed and even unsympathetic view of others. But even here it is essential to our analysis that this interference and influence be kept distinct from the structures of romantic love itself. A person may choose a lover, for example, for the sake of public approval, even applause. A man may fall in love with a woman because *everyone else* thinks she is beautiful, but—in addition to the gloomy prognosis such love deserves—there is also the question of whether the "everyone else" has in this case entered into the structure of the emotion as well. And the answer has to be no, not if it is love. Love must be solely a matter of the perceptions and fantasies of the lovers, and though the encouragement of others is surely not incompatible with love, indeed may even influence it mightily, it is never part of love, and this, perhaps, is the most dramatic single distinction between our own concept of romantic love and other emotions that might be called "love" in societies or contexts that do not have this rebellious subjective element—that our opinion (just the two of us) is all-important.

### Illusions (versus Fantasies)

If all of this is defensible as fantasy, what then counts as illusion? Illusions are *falsifications* of reality. They are not mere daydreams or idealizations or playful images but unreal, unreasonable, self-deceptive and ultimately destructive expectations. To love someone who is quite ordinary and to fantasize extravagantly is not illusory, but to have expectations that will inevitably lead to disappointment and dis-illusion-ment is indeed illusion. The most common and familiarly tragic illusions in love have to do with reciprocity—believing that one is loved in return when in fact one is only getting kindness or courtesy, loving for unreasonable reasons or reasons one knows to be (but will not admit to be) fallacious. I play a role, and I assume you're playing too: in fact, you're only "humoring" me. Sometimes such illusions are wishful misperceptions; sometimes they are calculated appearances, for example, when one allows oneself "to be led on," even while knowing better. One can fantasize that one is loved when one knows one is not. I can imagine without illusion what it would be for my favorite actress or writer to love me. But when we come to believe what we fantasize or imagine, despite the fact that it is self-deceptive as well as destructive, that is illusion. And it is entirely different from fantasy—at least from most fantasies—for precisely that reason.

Many illusions, also common but less widely recognized, are not so much part of love as they are illusions *about* love. These are the illusions most vigorously and rightfully attacked in *The*

*Women's Room* and by other feminists: for example, expecting to be loved "no matter what," or expecting to keep on loving without effort, without doubts, without change. Indeed, lovers are often intolerant of the slightest shifts in the delicate structures that make up their love; forget about turning into a frog —one of my friends has threatened to divorce her husband if he simply shaves off his beard. The idea that love lasts "forever" is an illusion, even if it lasts. "This time will be different," uttered not as a resolution but as a simple expectation, is almost always an illusion, and the idea that love is "everything," that it alone will transform one's life, guarantee happiness and protect one from all disappointment, is an illusion.

Where illusions enter into the love itself, they may range from simple negligence to finally fatal misperceptions. But what makes illusions *illusions,* not mere mistakes and not fantasies, is an element of *will* involved in them. Illusions are, in Freud's sense, *wishful thinking.* A mistake may be a mere misperception or lack of information, not knowing any better. An illusion, on the other hand, is a *willful* misperception, a forced expectation, not "on top of" but despite the facts and what one knows. This is why illusions are so explosive; they involve not just a falsehood but a falsehood that one already knows to be false. Thus we *want* the security of being loved without qualification—though we know better—and so we convince ourselves through a thousand legends and poems that "true" love is indeed unqualified. Knowing our own fickleness and emotional variability, we wish we could guarantee our feelings, lock them into an ironclad warranty with the grace of God as their guarantor—and so we make ourselves believe that love is "forever." We are unhappy with our lives and wish that in a stroke they could be changed. Thus our schizoid attitudes to romantic love in general; it is not that romantic love itself is an illusion, but rather that, at one and the same time, we wish for everything and know full well that those wishes and expectations are foolish. Thus our piety and our cynicism, both at once. Thus our foolishness, and too much of our poetry and philosophy.

Many if not most of our illusions have a social background, based in the myth of romantic love and the stories we are told from childhood. It is indeed, as some feminists have charged, as if there were a cultural conspiracy to keep us indoctrinated, not just with harmless and edifying fairy tales but with dangerous and destructive deceptions, which we can see through but yet believe at the same time. We are told that love must be one sort of thing, and we inevitably find it to be something less, and we are disillusioned. But the illusions of love should not be confused with love itself. Because we deceive ourselves into expecting everything from love does not mean that love in fact gives us nothing. Because we wish the impossible does not mean that we have to deceive ourselves, and because love doesn't last forever does not mean that love itself is an illusion and not worthwhile while it lasts. Love does have its fantasies, and inevitably some of these may turn out to be illusions. But this is not to deny the difference between the two, much less to show that love itself is an illusion.

Does it really matter to anyone else if you *aren't* the most wonderful person in the world? In what sense does it even matter to me? To love is to share the loveworld together, and that is itself a fantasy, a fantasy in which it is, as far as we are concerned, "just the two of us." And that is why, ultimately, you are the most wonderful person in the world. Apart from me, you are the only other person in there.

# "I'LL BE YOUR SLAVE" 15
## (IF ONLY YOU'LL GET UP ON THAT PEDESTAL)

*A little less love, if you please, and a little more common decency.*

KURT VONNEGUT, *Slapstick*

One of the clichés of love is the interconnection between love and respect. The fact that this often flies in the face of experience does not damage the cliché, of course, for, like all illusions about love, this one consists mainly of wishful thinking. It is not just an observation but a set of hopeful expectations—that in being loved we are guaranteed the respect that may evade us in everyday life. In fact, love is quite different from respect (which does *not* mean that you can love only someone you don't respect).

What is the connection between love and respect? How essential to love is a sense of equality (which is often confused with respect)? Women who have resigned themselves to a subservient lot in life (albeit as a "total" woman) expect by way of compensation their lovers and husbands to respect them and treat them as equals, because of love, but also as one of its preconditions. But there are still no small number of men who feel that love is *not* a matter of equality, though perhaps (also by way of compensation) still a matter of respect, and so the supposed equality of love often turns into a struggle for power and status, a question of "Who's boss?" in which mutual respect is famously absent. It is in love, but luckily not in war, that we have come to expect almost anything, as "fair."

The obvious fact of the matter, wishful thinking and egalitarian ideology aside, is that a great many love relationships are not either equal or symmetrical, and a great many love roles depend on a mutual sense of domination and submission, "S/M" relations (without leather and whips) in which one is the master and one the slave, in which power, status and responsibility, or the lack of them, provide the primary reasons for love. Is this love? And perhaps far more importantly, are these roles of superiority and inferiority to be equated, as many recent theorists have equated them, with male and female, masculine and feminine roles, whether allegedly "natural" or not?

### Love and Equality

Virtually every emotion that is concerned with other people involves a set of judgments that have to do with *status*. In fact the objective of many emotions is to increase our status vis-à-vis other people, at least in our own eyes, to set ourselves up as superior or, in the image of the Orient and Erving Goffman, to "save face." ("The term *face* may be defined as the positive social value a person effectively claims for himself by the line others assume he has taken during a particular contact" [Goffman, "On Face-Work," *Interaction Ritual*, Doubleday, 1967, p. 5].) In the emotions pity and contempt, for example, I set myself up as markedly superior to another person. In worship, envy and resentment, on the other hand, I see myself as inferior, to God in the first case, to someone more powerful than I am in envy or resentment. (One can feel envious or resentful of inferiors only in so far as something about them is enviable or impertinent.) Anger is an emotion that requires more or less *equals*, even as it asserts a certain superiority by virtue of the emotion itself. To become angry with a child is not only to assert one's moral authority, it is also to treat the child as a responsible person. (As opposed, for example, to being merely annoyed with him, as one might be with a mosquito.) Thus a favorite strategy of servants and teenagers is to make a superior "lose his temper," so bringing him *down* to one's own level. Jealousy too involves a confrontation of more or less equals (thus distinguishing it from envy), and so does hatred (thus distinguishing that emotion from contempt and resentment). It is the black knight whom the white knight hates—not the trolls and ogres, whom he merely despises, or the dragon, which he fears.

But what about love? In *The Passions*, I came down rather flat-footed in the position that love demands equality. One might feel affection toward an inferior, or idolize a superior, but neither of these is love. To "care for" a person is not to love him, nor is it love when one admires, adores or worships. (What is it to think of adoration as an emotion appropriate for a woman toward a man, but think of a man treasuring or cherishing a woman?) One argument against any significant difference in status between lovers is that it creates a distance that seems incompatible with the intimacies of love. The troubadour's imagery of *devotion*, for example, re-creates the detachment of a lord and servant in a purely personal context (the woman in this case playing the lord) and this in turn makes difficult if not impossible a sense of shared identity. The other person becomes truly Other—"The Beloved" (which is one reason that term is so obnoxious). Slaves cannot be lovers of masters, nor masters of slaves. (Affection or adoration, yes; love, no.) For someone to be your slave may be a great convenience, even flattering, but slavery and devotion is not to be confused with love.

Loving someone who is superior, loving God for example, is always a kind of *hubris*—the Greek sin of supposing oneself God's equal. (This leaves open the question of whether it makes sense to believe that God loves us.) There is quite prop-

erly a sense in which we can be *offended* by the revelation that
someone loves us, rather than simply amused or flattered or
indifferent, if we think of that person as markedly inferior.
Thus the gods did punish those mere mortals who sought to
embrace them.

The other side of making oneself a slave is elevating one's
loved one to some exalted status; "putting her on a pedestal" is
the common expression when the loved one happens to be a
woman. (When it is a man, he is adored or worshiped, but
why *not* on a pedestal?) What is wrong with "being stuck on a
pedestal"? Well, to begin with, as Gloria Steinem argues, "a
pedestal, like any small place, is a prison." But it is the height
of a pedestal, not its diameter, that is the objection against it.
Height is distance, and distance is antithetical to love. And
then there is the fear of falling. When a person is so idealized,
he or she cannot help but be disappointing. This is a point
made bitterly by feminists Shulamith Firestone and Marilyn
French, but of course it is a problem equally shared by adored
men. Simone de Beauvoir writes in one of her novels, "When a
god falls, he does not become merely a man; he becomes a
fraud." But, as we have already argued, idealization need not
involve falsification, and thus not be inevitably disappointing.
What is wrong with pedestals is the fact that they are indeed
elevated, and thus at a distance, limiting reciprocity and mutual expression. This didn't bother the troubadours, whose ladies were already effectively on pedestals—in a high tower
above the moat, according to the most common of our chivalric images—but then, I have argued that their devoted adoration should probably not count as full-blooded love either.
The higher the pedestal, the less chance for mutual expression.
Thus a woman rightly reacts, "When you idealize me so, I
don't know how I can respond to you." Not because she is a
prisoner (she can always jump), but because the distance itself makes response impossible, or inappropriate. Idolatry is
sometimes an admirable and inspiring emotion, and being idol-

ized can be both exhilarating and self-satisfying. But neither adoring nor being adored has anything to do with love. In fact (after the initial fascination at least) both may make love all but impossible.

There is a familiar objection to all of this, however, that must be put aside before we express reservations of our own. Some of our best-known romantic stories, "Cinderella," for example, are based on the premise that love involves lovers who are wholly unequal, a prince and a scullery maid, in this case. Or the countess falls in love with her chauffeur, fighting to defend her love in the face of the most socially embarrassing inequality. Aren't these clear counter-examples to the thesis that love is possible only between equals?

We have emphasized the notion of *personal* identity, in opposition to social roles and social identity, for precisely this reason. Indeed, what these examples show is precisely this opposition, for the inequalities are *social* inequalities, and the conflict—the source of the romantic elements of the story—is precisely the contradiction between these initial social inequalities and the personal equality that is required by love. ("Love does not find, but *creates* equals," writes Stendhal.) In the story of Cinderella, the prince not only marries the maid but raises her to the peerage, thus to live "happily ever after." King Edward VIII found it necessary to lower his social status to match that of the woman he loved, and Shulamith Firestone argues that this is the case for all men's love—"they fall in love to justify their descension to a lower caste." But the countess who cannot suitably elevate her chauffeur may well "lower herself" as well, and the adjustment of social status to match the personal requirements of love is not in itself a remark on the relative roles of men and women in love. The idea that, in our society, women more often move *up* to the social status of their lovers while men rarely agree to move *down*—if this is true—is certainly indicative of an asymmetry in *social* status, but not therefore in personal status as well. Indeed, it is part of

our domestic mythology that it is the woman, in love, who is
"on the pedestal" and women, in general, who are superior in
all matters of emotion and personal relationships. Whether or
not this is true, it shows quite clearly that personal status and
social status are quite distinct for us.

And so we agree: *Love requires equals,* and where there are
no equals, where one is the master and the other a slave, where
one is adoring the other, who is high and far away—that is not
love, whatever else it might be.

Romantic love is the great equalizer, as our grade B romantic novels are so fond of pointing out. It is sometimes said that
sex serves this function. This is sometimes true but just as often
not true at all. Taking off one's uniform may indeed bring a
person "down to size," removing at least the most visible trappings of social status and power. ("He looks pretty good with
his pockets on," according to an old Bogart line.) But sex can
also be used as a vicious weapon for creating inequality, for
degrading someone or making a person feel wholly inadequate.
It is love, not sex, that creates equals, though sex *in love* is one
of the primary structures of this equalization.

It is one of the dogmas of our pervasive egalitarianism that
one loves another "just as a human being"; there is a crumb of
truth in this wonderbread of modern humanism. The truth is
that equality is essential to love, but to insist that one does not
love a person for his or her social status does not entail the existence of some naked entity called "the human being," for a
person stripped of social status nevertheless retains his or her
character as a set of personal roles, and it is this character,
these roles, that are engaged in love. Cinderella cannot love
the prince *because he is a prince,* and neither can the prince—
who has class identity problems—love Cinderella because she
is a maid and a member of the proletariat. Love demands and
if need be creates equals. The girl and boy next door may take
this for granted, but nonetheless it is one of the structures of
an emotion which otherwise has no right to the name "love."

Some equals, however, are more equal than others. An emotion may require more or less equals but yet include a significant difference in status. Anger, I suggested, is such an emotion; on the one hand, it requires equality, or it degenerates into scorn or contempt, or worse, thinking someone "beneath contempt." On the other hand, anger includes a rather dramatic sense of self-righteous superiority, with the other as a moral inferior—at least for the moment. And in love, one of the most common configurations of roles is the pairing of domination and submission, which at its extremes becomes sadism and masochism. Now it is all too easy to confuse this configuration with a master and slave relationship; Jean-Paul Sartre does exactly this when he interprets love relationships and their dialectic to the "master-slave" relationship discussed most famously by G. W. F. Hegel in his *Phenomenology of Spirit*. But the point to be made here is that domination and submission are not the same as master and slave roles, and in the context of love these roles must nonetheless be complementary relations between equals. And we should also say—again—that these roles need have nothing to do with male and female, masculine and feminine. Whatever the inequities of our social life, our personal roles seem far less one-sided. The domineering wife is at least as old and familiar an image as the overbearing husband. Equality here is a personal, not a social or sexual concern.

One way of putting this quite simply is to say that the masochist acts his or her role *voluntarily*, not out of fear of some greater punishment, in which case he or she would merely be a victim of kidnapping. And even the sadist is wholly concerned with the feelings and reactions of his masochistic partner, which is why he is a sadist in the first place. (The Marquis de Sade, who knew about such matters, argued that the whole purpose of sadism was to assure a sincere response from one's partner. Pleasure can be feigned, he argued, but not pain.) But leaving aside the extreme case of sadomas-

ochism, emotional dominant and submissive roles play a part
in almost all relationships at one time or another, though it is
rarely the case that one person always plays the same role. In
different contexts, the roles often switch—and sexual roles com-
pose but one of the contexts within which these roles are
played. The person who is typically the dominant conver-
sationalist may well be the more passive sex partner, and the
person who is physically more aggressive may well be the one
who prefers to be hugged and stroked. In times of insecurity,
one or the other may well find baby talk and what in public
would be obnoxiously obsequious behavior the most comfortable role. Or else one may compensate for other inadequacies
by being boldly assertive, even commandeering, with which
the other may or may not comply. But the point to be made
here is that domination and submission are not only intrinsic to
love roles (and thus not to be condemned as such) but they
also presuppose a mutually agreed-upon scenario between
equals. Only equals can *act* inferior with one another and not
be.

### R-E-S-P-E-C-T

Love can be said with qualifications to be between equals.
But what about *respect*, which is so often taken as a *sine qua
non* of love and equality? "How can you love me if you don't
even respect me?" But one can, and does. Respect, common
wisdom aside, seems to have very little to do with love, although to be sure one would hardly want to be in love without
it. Respect is an attitude that is distinctively impersonal, anonymous, the very antithesis of intimacy. When you are told by
someone you love, "Well, I respect you very much . . ." you
know that you've had it, and you expect a disappointing
"but . . ." to follow.

It is most desirable if I love you that I also respect your professional ambitions, but it is a sad if long-standing fact that

love in no way requires this, and sometimes contradicts it. And in so far as I respect your career, for example, my opinion is no different from anyone else's, however important it may be to you and to us. You may at some point insist that I respect you "as a human being," but respect, like equality, has meaning only when it has a specifiable content, and in so far as "being a human being" has content at all, it is minimal content, making you just one of the multitudes, not someone special, not someone with whom and through whom I define my identity. When you are in love with someone, respecting him or her as "a human being" is very little, requiring some "common decency" perhaps but wholly ignoring everything that makes this particular person—as opposed to just some stranger or other—very special. In much the same way so-called *self-respect*, difficult as it may sometimes be, makes utterly minimal demands on the self, whereas *self-love*, by way of contrast, requires seeing oneself as much more than minimal or merely equal—as superb or superior.

Respect is an emotion that, if not egalitarian, at least requires an open mind, a sense of distance if not indifference. Respect is never exclusive, as love often is; respect is never intimate, as love *always* is. Respect is not necessarily even personal, as love must be. In fact respect refers far more to social and public status than to personal status. That is why the question, "Will you still respect me in the morning?" is so philosophically significant; what it makes quite clear is the conflict between intimacy and neutral social respect. If respect were so like or part of love, as we often suppose, this question would not even make sense. Years ago, intimacy was rare, respect quite common. Curiously, we are now promiscuous with our intimacy, stingy with our respect. No wonder then that often we now prize the latter far more than the former—and wish that love would provide what our busy competitive world will not.

Holding you in my arms, the idea of "respecting you" is wholly foreign, not because I don't, but because it is only when I watch you at work, think of you at a distance, away from and distinct from me, that the question of "respect" arises. But this raises a specter of conflict, with respect and equality too, which has too rarely been viewed as a problem in love. If respecting a person means, in effect, letting him or her out of the love-world, we can understand how an insecure relationship might well turn two lovers into antagonists, not mutually supportive but mutually threatening and wholly incompatible standpoints. The private world of love is threatened by the public world of respect. And the result, as many women have rightly complained, is the painful choice between love and success. But this is not an essential feature of love itself, as some feminists have complained; it is rather the somewhat pathetic feature of some men's insecurity and, consequently, some women's tragedy. (See Chapter 22.)

A similar conflict arises with regard to equality, which is more complex because equality, unlike respect, would seem to be part of love and the loveworld and therefore not opposed to it. And yet it is a familiar experience of the last several decades that fighting for equality *within* a relationship has a tendency to destroy love. Why? If love already presupposes equality, what could there be to fight for?

"Equality" is one of those political glow-words with very little determinate content, like "liberty." One gives it a content by giving it a context—for example, equal work time, equal pay, equal say in an issue, equal responsibility for some specific activity or equal power. And what counts as equality in a particular relationship may indeed be quite different from what counts as equality in another. The equality that is the precondition for love only consists in the demand that social differences do not matter, that both lovers are mutually willing to take up the various personal and private roles that make up intimacy. But as the notion of equality starts to become more "objective" and more concerned with social rather than personal status, as the private is measured by public criteria, the tacitly accepted roles within the relationship tend to be shattered. The quasi-political self-consciousness that replaces them undermines the intimacy of love. What was once a relationship now becomes a "partnership," which may well be more efficient, even a model of fairness and success in "having worked it out," but it isn't love. It is too dominated by foreign and critical observers, external measurements and publicly defined if nominally private roles.

The demands might all be completely reasonable. They may indeed force a relationship to conform to some more general and "objective" form of equity. But what follows too easily is the intrusion of external opinions and criteria which all but obliterate the delicate mutual understandings and adjustments of intimacy. And this is true of therapeutic advice regarding mutual communication (how much talk is "normal" or "healthy"), or the "correct" way to distribute the household chores, or the "normal" or "healthy" quantity and quality of sex a couple *ought* to enjoy. There are instances, of course, in which communication is so lacking, housework so inequitably distributed or sex so unsatisfying, that outside opinions are both welcome and necessary—but in these cases the intimacy that defines the relationship is probably already in shambles.

The division between the public and the personal, the concern for equality of the sexes in the public sphere (equal pay for equal work, equal access to jobs and careers, equal rights and responsibilities under the law), on the one hand, and the sense of equality that is the precondition for intimacy on the other, have been commonly confused by both feminist theorists and anti-feminists alike. Shulamith Firestone is just one of many theorists who have argued that romantic love and "the relegation of love to the personal" are part and parcel of the manipulative ploy to "keep women in their place" and to rationalize, even idealize, their class inferiority. But love is by

its very nature personal, and if indeed it isolates women in romantic relationships it isolates men in exactly the same way.
That is what we mean by a "personal" relationship. The mistake is to think that the *over*emphasis on the personal which is
foisted upon women, to the exclusion of public roles and interests, is a feature of romantic love itself, and that the indefensible inequality in the public sphere necessarily has its counter-
part in the personal sphere as well. But these are quite distinct,
and to treat them together as a single problem may mean blur-
ring the very different strategies that are required to deal with
each of them.

Romantic love requires equality; it excludes what we usually
call "respect." But within the equality of a relationship, dramatic variations in status are both possible and common. Indeed, to impose external standards of equality in a relationship
may well be to destroy it. But so, too, to impose external criteria for roles of any kind may well mark an intrusion which
undermines the very distinction between the personal and the
public which love presupposes for its existence. Love is, first of
all, a kind of personal freedom. And without that, neither love
nor equality means much at all.

# "WHY NOT GET ANOTHER GIRL?" 16

*In her first passion woman loves her lover,*
*In all the others all she loves is love,*
*Which grows a habit she can ne'er get over,*
*And fits her loosely—like an easy glove,*
*As you may find, whene'er you like to prove her:*
*One man alone at first her heart can move;*
*She then prefers him in the plural number,*
*Not finding that the additions much encumber.*

BYRON, *Don Juan*, III, 3

More than one anthropologist tells the story, though it may be apocryphal, of the Western visitor sitting around the communal fire in one of those societies we call "romantic" who know nothing of romantic love, telling one of our chivalric adventure stories. The brave knight whom he describes battles pirates, climbs glass mountains, slaughters ogres and slays dragons—all in order to rescue his maiden fair. After which the natives, amused and confused, ask simply, "Why didn't he just get another girl?"

It is a question that bores deep into our conception of romantic love, for if there is one feature that seems undeniable, it is the *particularity* of our lovers, and consequently their *irreplaceability*. It may not be true that "I'll never love anyone but you," and it may not even be true that I can love only one person (romantically) at any one time, but the fact that we love one particular person is essential to our conception of love, which is unimaginable without it. But why should this present a problem to us? Well, for one thing, because this seems not to be true of many other emotions: I can be angry indiscriminately with everyone who comes into my office, and that does not mean that I am not really angry. A person can be embarrassed constantly but is thereby no less embarrassed on any given occasion, and a person may be perpetually aggrieved at a large number of different losses without thereby being any less aggrieved at any one of them.

So why not love? It is worth noting, with anthropological fascination, how we are so suspicious about a person who loves several similar people in succession. Even if the sequence is quite limited—for example, a man or a woman who has three or four marriages over many years—we wonder whether he or she could really have loved them all. We have this sense that one can only *really* love once, and for every love after the first, we can wonder, "Do you really love me, or are you still in love with X?" Indeed, we have all had that experience which in high school we called "love on the rebound," when it was clearly obvious—to everyone else but us—that we were still in love with the last one, and our present lover was just a stand-in, a kind of compensation. Or if Freud is right, could it be that *all* of our lovers are "stand-ins," and we ourselves too? When the sequence involves a rapid turnover, the puddle-to-puddle romances of a Don Juan for example, our suspicions become the conviction that he could not possibly love *any* of them. But why? (We wouldn't doubt the claim that he really *hated* them all.) Thus Albert Camus suggests that what Don Juan really loves is the Platonic ideal, *Woman*, and he is poorly served by the many women he woos, who are merely imperfect instances of that ideal. Freud suggests that they all may be unsatisfactory sublimations for the primordial fantasy he has of his mother. But whether the sequence of lovers is extremely limited or extravagantly long, the idea that we can love only one particular person is thrown into question. And do we in fact love a particular person at all, or do we rather, as Freud suggests, love a certain *type*, of which this person is an instance? This means, however, that he or she might be replaced by another instance of the same type, and we might be replaceable too.

This heretical query becomes urgent as soon as we see that love is *for reasons*. Indeed, the fear of replaceability is a powerful motive for the pious defense of love as the love of a "soul," of a "unique individual" rather than a person with properties who might be replaced by another person with similar properties. If indeed we love for reasons, and a lover loves beauty or money or fame, why not shift one's love to someone else who has more beauty or money or fame? The high school cheerleader falls in love every season with the new football quarterback, while the bass drummer in the band falls in love with the head majorette of every visiting team. A woman who married a man "because he would take care of me" leaves him for another man who will take better care of her, and a man who married the most sexually exciting woman he had ever known finally leaves her for someone new and more exciting (if only because she is new). These infidelities strike us as proof that one has not really loved at all, but why?

Now, granted that we do not generally go about exchanging lovers like sparkplugs, requiring only another of the same model and size, the reasons for this are not always obvious, which is why we feel compelled to invent reasons of a more than suspicious variety. For example, we claim that love can be "true" only in a single instance (for each of us) despite the fact that this has virtually no confirmation in our experience and is refuted every time we fall in love again. For example, it is said that love is particular because love is a "commitment," which is not true of love (see following chapter) and not yet an explanation in any case. (Why would one need to make a "commitment" unless the possibility of loving someone else is already recognized?) For example, it is insisted somewhat piously by the defenders of "true" love from Ann Landers to

Victor Frankyl that every person is different, and so every
lover unique, and thus *as a matter of fact* irreplaceable. But
the fact that no two people have the same fingerprints or den-
tal work is never a reason for loving, and mere uniqueness—if
it's true—is not the reason for our particularity. Even if the
reason for loving is so central as "You're the most wonderful
person in the world," the truth is that someone else, if loved,
might be the most wonderful person in the world too. Indeed,
it is not uncommon for men and women who have had many
lovers to insist that they all, with several discreet exceptions,
have been "the most wonderful people in the world."

In response to these fatuous explanations, not surprisingly,
the cynics have come back with an explanation of their own.
Could our insistence on exclusivity and irreplaceability in love
possibly be a matter of simple insecurity? Could it be that
most of us feel sufficiently lucky to find even one lover, and so
we wish to close the doors to the possibility that he or she
might find another? Could it be that the particularity and irreplaceability of lovers is just another illusion in the mythology
of romantic love, making a matter of morality out of what in
fact is a matter of personal weakness and insecurity? After all,
ending a love affair is painful, and starting a new one is full of
traumas and risks. Could it be, then, that our emphasis on
"fidelity" in love is no more than a rationalization for being
satisfied with what one has, and minimizing life's risks? The
answer is no—but what are we to say instead?

Curiously, the problem of replaceability was raised explicitly
by Plato in the *Symposium*. Plato's very proper commentators
have preferred to focus on his complex doctrine of the soul and
*eros*, of course, but there is a much more amusing argument
that emerges from Socrates' weighty dialogue with the muse
Diotima: a defense of promiscuity that might raise an objection even from Don Juan himself. What turns us on, according
to the oldest Platonic lover, is the beauty of the other person.

But soon we see that this beauty is not unique to this one person, but common to others as well, and so it is the beauty itself we desire, not that particular person who exemplifies it. One is the same as another, and what one comes to realize is the naïveté of thinking that love is exclusive. Of course, ultimately, one comes to appreciate that it is not even beautiful bodies in general that one loves, but the Heavenly Form of Beauty itself. The desirability of particular persons drops out of the emotion, and one joins Socrates as a philosopher, a lover of beauty as such and, as Socrates so brutally demonstrates at the end of the dialogue, virtually indifferent to the feelings and beauty of his lovers. But the secular message is clear: particular people don't ultimately count; it is the Form that we love, Beauty itself.

A different form of the same argument permeates Sigmund Freud's theories. Let's not yet worry about whether the person whom we all *really* love is our mother or father and the person we seem to love is only a stand-in for the tabooed parent. Whether or not we agree with this popular "Oedipal" doctrine, it is clear that, on all of Freud's accounts, what one loves is not so much a person—the phrase "object of love" comes into modern parlance largely with him—as a cluster of properties and characteristics. These may or may not be "real." They may or may not succeed in satisfying the needs that require them. But the point is that the identity of the love "object" is seriously in question. Freud routinely talks of both love and sexual attraction in terms of "attachment," but what is clear about these attachments is that they are almost always (except for the originals) makeshift and undependable. The person one loves is a constellation of properties defined by one's own psychic needs and is therefore imminently replaceable, were it not for the severe restrictions imposed upon sexual exchanges by "civilization," that is, European middle-class morality and marriage.

Returning now to the orthodox "Oedipal" doctrine, if what one really wants is one's mother or father, then it is clear that

getting what one wants is, for most of us, utterly impossible.
But even this needs to be made more problematic, for Freud is
quite clear about the fact that it is not one's actual mother or
father that one wants, but rather some ideal fantasy, which
may or may not be faithful to the way one's parent was once
but is not now. It matters little whether the fantasy ever was
"true," so long as it is indeed not true now. The point is that it
is not even accurate to say that the person one really loves is
his or her parent, for the parent, as much as or even more than
the surrogates one auditions through life, is not the ideal that
is required. Not only are lovers replaceable; they are all exchangeable like so many makeshift and ill-fitting parts to a fantasy that will never in fact be fulfilled. Even the parent at the
back of the fantasy is nothing but a representative of an ontological ideal, like a "perfect gas" in a physics textbook, a mere
approximation, and never real at all.

Philip Slater brings the Freudian position up to date, mixing
it with a quasi-Marxist scarcity model of bourgeois society. He
argues:

> Since romantic love thrives on the absence of prolonged
> contact with its object, one is forced to conclude that it is
> fundamentally unrelated to the character of the love ob-
> ject, but derives its meaning from prior experience. "Love
> at first sight" can only be transference, in the psycho-
> analytic sense, since there is nothing else on which it can
> be based. Romantic love, in other words, is Oedipal
> love. It looks backwards . . . it is fundamentally inces-
> tuous. . . .
>
> *Pursuit of Loneliness,* pp. 86–87

Of course it is wholly fallacious to leap from the fact that "love
at first sight" cannot be based on merely present experiences
with this brand-new, unknown person to the conclusion that it
must be based on residual Oedipal love. Early friends and sib-
lings, recent fantasies, past lovers, a collage of images from

movies and magazines all contribute to the outline of an ideal lover which this new person just happens (or seems) to fulfill. (See Chapter 8.) But the point is still that the person one loves is indeed just a stand-in, and therefore replaceable by someone else having essentially the same (romantically relevant) features.

In response to this dangerous cynicism, we are assured that "marriages are made in heaven" (small compensation when we have to make them work here on earth). We assure each other that "we're perfect for one another"; but of course we are not. And even if we were, why think that no one else could be "perfect" too? But if you're dispensable to me, then it follows (even when I'm not in a rational mood) that I'm not indispensable to you either, and so we both accept the myth; better than facing that insecurity. One may even be so cynical as to suggest, as in an old Abbott and Costello routine, that it is better to fall in love with an ugly person. "Then you know you won't lose her," says Lou. "But what if you do?" asks Bud. "So who cares?" says Costello.

There is a term in law, which philosopher Ron de Sousa has interestingly introduced into philosophical discussions about love: *fungible*. (Try to ignore the mycological connotations.) Fungible goods are those which are exchangeable for others of the same kind. If the repair shop damages my radio beyond repair, it has legally discharged its obligations to me (would that it were always so simple) if I am given another radio, the same make, the same quality. Of course it doesn't have to be *exactly* the same, but I'd hardly get to court if I complained that the new one doesn't have the pencil scratches I'd accidentally scraped on the last one. Fungible goods satisfy certain conditions, and though people are not "goods," perhaps, we still might ask to what extent people—as lovers—are fungible in much the same sense.

To say that people are fungible is not to say that there are no differences between them, but only that, regarding this particu-

lar emotion in this particular circumstance, they are replaceable, satisfying all psychological conditions for the emotion.
If I am sad because I've lost my watch, you can satisfy me and
end my sadness by giving me another just like it—the watches
are emotionally fungible. But what if that was the watch that
my grandfather gave me? Then the new watch, even if exactly
the same mechanically, etc., will not satisfy me, and it is not
emotionally fungible. But here we see one good explanation
for the irreplaceability of lovers, without metaphysical or
moral embellishments. Lovers do not merely satisfy pre-existing needs and sentiments; they create (that is, we create) sentiments particular to the love, which are therefore difficult, if
not impossible, to replace.

Suppose a man loves a woman for her money; he enjoys seeing her mainly because she has money though he also enjoys
her sense of humor, her love-making, and the things they cook
together (but none of these would be special *about her* if she
didn't have the money). It is clearly predictable that he would
be willing to leave her for someone else with money, although,
because of the inconvenience, he may well require much more
money, or something else besides, before he makes a move. We
might despise such a man, but the point is that, given the
rather limited reasons for his love, his lover is emotionally fungible in a rather obvious way. The same holds true of, let us
say, a woman who loves a man for his magnificent body and
love-making. We will readily expect that she will transfer her
love to another man who has a more magnificent body and
makes love better. But as the reasons for love become increasingly personal and not simply pre-existing aspects of a person
but interpersonal creations of the relationship itself, we can see
that this easy transferability becomes far more difficult. Time
together cannot be transferred, nor can shared experiences and
mutually defined roles, habits and expectations. For example,
we build up a history together. ("We've been through so much
together.") It is virtually impossible to find someone else with

whom you also share that history. So powerful and obvious is this particular dimension of love that couples almost immediately start manufacturing a history, even before they have one. ("You were at the Segovia concert too! Well, maybe we even met there; where were you sitting?") Even when it is clearly too soon to forget we are already asking, "Do you remember the first time we . . . ?" and "How long has it been?" History is perhaps the best possible insurance against dispensability.

And yet we tend to make too much out of this. Obviously, if one thinks of having "invested" twenty years in a relationship, it is much harder (in terms of capital loss, perhaps) to leave. But even if histories aren't replaceable, that doesn't make them final or definitive. Our shared history may at most be *a* reason for my loving you, but it would be a peculiar case indeed in which that alone would suffice. What that history represents is more likely our identity together, and the quality of our present emotion depends then not on the history but on the nature of that identity *now*. *Having* loved someone is almost never a sufficient reason for loving them now.

The notion of time together, a shared history and identity, jointly created roles and a life together certainly explains why we do not easily transfer those relationships and emotions that are most valuable to us. Even if love is for reasons, a couple can compile and create so many good reasons that replaceability is all but out of the question, so long as we do not slip from that extreme improbability to the illusion of some metaphysical guarantees. But this does not yet answer our original question, which is—regarding the knight in love with his fair maiden, whom he has met only once and whose presence is signified only by the locket he wears attached to his armor— "Why not get another girl?" His own virtues of courage and perseverance must be set aside in considering this question, of course. (Mere obstinacy may inspire love, but it must not be confused with it.)

The question of replaceability has two facets, which must be kept separated. First there is the question of whether repetitive love can be genuine love, as repetitive anger is genuine anger and repetitive embarrassments are real embarrassments. Our answer here must be yes, that a person who loved a sequence of people for more or less the same reasons might nevertheless be in love every time, given a certain reasonable limit, of course; even an angry young man can be angry only so many times before we are willing to dismiss his anger across the board. So, too, Don Juan can have only so many lovers and still call it love. (Thus Byron's Juan, who has only a few, might genuinely be called a lover, but Mozart's Giovanni, with his "1003 in Spain alone," surely could not be.) But the second aspect of the replaceability question yields a very different answer: is romantic love as such a matter of fungibility? Can the knight indeed find himself another girl? The answer is, *of course* he can. Where there is not yet a "relationship," there are not yet those interpersonal bonds and reasons for particularity. Not only fair maidens, but knights and dragons, too, are a dime a dozen, and there are not yet intrinsic reasons why this one should be any more preferable than that one, why this love cannot be replaced without loss with another.

What we sometimes call the "depth" of love (too easily confused with its intensity) is in fact a measure of the ease or difficulty with which it can be transferred. Though "depth" need not depend wholly on time (some people can form a lifetime bond in only a few days), it does depend on the kinds of reasons for love and the likelihood of re-creating these reasons in another relationship. But there is nothing pathetic or insecure in this, as the cynic suggests, nor are there the specious metaphysical assurances demanded by the defender of "true love." Even in the most irreplaceable relationships, there are no guarantees, but it is a sign of how badly we want these that, when threatened, almost any argument for irreplaceability will do. ("But no one else will ever be able to rub your back the way I do.")

The lesson of "Why not get another girl?" is not, however, to remind us of our vulnerability, and certainly not to give another forum to the tiresome debate between the pious and the cynics. It reminds us, rather, of the fact that love is always a kind of achievement, a mutual building together, and it is this, nothing else, that keeps love alive. There may be any number of other forces keeping "the relationship" together, of course— the inconvenience of moving out, the embarrassment before one's friends and family, the legal liabilities that one would prefer to avoid—but in love there is but a single source of security, and that is the world we have built and are building together, and how good it is.

# DECISIONS, DECISIONS 17
## (AND "COMMITMENT")

*CHOICE. If you're looking for a simple truth to live by, there it is. CHOICE. To refuse to passively accept what we've been handed by nature or society, and to choose for ourselves. CHOICE. That's the difference between emptiness and substance, between life actually lived and a wimpy shadow cast on an institution wall.*
TOM ROBBINS, "Meditations on a Camel Pack,"
*Esquire,* July 1980, p. 38

Love is a *decision.* A decision *to* love, and a decision about *whom* to love, and how, and when, and why. Romantic love is an emotion of *choice.* It may not feel like a decision; indeed our language and literature are filled with fine phrases and allegories in which love appears to be everything but a decision—a force, a disease, a gift of God, an imposition, a need, palpitations of the heart, the unwanted prick of Cupid's arrow. In fact everything about love is made to seem circumstantial, inexplicable, "spontaneous" and a matter of luck or misfortune. So in what conceivable sense can love be based on decisions and romantic love be a matter of choice?

If romantic love—and emotions in general—must be considered to be learned systems of roles and judgments, taught to us by our culture, then three different levels of decision, choice and responsibility can be demonstrated, three senses in which love must be seen as one's own "doing," no matter how chancy or spontaneous it might seem at the time. *First,* because they are systems of judgments, we are responsible for our emotions, which we "make" just as we "make judgments." As roles played, we are responsible for our choice of roles, as well as how well they are played. (The "art" in loving.) We rightly judge that our emotions are with or without justification or warrant. We get angry with or without provocation, with or without reason. We do or do not have a right to be jealous. And we love well or badly, wisely or foolishly, "deeply" or with one foot out the door and one eye open over our shoulder. Of course, to say that we choose our emotions is not to say that one can simply, by *fiat*, decide to fall in love or get angry. (There has to be someone with whom to fall in love or get angry, for example.) But that does not mean that we do not choose them, make essential decisions about them, or that we should not take full responsibility for them.

*Second*, there is an important sense in which a society as a whole "chooses" its emotional world, appropriate to the circumstances, usually, and only rarely as the explicit choice of any one person or group. It is a collective choice, perhaps never stated as such by anyone, but it is a choice nonetheless. Thus it can be argued that some much-studied Eskimo tribes have "chosen" their emotional life of resignation appropriate to the extreme discomforts and dangers of their environment. We often make such judgments about ethnic groups, though rarely in print, suspecting what we do not say: that cultures collectively choose their temperament just as surely as they do their cuisine. The chivalric age chose to invent romantic love as compensation for a society disintegrating, and the Victorians reaffirmed that choice, as Marx and Engels anticipated, because it served the purposes of the "nuclear" family, which in turn served the purposes of capitalism.

Of course as individuals we do not have this sense of collective decision making. Not only do we see our emotional world as a *fait accompli* but we do not see it as a decision at all, rather as a psychological "need." Thus psychiatrists slip happily from a discussion of infantile dependency and motherly affection to their fallacious conclusion that we all need (even "all we need") is love. Natural-love theorists trace it back to the birds and the bees, and philosophers propound on the nature of "human nature," projecting our culture's collective decisions onto "humanity" writ large. But the truth is that, in so far as romantic love is a need at all, it is a need which we have created—like catsup and sparkplugs. What we so easily attribute to the wisdom of Mother Nature might better be looked for at the movies.

One could argue, of course, that there is a genuine "need," that "man" is a social animal and needs other people, and here we have no choice. Perhaps. Even so, it is an entirely open question, after early infancy, whom one needs and how. Why not family? Why look for a stranger from outside the tribe? And as we read about the nature of exogamy and its economic and political explanations in everyone from Margaret Mead to the Marxists, the matter is clear. Whatever our primitive need for other people, or the sociobiological analogs of exogamy, the "needs" that make up romantic love are cultural inventions, the created structures of certain kinds of societies, a collective choice, not biological or psychological determinism. And what we have collectively chosen, because it is chosen, might always be reconsidered.

*Third,* regarding romantic love in particular, we *choose* our lovers. We often hide this fact under metaphysical disguises such as "we were made for each other" and "looking for Mr. Right," but no matter how predestined we now seem in retrospect, no matter how "lucky" it was that we both showed up in the same place the same time and no matter how "remarkable" that we both enjoy Mozart (after all, millions do), the simple fact is that we were complete strangers, from opposite ends of the country, with different religious backgrounds, entirely different upbringing and quite different expectations and demands. Both of us had histories of friends, lovers and would-be lovers from whom we could have chosen (and did). But we *chose* one another. I decided to love *you*. (In fact it was after I had chosen you that I decided to *love* you. Some people decide first to love and then go out into the world to find the *you* to love.) If we are so good together, that is in part because we have made that decision, and if we break up we will not be able to say, "We were wrong for each other," and leave it at that. We chose that too. Love is not predestination but a process, and some of the daily decisions that make up that process are divisive rather than unifying.

The enormous emphasis we place on choice in love is evident in two extreme examples. First, we are fascinated by forbidden love, love that breaks the rules and oversteps the bounds, that flies in the face of reason, convenience and even life itself. The same old examples keep appearing—Romeo and Juliet, Lancelot and Guinevere, Antony and Cleopatra, Rick and Ilsa in *Casablanca*. It is the fact that such love does not fit into any predictable social pattern, disrupts those patterns (even if love then forms a pattern itself), that displays what is too often called love's "irrationality" but is better understood as the extreme assertion of individual choice. Emma Bovary hated her husband, who was "right" for her but not her pick. But she loved her lovers, both of whom were disastrous—but her own choices.

The second example is our absolute horror of the idea of arranged marriages. The idea of forced intimacy, arranged by contract in advance by possibly wise and understanding parents or a professional matchmaker, based on similarities and complementarities of background, class, abilities, needs and temperaments, fills us with repulsion. An utterly rotten love affair, on the other hand, established on a basis of mutual misunderstanding and immaturity, founded on illusions and held together by mutual obstinacy, seems to us to be just the luck of love, the chances one takes—but at least it is freely chosen. My point is not to argue the preferability, much less the "sensibility," of the one over the other, but rather to show just how extreme is our preference for personal choice, even over the likelihood of happiness and security.

Choice usually refers to the realm of deliberate action, and it is distinguished from what happens to us, what we cannot control. But the vast region that lies between deliberate, intentional, overt action (e.g., attempting an assassination, signing a contract or doing the broad jump) and events of which we are clearly victims (being hit by a meteor or a lawsuit, having a gout attack) lies largely uncharted. Freedom and unfreedom are limits, abstractions. Even intentional action has its involuntary and mechanical components: the workings of the brain, the way one was toilet-trained, the immediate circumstances and the machinelike "action" of muscles and nerves, operating in mindless sequence though perhaps initiated by what older philosophers used to call "an act of will." And even our victimization is liable to blame: for luxurious living, for being too ambitious, or just for "being there" at the time. "There are no innocent victims," wrote Jean-Paul Sartre during World War II in France. His charge is extreme but, with regard to emotions and other "acts of mind," I would have to agree. Nevertheless, to say that our emotions are aspects of our freedom is not to say that they can simply be willed, *de nihilo*, from nothing, without restriction or limitation.

To say that love is a decision, therefore, does *not* mean that, with a snap of the fingers, one decides to love, as one might jump off a bridge (assuming, of course, that one is already on a bridge). Literature is full of such attempts, of course—the homosexual Daniel and pregnant Marcelle in Sartre's *Age of Reason,* for example—and they are inevitably failures. But this does not prove that one cannot decide to love, only that one cannot *simply* decide to love, regardless of the circumstances, one's already partially formed personality and emotions already established. There must be the person there who can serve as a plausible candidate for love—not likely between a woman-hating pederast and a much-pregnant woman. The circumstances have to be appropriate; one falls in love during a dinner more easily than during a funeral, but more easily then than during an Internal Revenue audit or an hour's wait at the dentist.

If much of love is fantasy, then one key to love is imagination. Imagination is a free act of mind, beyond question, but one can't simply imagine anything, at any time, conjure up an image as God could create an entire menagerie, with a simple act of will. One needs knowledge, time and the ability to will; it is hard to be properly indignant when you don't know what's going on. And it is hard to imagine, when you're in love, how this same so wonderful person could someday be a stranger again—or an enemy. The freedom we realize in imagination and emotions provides itself with its own limitations, its own barriers, beyond which it cannot or will not proceed. When I'm in love I forbid myself to imagine what I am told are your fatal flaws, and it is difficult if not impossible to make yourself love someone who already disgusts you. (Someone you hate, on the other hand, a good respectable enemy, is quite another matter.)

Our emotions are bounded by circumstance, by other emotions and by their own inherent limitations. But given a set of circumstances, and a psychological circumstance too, one can choose any number of different emotions. A relative dies; I can rationalize (a way of choosing) any number of different emotions—not only grief but anger, relief, indignation, renewed affection or even jealousy, or any combination of these. And given that I find myself in a "relationship," already filled with sexual excitement and mutual admiration, having gone on so long on a strictly day-to-day or week-to-week "casual" basis, it now becomes an urgent question (perhaps because I decide that it should be) whether I will continue to view all of this as a passing convenience, or make it into something "more," or

make sudden demands which might, in effect, be tantamount
to choosing that the relationship end immediately. I cannot
make such a choice in a vacuum, without a "lover" in question
to be loved; I cannot choose to love someone who bores me and
I cannot choose to love when I am overburdened with other
responsibilities. But, given some such relationship or a reasonably perceived possibility of one, I cannot help but choose, one
way or another. Choosing to postpone the choice and continuing on a "casual" basis, of course, is a choice too and, under the
usual circumstances, by no means the easiest of the alternatives
to maintain over time.

A decision need not be deliberate, thought out or thought
about; it need not even be conscious. It need not occur at a
given moment; often it does, but often it only seems as if it oc-
curred at a moment—midnight Sunday—when in fact it was in
the process of formation for weeks or even months. The dominant model for decisions is the razor's edge—this way or that—
which fits well enough when we are deciding where to go for
dinner or whether or not to enlist in the army. But one also decides in a step-by-step way, like a Sunday afternoon drive in
no particular direction which ends anyway at a favorite spot,
after a series of insignificant choices of roads. Love may on occasion depend wholly on a "leap" (the active component of
the "falling" metaphor); but more often it moves on a long
series of decisions, one or two of which may well try to take
the credit for all of them.

If love is a matter of choice, then how can we explain the
fact that it so often seems like an obsession, not a matter of
choice at all? Why is love so intractable and tenacious, even in
(especially in) the most trying of circumstances, for example,
when love has gone sour or is still unrequited? But obses-
siveness and intractability are not marks of passivity. If I may
use an economic metaphor (which has its admitted limitations
in these romantic concerns) I would say that love, once chosen, involves an *investment* that is not easily withdrawn. All
emotions, I have suggested, involve self-esteem and the refor-

mation of self; love, in particular, is the formation of a shared identity, an identity tied up with, defined with, through and by this particular other person. To drop out of love is not therefore a casual decision, whose consequences are mere inconvenience or embarrassment. It is literally a part of one's self that is at stake. The intractability is not so much an inability to extricate oneself as an extreme *unwillingness* to do so, because the emotional cost is too great. Again, the difference between "cannot" and "will not" is not always clear, particularly in the realm of emotions. But as a historical corrective to the emphasis on passivity, at least, our own emphasis should be on the latter.

### Good Decisions—and Bad

Like any other decision, love invites evaluation. Love is for reasons, and these reasons can be reviewed, as good or bad reasons, wise or foolish, rational or irrational. The language of "falling" in love tends to preclude such evaluation; one does not fall down well or badly, unless of course one is a clown or an acrobat. But we obviously love wisely or not so wisely. We choose our lovers well or badly. For right reasons and wrong.

This does not mean, however, that one can always or even usually construct a tally of reasons pro and con in order to decide, once and for all, whether to love or not to love, and whom. Reasons cannot always be quantified—much to the dismay of many utilitarians and other philosophical accountants—and therefore cannot be added up and weighed against one another. One can imagine sitting down to make a list, "counting the ways," in effect: "How do I love thee" on the left, "How I don't" on the right. And on the right (let's suppose it's a mean-spirited morning) one compiles a list of charges that would condemn a person in vagrancy court for life; on the left, one can only think to write, "Still, I want you." What is our verdict? To throw away the calculations, of course.

If emotions are judgments, it makes perfectly good sense to

evaluate them in terms of justification and reasonability, as we often do in everyday life. There may not be any ironclad decision procedure for us to pronounce final judgments *about* them (judgments about our judgments, in effect), but nevertheless there is something to say. It is often said that "love is irrational," and sometimes so it is. But it is essential to understand that emotions in general can be *ir*-rational only to the extent that they are also *rational,* in other words, based upon *reasons.* And it does not even make sense to say that the reasons for love are *always* bad reasons. Nor is it true, as our tally above might suggest, that we love *despite* our reasons. Reasons are reasons only in so far as they are the reasons one actually loves. Not just rationalizations. And though our reasons are often inarticulate and certainly unquantifiable, they are nevertheless our reasons, and often good reasons besides.

What would it be for a reason to be a bad reason? We have already explored several of these in previous chapters. A reason can simply be false. If I love you because we're sexually compatible or because we both love the Rolling Stones, my reasons are bad reasons if we aren't, or if you don't. A reason can be unreasonable, for example, if I've decided to love you because you've made one of those rash assurances that desperate lovers sometimes make, e.g., "I'll love you forever, no matter what." Two reasons can be contradictory, for example, if I love you because of your driving ambition and I love you because I love relaxing at home with you, day after day after day. Reasons can be trivial (although this must always be judged in the "eye of the beholder"). A reason might be true, reasonable and significant but not a real reason at all, in other words, just a rationalization. It sounds like a reason, indeed a good reason; but it is not *my* reason at all. (In her new novel, *Bleeding Heart,* Marilyn French describes a woman who feels compelled to continue to love her husband because he is "a good father." Indeed she even convinces herself, but in fact, in her own judgment, this is not a reason for loving him—though perhaps it is one for staying with him.)

Over and above these rather straightforward types of "bad" reasons is a category that concerns us far more in love but often escapes the theoreticians of love who underestimate the complexity of emotions. There is a criterion of worth which is more or less internal to our emotional worlds—the loveworld in particular—namely, the worth of the roles and consequently the self as constituted by that emotion. One might love a person for all of the "right" reasons but yet feel bored, suffocated, weak, unproductive, sexless or just plain guilty because of it. And one can love for all the "wrong" reasons and feel exhilarated, daring, adventurous and, in general, extremely good about oneself. Choice of the "wrong" lover can ruin your life, or at least several months of it, but in return for that disaster one might suffer grandly, feel nobly sorry for oneself, publish beautiful poetry, develop an exquisite sensitivity. On the other hand, the "right" relationship may be just that—two pieces of a puzzle that fit precisely, and that's the end of it. Nothing to build. No conflicts, nowhere to move. Nothing to complain about. These are extremes, but they pose a familiar dilemma— that what seems "irrational" in love depends on what you feel about yourself and what you want as a life: drama or stability, excitement or routine happiness. Stendhal enjoys condemning his characters to death as they fall in love, or otherwise minimizing contact between them and maximizing desperation. Tolstoy, on the other hand, portrays love and durable happiness hand in hand, despite his own unhappy marriage, which may be why Natasha and Prince Andrei are so much more persuasive than Natasha and Pierre, blissfully married.

Rationality, in love, is relative. Moralists beware, for the commandment to love has no set reasons. But this does not mean that love is beyond reason, or reasons. It does not mean that love is arbitrary, whimsical or "illogical," though it can on occasion be so. Love, like all emotions, has its "logic," its schemes and strategies, its reasons and fallacies. The problem, for each of us, is to see what these are.

### Deciding What?

What do you decide when you decide to love someone?
First, of course (though not always first in time), you decide
on a person, a candidate, presumably someone palpably "lovable." This is true even if one is simply "in love with love," a
clichéd idea (e.g., Byron, *Don Juan*, Canto III) which tends
to hide our more significant obsession with the choice of lovers
itself, no matter how unpredictable, whimsical or frequent. Indeed, the whimsical unpredictability of this choice (though
not its frequency) is part of our paradigm of romantic love,
and though it may in the final analysis be true that people are
more likely than not to marry the boy or girl next door (or in
the nearby vicinity) our romantic heroes and fantasies will
continue to be the sudden stranger, the forbidden love, the unexpected. Of course one usually chooses to love from among a
field of candidates already available, most often, perhaps, in a
field of only one or two. But our obsession with love makes
equally significant those who go out into the world with the
loveworld already constructed, looking only for the first lovable person who will fit within its already tight-fitting roles.

Confining ourselves to the more usual instance, however, in
which one decides to love a person one already knows and perhaps knows well, or chooses between two more or less "casual"
lovers, what is it that one decides? What does *not* happen, as I
want to argue at length in the following section, is that one
"makes a commitment." What does happen is that one makes a
decision within a context, open-ended for the future but based
entirely in the present, that one will continue to foster the circumstances and the context in which love will flourish, in
which shared interests can be developed and a shared identity
is most likely to grow without external threats and avoidable
uncertainties. Minimally, that means deciding to be together
enough so that love is not mainly memory, so that bonds can
be forged out of shared experiences, and differences can be

defined and defused in repeated confrontations. It means sticking around when "the going gets rough," but not "no matter what." It means a selective deafness—not listening to alternatives, a kind of blindness, as the cliché declares, to facts and faults that might otherwise turn us away. It means making plans together. It means that one stops thinking in terms of self-interest as the criterion for making decisions. It means, paradoxically, ceasing to think in terms of self-esteem, even though the strategy of love itself is to maximize self-esteem. (The way to feel best about yourself is to stop trying to think about how you feel about yourself.) It means forgetting about one's "independence" as the ideal of self-identity. It means making an investment—by way of a telling confession or by intermingling our books and records on the shelves—such that it will be all the more difficult to back out later. But—and this is essential—it is not the difficulty of backing out in the future that is essential to the decision but rather the expression of confidence in the present. In this difference, so easily blurred in all talk of "commitment," lies the difference between positive decisions *to* love and negative and almost always self-destructive setups for future resentment and spite.

The decision to love, in other words, is a decision to foster a set of conditions conducive to love, encouraging but not requiring the formation of mutual interdependency and shared self-identity. It may include the exclusion of all other relationships (at least, other sexual relationships), but it need not. What it cannot do is allow other priorities to intervene, no matter how urgent, which conflict with the primacy of the new self-identity being formed. But because love is a continuous process, a sequence of constant decisions rather than a simple or single scenario, what one mainly chooses in choosing to love is not so much love itself as a set of circumstances conducive to love. What these are, of course, varies with the individual case. (For some people, deciding to live together is a way of fostering the conditons of love; for others, deciding not to live together may be the better way of fostering the conditions of love.)

### *"Commitment"*

It is at this point that the common belief that love is a commitment ought to be confronted head on. Love is not, I want to argue, a commitment. It is the very antithesis of a commitment. The legal tit-for-tat quasi-"social contract" thinking of commitment talk fatally confuses doing something because one *wants* to do it and doing something because one *has* to do it, whether or not one wants to at the time. Immanuel Kant, the philosophical father of *duty* in general, conceived of the "moral worth" of an action strictly in terms of the extent to which we felt we *ought* to do it, regardless of our desires. In rejoinder, we might say that the *emotional worth* of an action is determined precisely by the degree to which we *want* to do it, regardless of our obligations. And that means that an act of love—and ultimately love itself—is the very opposite of a commitment of any kind.

Romantic love is founded on voluntary choice, even whim. We fall in love with a total stranger. A married man or woman. The son or daughter of the enemy. The Queen. A god. And the greater the danger, the greater often is the desire. But to evade or deny these dangers and uncertainties, and ultimately deny the desire itself, we seek out guarantees. We want the assurance we thought we had as children, the supposedly unconditional love of our mothers. (This is overrated too; very few mothers love their children "unconditionally," but that is another story.) The whole point of romantic love is that it is *not* based on such presumed assurances, but then we turn around and try to make love imperturbable, guaranteed if not by God, then at least by the sanctions of the state. Marriage, for many people, is not so much an expression of love as a request for guarantees, by way of sanctions, social approbation and the threat of legal harassment. And short of marriage, we invent the quasi-legal concept of "commitment," in order to set up a set of *moral* sanctions at least, thus turning love, which is a continuous stream of decisions, into a promise, an obligation, an act of prevention rather than a desire.[1]

In his *Discourse on the Origins of Inequality*, Jean-Jacques Rousseau formulated the distinction that now forms the heart of the *Cosmo* cosmology—that it is commitment that distinguishes casual sex from love. A commitment, of course, need not be made explicitly—and here is where the confusion begins. It may be understood as an inference from a declaration of love. It may be assumed—though rarely these days—just from the sexual relationship itself. But whether stated or inferred or simply assumed, a commitment is a kind of promise, a promise *to* someone to *do* something. But when does one make a promise without actually saying anything? To whom does one make this promise? And what, specifically, is it a promise to do?

A promise need not be stated as such, it is true. You ask me if I will take care of your children when you're away, and I nod. I have promised. Indeed, one gets into all kinds of obligations by tacit acceptance of a situation, not only with lovers but with strangers as well. Walking around a ladder, I am called to by a fellow at the top, asking me if I will hold it steady while he reaches for his cat. I grab the ladder, saying nothing; I have just assumed an obligation, and the fact that I change my mind in a moment makes not one bit of difference. Obligations and commitments are much clearer in such situations than in love, where intimacy and familiarity often allow us to neglect or ignore courtesies and responsibilities that we would owe to any stranger. But it is true that one makes commitments and accepts responsibility just by virtue of certain circumstances and relationships, and it would be most surprising if this were not true of love. (Thus love is not, in case you ever wondered, "never having to say you're sorry.")

---

[1] The boundaries between morality and legality are often smudged in our society, especially in the realm of sex, love and marriage. Thus it has become apparent in the courts that a moral commitment does have legal consequences similar to marriage. But marriage itself is more than a commitment, of course.

The problem is that, though a mutual commitment need not be actually stated as such, it must be mutually agreed upon, and explicit at least in that sense. Sometimes the agreement can be assumed without ever being mentioned; in an earlier generation, it could be assumed that two people in love would be sexually "faithful" to one another. Even so, it is clearly and unquestionably mutually understood. But to have the idea that being in love itself constitutes such a commitment, even if nothing is spoken or implied, is to move much too easily from the fact that not all commitments need be stated as such to the idea that there need not be an explicit agreement at all. And in so far as there are such agreements, tacit or stated as such, these are in no case the commitment *to love*. They are rather obligations understood and undertaken by the nature of the relationship, or by living together, or by mutual expectations that have been clearly assumed. Love itself is not a commitment, nor can it be committed.

I have said that love is a decision to foster a certain set of conditions conducive to love. But this decision is not a promise, and in particular it is not a promise to my lover. If I change my mind or find my emotional enthusiasm flagging, there has been no moral breach, no broken promise, no commitment unfulfilled. One might argue that I have made a commitment *to myself* but, although we often employ such expressions to express our resolutions, there is no such commitment. My commitment to you can be canceled, with your say-so; but changing my mind about a commitment to myself and giving my say-so to the change are one and the same act, which means that it makes no sense to talk about "commitment" to myself in the first place.

When I say "I love you," I am indeed setting up a set of expectations, implicit agreements and promises (see the following chapter). But what I have promised is to foster a set of conditions; I have not promised—I cannot promise—to love you in the future. I can be rightly accused of betraying your trust if I willfully make impossible those conditions (for example, by running off and marrying someone else), but not for ceasing to love you. I can promise you almost anything, except love.

The essence of romantic love is a decision, open-ended but by the same token perpetually insecure, open to reconsideration at every moment and, of course, open to rejection by one's lover at every moment too. One might reject romantic love—as too risky, as too insecure, as too unstable for a foundation of interpersonal relationships. In its place, one might well suggest a system of contracts, for five or ten years, complete with guarantees, promises and sanctions. But that is not romantic love. I can promise revenge: I can't promise to be angry. I can promise to stay with you, but not to love you.

To love is to protect a set of conditions, to take on responsibilities. But one accepts that set of conditions and those responsibilities because one *wants* to, not because one is *obliged* to. There may be obligations that require us to stay together in spite of love or the lack of it—but these are not to be confused with the conditions of love. There may be reasons for making a commitment—security, respectability, friends, to prove something, "for the sake of the kids"—but love itself is not one of these reasons, nor are commitments alone ever reasons for love.

Our society has gone litigation crazy, but the one area that is or ought to be immune from the ubiquitousness of the lawyers is love. It is the very nature of contracts that they are public and explicit, and that they are independent of our desires and emotions. But love *is* an emotion, and thus the very antithesis of a contract, even when it is made explicit. Would you really want me to say, "I promise I'll stay with you, no matter how I'll feel?" Could I promise, even if I wanted to, that I'll love you in three years, under circumstances wholly unknown and perhaps even unimaginable? Love is not only a decision, in other words, but a lifetime of decisions, and that is why it cannot also be "commitment."

# "I-LOVE-YOU"[1]  18

*I-love-you has no usages: Like a child's word, it enters into no social constraint; it can be a sublime, solemn, trivial word, it can be an erotic, pornographic word. It is a socially irresponsible word.*

*I-love-you is without nuance. It suppresses explanations, adjustments, degrees, scruples . . . this word is always true (has no referent other than its utterance; it is a performative).*

ROLAND BARTHES, *A Lover's Discourse*

I love you."
 What does that mean? Of course you know, but tell me.
 A description of how I feel? Not at all.
An admission? A confession?
No, you don't understand, after all.

"I-love-you" is an action, not a word. It is not a short sentence. Of course it *looks* like a sentence, made up of words, but sentences can be transcribed and transformed. "I-love-you" is more like the word "this" or "here"; it makes sense only when spoken in a very particular context. In writing, in a letter, it has meaning only to you, and only while you can still imagine my speaking it. To anyone else, and after a while to you, it means nothing at all; like the word "here," just sitting on the page like an old coffee stain. Hardly a word at all.

"I-love-you" has no parts, no words to be rearranged or replaced. "You-I-love" is more than merely clumsy, like "Me Tarzan, you Jane." It is something like staking a claim. "John loves Sally," said by John to Sally, is absurd. "I-love-you" allows for no substitutions, no innovations. It stands outside

---

[1] With appreciation to the late Roland Barthes.

the language. It says nothing. If it *is* misunderstood, it cannot be explained. If unheard, it has not been uttered. And when it is heard, it no longer matters that you didn't mean to say it in the first place, that you "just blurted it out." You *did* it, and it cannot be undone.

"I-love-you" does not *express* my love. It need not already be there. Perhaps I didn't feel it until I said it, or just before. But then, in a sense, I didn't *say* anything at all.

One of the perennial misunderstandings about language is the idea that all sentences *say* something; words refer and phrases describe. But language also requests and cajoles, demands and refuses, plays, puns, disguises as well as reveals, creates as well as clarifies, *pro*vokes as well as *in*vokes, *per*forms as well as *in*forms. We *do* things with words, in words done by the late Oxford philosopher J. L. Austin. With words we make promises, christen ships, declare war and get married, none of which would be possible without them. Our sentences mean what we *do* as well as, or rather than, what we say. They bring things about as well as tell us what has already come about. And the meaning of "I-love-you" is to be found in what we *do* with it, not in what it tries to tell us.

If we so easily misunderstand language and persistently refuse to look at love, then of course we will miss completely the significance of the language of love, if, that is, it is a language. Or is it, as Barthes suggests, a *cry?* "I-love-you" mainly makes a demand. So when I say it you react—not "How curious that you feel that way" but rather "But what do you want me to do?" Its meaning is aimed at you, to move you. (A "perlocutionary act," Austin called it.)

I say, "I have a headache," and you say, "Poor Boobie." Perhaps you kiss my forehead, and I'm most grateful. But if you say, "Me too," I don't think, "What a coincidence"; I feel slighted. You've misunderstood me. Suppose I say, "I love you," and you kiss my forehead. I'm offended. That's not a reply but an evasion.

I say, "I love you," and I wait for a response. It can only be one phrase: "I love you too," nothing less, nothing more. Perhaps, "Me too," though it is ungrammatical and a serious confusion of pronouns, but it is also less than the proper formula. If you say, *"Je t'aime,"* you have not done it either; instead you are showing off.

I could be silent and just love you. And perhaps you'd know. I don't have to say, "I'm so angry with you," when I've been yelling at you for twenty minutes. I don't say, "I'm sad," when I'm crying. And yet I feel compelled to say, "I love you," even when it's obvious I do. "Nothing says I love you like 'I love you.'" But it is more than that too, more than something said.

The power of words, or at least certain words, sometimes is awesome. "I-love-you" is a magical phrase that ruins the evening. Or changes love into something more, even when it was love before. It is not an announcement, no R.S.V.P. No "if you please." It *demands* a reply; in fact, it *is* this demand. And a warning, and a threat. It is an embarrassment, first to me, but soon to you. It makes me vulnerable, but you are the one who is naked. I am watching your every move. Counting the fractions of a second. What will you do?

"I love you"; "what a terrible thing to say to someone." Terrible indeed.

"Tell me you love me."

"What are you expecting from me? You know I love you."

"Then say it."

"I don't want to say it."

(The evening's already lost, but I pursue.)

"If you love me, why not say it?"

"Oh. I don't know; it just changes everything."

"How can saying what is true change anything?"

But it does. "I-love-you" doesn't fit into our conversations. It interrupts them. Or ends them.

"I-love-you" is language reminding us of the unimportance of language, language that destroys language. It is language without alternatives, without subtlety, like a gunshot or the morning alarm. And then it's gone, not even a memory, and has to be done again.

But once said, it can never be said again. It can only be repeated, as a ritual, an assurance. Not to say it, when it's never been said, is no matter, a curiosity. But not to say it, once said, is a cause for alarm, perhaps panic. One commits oneself to the word, and to say it again. What else follows? Perhaps nothing.

Barthes says it is "released," but I say, *shot out*, like a weapon. Released like an arrow, perhaps. And if I make myself vulnerable in saying it, the real question is what it will do to you. I'm still watching you. Still counting the fractions of a second. What will you do?

I say, "I hate you," and you quite rightly ask "Why?" But I say, "I love you," and "Why?" is completely improper. A reasonable question, but a breach in the formula. You have turned the weapon back onto me, so of course I reply indignantly, "What do you mean? I love you, that's all." And I again await your reply. A second chance, but no more.

I say, "I love you," and you answer, "How much?" What are we negotiating? Perhaps you are saying, "Well then, prove it." And, having said the word, I am bound to. Nevertheless, your reply is insufferable. You're acting as if I actually *said* something which can now be qualified, quantified, argued for and against. But I didn't. I just said, "I love you." And that is, in terms of "How much?" to say nothing at all.

"I-love-you": a warning, an apology, an interruption, a plea for attention, an objection, an excuse, a justification, a reminder, a trap, a blessing, a disguise, a vacuum, a revelation, a way of saying nothing, a way of summarizing everything, an attack, a surrender, an opening, an end.

I say, "I love you," and I no longer remember the time I was with you when it was not said. And we will never be together again without it.

# THE IMPORTANCE 19
## OF BEING HONEST

*When my love swears that she is made of truth I do believe her,
though I know she lies.*

SHAKESPEARE, *Sonnet* 138

In 1976, Jimmy Carter provoked far more debate over his
qualifications for the presidency with an interview for
*Playboy* than he did with his various proposals concerning foreign policy. In essence, he *confessed:* "I have felt lust in
my heart." Libertines chuckled that lust should be so limited; conservatives were horrified that the subject had been
broached at all. But the point, of course, was *honesty.* Jimmy
Carter, he and his aides assured us, would not lie to us, even
about his private sins, small as they were. Honesty, it seems,
has emerged as something like our ultimate value, the single
most important mark of character. The Watergate follies have
given renewed emphasis to this ancient virtue, but, where love
is concerned, one would think it has never even been ques-
tioned.

My students, for example, display unembarrassed conform-
ity in their agreement that people in love must be "totally honest" with one another. Trust, they say, is the essence of love,
and a relationship without it—that is, without *complete* trust—
"cannot be worth much." If this were so, however, no love
would be "worth much" since total honesty and complete trust
are impossible. To expect them as a matter of course, to demand them as the precondition of a relationship, is to adopt
what may be today the most dangerous single doctrine of the

myth of romantic love, the myth of "total openness," which is confused with trust and glorified under the banner of "honesty."

Now, of course I would not deny that love and trust stand in a particularly intimate connection with one another. James M. Cain, in *The Postman Always Rings Twice*, tells us that "when fear gets into love it just isn't love anymore; it's hate." This may be a good summary of the incompatibility of love and terror, love and *dis*trust. But the antithesis of distrust need not be trust, and the opposite of wholesale lying is not "total" honesty. Not telling is not necessarily deception, and deception is not always antithetical to love. Which raises the question of why truth and trust are so emphasized—I would say overemphasized—in most discussions about love. Why so much concession to what I call *the urge to tell,* as if in itself this were a virtue without which love cannot be? The truth of the matter seems rather to be that truth is a complex and negotiable issue and honesty is sometimes an obstacle rather than the essence of love.

To begin with, truth and honesty are never total, unqualified or absolute. At the extremes of human endurance, one can always discover a context in which a lie—albeit a "white" one—would be generally agreed to be justified, if, for example, a gangster threatens to kill both of us if I tell you where I've been tonight. But we need not go to the extremes to see that trust and honesty are not always virtues. A person who feels the urge to "tell all" will more likely be a bore than a saint, and we all know people who tell—under the guise of honesty and openness, of course—as a way of manipulating people, even as a way of destroying them. The urge to tell is not always motivated by virtue; it may also be a demand for attention, a way of trapping someone into a covenant that he or she would rather have avoided, a way of shifting the burden of guilt from oneself to another:

"I have a confession to make."

"Oh, you don't have to tell me if you don't want to."

"No, but I do. I feel I ought to tell you."

"Well, okay. [*Joking*] What monstrous crime have you committed?"

"I've been sleeping with so-and-so, your best friend."

"You what?!"

"Now don't get upset. That's why I'm telling you."

"How *could* you!"

"What are you getting so angry about?"

"You're telling me that you've been sleeping with my best friend, behind my back . . ."

"That's why I'm telling you now; I want to make a clean breast of it."

"But how could you? How could you?"

"You have no right to get so angry. You're making me feel guilty about it, and that's why I'm telling you, after all, so that I don't feel so guilty anymore. I'm just being honest; why can't you be understanding? This fight is all *your* fault, for being so unreasonable."

The urge to tell: it's more complicated than it looks. Lying, of course, need not involve the fabrication of actual falsehoods; it may sometimes be keeping silent or, as Camus writes (concerning his novel, *The Stranger*), "Lying is not only saying what is not true; it is also and especially saying more than is true and, as far as the heart is concerned, saying more than one feels."[1] And, we may suppose, saying *less* as well. As often as not, truth takes the form of confession, and it is the wisdom of Christianity, Freud too, to appreciate just how strong the urge to confess seems to be. Confession erases responsibility for sins. Not confessing multiplies them. And if it is easy to think of counter-examples to this simple two-part principle, it is just as important to realize how many of our "sins" are not

[1] Introduction to *The Stranger*, 1955 ed.

*crimes* at all but rather acts of an uncertain character, whose worth or blameworthiness depends wholly on absolution or approval, and it often doesn't matter much by whom.

In relationships, of course, it matters very much by whom, since it is indeed part of the essence of love that the opinion of one's lover counts far more than the opinion of anyone else, at least in matters that pertain to love. (If this sounds circular, of course it is.) Thus "telling all" is not an expression of love if the "all" doesn't pertain to the love. Recounting in tedious detail the events of the day may or may not become a part of love's daily ritual, but it has nothing to do with trust, honesty or openness. (In fact it may be evasion.) Not telling one's lover about one's past in certain circumstances may be awkward (the appearance of an old lover; the arrival of a letter from one's buddies in prison). Not telling one's spouse, for example, that you have been fired from your job may, to say the least, be a bit odd, though, according to some recent reports, this is a quite common reaction among professionals who have been "laid off" for the first time in their lives. But it is not a breach of love.

When is honesty relevant to love? Well, in romantic love, honesty about *sex* seems essential. One might not be dishonest when one fails to tell one's mother or brother about one's extramural sexploits, but, it will be argued, not telling one's lover would surely mark the ultimate breach of trust, and therefore a betrayal of the relationship itself. But something quite odd has happened in this regard; first, where sexual "fidelity" used to be considered an automatic presupposition of any "serious" relationship (in fact it tended to define such "serious" relationships), it no longer is. Most of my students make a firm distinction between relationships in which there has been some explicit agreement not to "see" other people and those in which there has not. The idea of an "implicit" or "tacit" agreement to that effect—usually nothing more than the fact that neither person has "seen" anyone else for a certain period of time—is not taken as morally binding. Once, sexual fidelity was considered one of the non-negotiable rules of romance, and sex with someone else was called "cheating." Now the rules are shifting, and many of my students even feel that other affairs are *desirable*, not only for their intrinsic pleasures, but as a way of testing the boundaries ("fetters," one student called them) of a relationship whose sexual parameters have not yet been settled. Telling, or not telling, is part of the test. Honesty, in other words, is now a negotiable tangent to love, not part of it.

Second, and consequent to this shift in presuppositions, is a most curious phenomenon concerning the importance of honesty. Sex itself is not considered so much a breach or betrayal of the relationship as the lying about it. "Well, at least you could have told me" is the most common phrase indicating this shift from the significance of sex to the importance of telling about it. In the wake of Watergate, the cover-up is considered far more deleterious to the relationship than the "crime" itself, whose status as a crime may even be in doubt.

With this shift in values (and I do not see it at all as a shift in the value of intimacy or "relationships" as such) the seeming abyss between casually thinking about sex with another person and actually having an affair closes up, and the problem of truth for Jimmy Carter and for *Tess of the D'Urbervilles* becomes essentially the same: to tell or not to tell? Tess had an affair and a baby; Carter only had thoughts. Tess lost a husband because she told: Carter almost lost an election. Why is honesty so important? And isn't *total* honesty, even on the most superficial analysis, absurd?

Consider this: when we're making love, and you bite my ear the way you do, I once flashed in my memory to a girl friend I had as a teenager, and the way we used to "make out" at the drive-in movies. This first association leads to another; we never actually "slept" together, which I've always regretted, and for a moment—just for a moment—I imagine, not wish, that you were she. Should I tell you?

The advantage of this example, over an actual affair, is that the likelihood of your "finding out" from someone else is indeed minimal. Too often the "tell or not to tell" dilemma is couched in the crude consequentialist terms of "what if she/he finds out?" thus missing the most interesting and important aspects of the problem. Sissela Bok, for example, in her book, *Lying*, sticks fairly close to this consequentialist account, which may be appropriate to lying in politics, perhaps, but is at most a secondary issue in personal relationships. Now if one takes telling the truth to be an absolute principle, at least in a love relationship, one will, whatever the consequences, tell. And just to make the dilemma clear, let's suppose that your lover is sufficiently sensitive that telling will, if not end the relationship altogether, put a serious crimp in it. If one holds an absolutist (or what philosophers sometimes call a "deontological") view about not lying, then the relationship be damned; the truth must out. But most of us would probably see this attitude as something akin to insanity. To tell the truth is not *always* a virtue.

In reaction to this absolutist position, however, too many theorists too easily shift to a wholesale consequentialist position: telling the truth is right or wrong depending on the consequences, namely, whether it will (in the long run) improve or endanger the relationship. Thus questions tend to focus on the likelihood of the other person finding out from someone else, or the discomforts and dangers of trying to hide the truth without inadvertently "blurting it out," the plausibility of the truth being accepted with good grace by the other, the pain of feeling guilty, the pain of a confrontation, and so on. These are, of course, relevant, and the decision to tell or not to tell is largely determined by them. But the urge to tell is more than this utilitarian calculation of feelings and consequences. It is also a question of motives and a shared identity.

I have already pointed out the ease with which telling can
be turned into a kind of weapon, a "so now it's your problem"
kind of strategy. Indeed, in the example we've chosen here,
telling is so likely to be harmful that one can only suspect that
malicious motives are indeed involved. What else would be?
A desire to be cute? Sharing a bit of nostalgia? "Just being
completely open with you"? Much more likely, "I just want
you to remember that you aren't the only one that's excited
me" or "Let me interrupt you in your moment of passion to
shift the emphasis wholly to me." And if one does feel guilty
about such thoughts (our linear model of the mind too easily
makes us feel as if we can and should have "one thing only" on
our minds at a time) it by no means follows that one ought to
tell, even if (as may well be the case) telling will expiate one's
guilt. With our new psychological frankness, we too often tend
to think that telling is always justified, "letting out one's feelings"—in the name of honesty, of course. But it is not. Telling
one's thoughts and feelings is not the trump card in our morality that we have recently tended to make it. And the idea
that, whatever else one has done, one cannot be faulted for
confessing is a dangerous and often vicious strategy that ought
itself to be rejected as morally reprehensible. (One psychiatrist
described his experience in a contemporary "let it all hang
out" type of encounter group this way: "They were a lot of obnoxious people when they went in and they were just as obnoxious when they came out, except that they didn't feel guilty
about it any more.") And lovers too find honesty a cure for
guilt—in the name of righteousness, but often as a way of
punishing one another.

The honesty dilemma has much to do with the mutual identity that is part of love. On the one hand, each of us wants—
needs, demands—to be very special, uniquely special to the
other person, and in today's ethics the other's thinking about
someone else might be just as much (or more) of a threat to
that sense of identity as his or her actually sleeping with some-

one. But on the other side there is the need for approval and acceptance of one's lover, and this includes—in the confessional mode—absolution for one's own transgressions, no matter how minor, which one fears might raise an obstacle to that shared identity. But to gain absolution means to threaten the other person's sense of uniqueness. And this is the dilemma. One tells in order to remove these obstacles in one's own thinking—in order to be absolved, to be told, "It's okay." But this makes the telling for the benefit of the teller—even when it is not malicious or manipulative. Concern for honesty as such is secondary, and one is concerned for the feelings of the other person only indirectly, in so far as he or she will be hurt by the confession, and in so far as the relationship itself might benefit from one's own renewed peace of mind. This is not to say that honesty is selfish. Nor is it to say that the urge to be honest itself is never a motive. But at least some of the time "honesty" is a virtuous way of referring to a verbal strategy whose main interest is always the comfort of one's own emotions, a means of resolving ambiguity, if not shifting the discomfort onto the other person, and then the enemy of love.

Honesty is a virtue, of course; what I am arguing against is the current idea that honesty is everything and excuses anything, even (especially) cruelty and irresponsible criticism ("I'm just telling you how I feel"). But honesty isn't everything. If what is at stake is sexual infidelity as such, it may be, as one of my (married) friends put it, that the only answer is "not to do it in the first place." Perhaps, but if the transgression is in the realm of a random thought rather than a premeditated deed, the problem of honesty arises with obstacles that can hardly be avoided, even if we're tempted to say that they are, in themselves, not very significant. The strict absolutist position would be that one still ought to tell, if there's anything to tell. The consequentialist would say that of course one should not tell, since no good could possibly come of it. But even the consequentialist seems to leave out something essential, namely the notion of shared identity itself, which is something more than mere "consequences."

The whole problem of trust can be viewed from the other side. This is one of those cases where the Golden Rule, "Do unto others as you would have them do unto you," makes considerable sense, not because it is a moral absolute, but rather because reciprocity is indeed the touchstone of love, whether or not it is so central to other human relationships as well. Instead of beginning with the question, "Should I tell or not?" therefore, let's see what happens when the question is phrased as, "Would I rather be told or not?" When the emphasis is on the telling, our attention tends to focus on such pragmatic questions as "Will he or she be hurt?" "How much?" and "What are the odds against being found out?" But when the emphasis is on being told, the focus tends to be less pragmatic and more concerned with the sensitivity of the relationship itself. The other person becomes less of an "other," to whom the truth is to be told or from whom it is to be hidden. And one sees oneself less as the victim of a possible deception and more as the consciousness through whom a relationship comes to have meaning.

Shakespeare clearly saw this difference. ("I believe . . . though/I know she lies.") Given the inevitability of lies, "white" or otherwise, the problem becomes not whether to tell but what to believe, and love, valuing itself more than some abstract value of honesty, is perfectly willing to forgo the evidence in return for an untrammeled sense of trust. But one does not love because one trusts; one trusts because one loves. And what one trusts is not *to* be told but its very opposite, *not* to be told, when the relationship is more important than the truth. (In *Casablanca*, Victor—who knows, asks Ilsa—who knows that he knows—"do you have anything to tell me?" She says "no." And there is no doubt that she is right.)

Suppose I ask, "Would *I* rather *be* told or not?" Our first tendency is to blurt out, "Of course," but this is perhaps misleading. I can't opt voluntarily for being lied to, if for no other reason than the logical oddity of my agreeing to accept something whose very nature presupposes my ignorance or lack of acceptance of it. And of course, if the dilemma is put in terms of "There's something you ought to know; do you want to know it?" the answer is rapidly forthcoming. But the reality of the circumstance seems more like the following: What I really prize—and what thus provides the criterion by which I form my preferences—is my love for you and yours for me. And what I know is this—that as "liberated" as I am and as much as I accept "intellectually" the likelihood of your at least desiring —if not consummating—sex with someone else from time to time, I know that I'd make more of it than I should, perhaps using it against you, in any case feeling unnecessarily hurt and neglected. And so I'd rather not know. It's not that ignorance is bliss, but rather that omniscience is a drag. Love can't stand distrust, so I *decide* to trust you—even if I don't. What I refuse to know might not hurt me.

To make things more complicated, however, I can't really *tell* you this preference of mine. "Do what you want, but I don't want to know" is itself an example of the manipulative use of telling one's feelings, and it puts pressure on the other person of a curious kind. It gives permission (and the very act of giving permission is a kind of power game, a way of staking out emotional territory). At the same time it forces the other person into an uncomfortable situation, of not being allowed to tell, which includes, therefore, an inability to declare one's innocence too. It's sort of like "Have you stopped beating your children?"—a question that indicts no matter what the answer. One is presumed guilty. So the preference not to know, and to ignore whatever evidence or rumors might lead one to know, is a decision that I can make but shouldn't tell you. And this, I might suspect, is the optimal strategy for you too. But we can't tell each other this, either, and for the same reason.

Immanuel Kant, who made lying one of the central examples of his absolutist "categorical imperative," advanced the following argument against lying in general: if everyone lied, no one would have any reason for believing anyone else, and communication as such would become impossible. Now whether or not the argument works on behalf of the general principle, it certainly makes sense in personal relationships. "If I suspect that you've lied to me even once," proceeds our paranoid romantic consciousness, "I will never be able to trust you again." It is in this sense that trust is essential to love, not in the positive sense that to love is to trust but in the negative sense that it is difficult to feel comfortable with someone whom you don't trust. But this doesn't make trust as such a part of love; at most it means that sufficient *dis*trust makes love difficult, and it is an open question whether distrust actually makes love impossible. The fact that we tend to see these two as mutually exclusive and exhaustive opposites only confounds our appreciation of the problem—and thus leads us to make absurd claims about the need for "total" honesty, as if there couldn't possibly be love without it. But if the criterion (as in Kant) is the ability to trust (and therefore love) at all, it must be said that the breach of trust may often be created by honesty rather than by lying; Kant's argument might just as easily be turned around as a way of showing that "total honesty" is morally impossible; if both of us were totally honest, there could not possibly be any relationship at all, if for no other reason than because we would continually bore or offend each other past the limits of endurance.

The upshot of this discussion is that honesty is overrated, which is not to deny, of course, that it still is a virtue—most of the time. Given the flexibility and uncertainty of contemporary ethics, it is surely desirable to be clear and honest about the boundaries of a relationship, making explicit when necessary certain limits and expectations beyond which the relationship is no longer viable. But within those limits and expectations, honesty and declarations of trust have become more of a strategy and a weapon than a virtue, less an expression of love than a technique of expiation that may itself be more of an obstacle to love than the sin for which one feels guilty in the first place. Love depends on shared identities and roles, many of which are better engaged in silence. To spell out the forms of our mutual engagement is often to trivialize them; to make them subject to a debate will sometimes destroy them.

We talk too much. (Too many books too.) Descriptions of love easily become accusations, and confessions are more damaging than what they're confessions of. Some questions can be "talked out," and explicit descriptions of what's going on can sometimes improve a relationship immensely, even in those areas where talk was formerly considered out of place, in sex particularly. But we have to reject the idea that the "heart-to-heart" talk is the essence of love, as well as the idea that honesty excuses everything and that "talking it out" will solve, instead of make worse, most romantic problems. We tend to think of what we *say* as somehow more definitive than what we do, ignore the most obvious gestures while waiting for something to be said. It is true that words tend to give a definite and explicit form to roles and to rules that were formerly vague and implicit. But to think that definition and explicitness are always virtues is to lose sight of what is most essential about love, that sense of shared identity and affection that precedes and may be trivialized by verbalization. Sex (and music, flowers and food) are better than words as the language of love. Romantic conversations, but not love itself, are so typically joyless. And "Platonic" love, if it is love at all, tends to be more pretentious than gratifying. (Socrates sent the flute girl away, which may be how he missed the point.)

In *The Passions*, I too joined the pious in declaring that love included "unqualified trust" (p. 338). But this emphasis on absolute trust and honesty tends to ignore the fact that trust is negotiable, like almost everything else in a relationship, and that trust may indeed be sacrificed to the passion itself, if need be. In fact distrust in moderation may serve the cause of passion more than honest revelation.

A few weeks ago you saw your old boy friend, and despite every assurance from you that there was no danger, I put myself into a holy twit. Why? Not because I didn't believe you or trust you, but because it was an opportunity for me to use a modicum of suspicion to inflame my passion for you, to remind myself how much I'm in love with you and how I'd hate to lose you. It was a way of making sure I didn't take you for granted, of not treating "trust" as one more virtuous euphemism for boredom. And here, even *distrust* can function for the benefit of love. In fact, if a person never worries, never gets suspicious, never wonders, would we not wonder whether he or she is still in love, rather than merely comfortable?

It is probably true that we say, "I trust you completely," precisely when we don't, not as a lie, perhaps, but as a kind of wishful thinking, for example in those early moments of a relationship when one is desperately seeking an excuse to leap into an attitude whose structures will probably not be supportable for months to come. Sometimes "trust" is another way of announcing a decision to try.

And of course sometimes "I trust you" is a *warning*.

Sometimes *not* telling presents a special kind of problem; if I don't tell you (something that will hurt you) because I am protecting your feelings, does that mean that I am denying you "as an adult," paternalistically deciding *for you* what you ought to know and what not? If love is a relation of equals, this may indeed be a problem. And even if you *say*, "I can handle it," but I know pretty well that you can't, the problem is not resolved. If I don't tell, I'm not treating you as a fully self-sufficient autonomous adult; if I do tell, I've taken you at your word but hurt you and, consequently, us. What does the myth of "total honesty" say here? Do the consequences count for more than the way I feel about you? Is it so obvious, as my students seem to think, that if I can't be "totally honest, the relationship can't be worth much anyway"? Or could it be that honesty and trust are the *complications* of love, rather than its essence?

A recent acquaintance married a Japanese girl. He spoke no Japanese; she spoke no English. (With no third language between them.) And yet, as they acquired some mutual understanding, what became obvious was that their increased ability to explicitly express their emotions and state demands rendered the relationship not more intimate but less so. What Americans call explicitness she considered vulgarity and lack of style. A hint at most should be sufficient; anything more is a sign of gross insensitivity. What we call "making things clear" she considered a sign of disrespect ("Do you think I'm stupid?"); what we call "honesty" she called stupidity. It is an extreme example, but it separates, as we rarely do, the difference between love and contractual verbosity. Where love is concerned, honesty may be of very little importance. Which is not to say, however, that *dis*honesty has any place either. Sometimes, wisdom in love is just knowing when to shut up.

# BEHIND CLOSED DOORS: LOVE, SEX AND INTIMACY 20

*Dear Ann L:*
*My husband and I don't talk any more. I feel so far away from him. . . .*
*Dear ——: The results of a six-year study done by Dr. Ray L. Birdwhistell, an authority on non-verbal communication, should make you feel better.*
*In an effort to determine exactly how much conversation went on between married couples, Dr. Birdwhistell installed microphones and tape recorders in the homes and cars of selected pairs who had been married fifteen years or longer.*
*The results showed that couples who considered themselves happy spent 27½ minutes a week in conversation. The reason the figure was that HIGH, Dr. Birdwhistell said, was because the couples selected for the study coincidentally went visiting a lot, and they had to give each other directions.*

ANN LANDERS
Washington *Post*, September 5, 1979

Love, sex and intimacy are so closely bound together that it is only with an effort that we can pry them apart. Love and sex, of course, are easily distinguished—perhaps too easily—whether or not it is also true that sex is better with love.[1] But when we add the ingredient of intimacy, it

---

[1] Russell Vannoy, in *Sex Without Love* (Prometheus, 1979) argues that it is not.

is as if we've formed the perfect compound, sex providing the physical dimension of intimacy as the ultimate expression of love. But it is essential too that we distinguish between love and intimacy: unrequited love is love in which the issue of intimacy does not yet arise, and hatred can also be an extremely intimate emotion. Thus intimacy is not strictly necessary for love nor is it exclusive to love. Nevertheless it is hard for us to conceive of love without it.

What is intimacy? We think that we know but much of what has been said about it is, as I shall argue, dangerously confused. Too often intimacy is confused with vulnerability, sex alone or simply atmosphere. Sometimes intimacy is said to be an experience. Sometimes it is supposed to be a state of being, sometimes an activity or a kind of action. What I want to argue in this chapter is that it is essentially the experience of shared identity, the main metaphor for which is "closeness," for which sex provides the most readily available expression. "Feeling intimate" is sensing that breakdown of barriers and individual independence that is most commonly identified with intense sexual ecstasy and oblivion. "Being intimate" is a generalization of that experience, and sexual activity is but one among many actions and activities that contribute to that sense of "union." But intimacy, like love itself, has recently been shifted from the realm of sexuality, which has become all too common and routine, to the realm of the verbal, which has come to be the heart of intimacy, by way of "disclosure" and confession, "telling all" and perhaps being embarrassed by it. Therefore, though both sexual and verbal expressions are essential to romantic love, I want to spend most of this chapter emphasizing the first and de-emphasizing the second.

What is sex? An odd question, to be sure. If *anything* in the love-chat business is simply obvious and not worth defining, it is sexuality. But if love is not a mystery, perhaps sexuality ought to be more of one. Why should this physical activity—no matter how invigorating or pleasurable—be given such importance? On the basis of sexual attraction and sometimes little else, we fall in love, give a total stranger an extravagant place in our lives, shunt aside old friends, family and colleagues, and make commitments that may outlive our sexual enthusiasm. Why? We make no such fuss about our professional relationships, for example, whose significance is more a matter of convenience. We do not fall in love so readily with those with whom we share lifelong (non-sexual) interests—a favorite co-worker or tennis opponent. Why sex? And why is it so difficult, even in these "liberated" days of "casual" sex, to treat sex casually, like having lunch together—or just seeing a movie?

If one thinks of sex, as many do, as a merely pleasurable "natural" activity, the significance of sex will evade us, and the connection between sex and love will remain either a mystery or a curiosity. But if we conceive of sex as *expression*—and not the expression of love alone—then its importance becomes more evident. Romantic love, like most (but not all) emotions, involves an essentially *embodied* conception of self (which is why the concept of beauty, too, is so important to it). Romantic love is not an emotion that is possible between "two souls" or "pure consciousnesses." It is an emotion in which "the body is the meaning," according to the French philosopher Maurice Merleau-Ponty, and sex is "the projection of a person's manner of being into the world" (*Phenomenology of Perception*, p. 158). As intimacy lies right at the heart of love, sex as the expression of "closeness" is as essential to love as the desire for revenge is essential to anger, or covetousness is to envy. The urge to touch is the concrete expression of the more abstract desire to share the lover's self; the desire to hold and be held is the physical equivalent of the interlocking of two identities, distinct and different but now perfectly together. One might even say that sexual desire *is* love, by way of hyperbole, so long as one does not fallaciously conclude from that that all sexual desire is therefore love. The missing ingredient here is intimacy, for what determines the relationship between sex and romantic love is the desire, central to love but not necessarily to sex, to *be* together. For sex itself, now to complete our triangle, is not intimacy. Indeed, sex can be used precisely in order to deny or destroy intimacy. Even, sometimes, in love.

### *What Intimacy Is Not*

Intimacy is not sex, and sex is not intimacy. It is true that one cannot be physically closer than in sex—unless one is a thoracic surgeon—but physical proximity is only sometimes an expression of intimacy. It is noteworthy that our euphemism, "to be intimate," is a polite way of saying "having sexual intercourse," but what this signifies is only that sex *sometimes* symbolizes intimacy—which no one would deny even in these promiscuous times. But one can have sex and not be intimate at all; in fact, sufficient attention to technique and sensations is a popular way of *avoiding* intimacy, as Rollo May and his colleagues are so fond of pointing out to us. Intimacy is possible without sex, of course, as in one of those often re-enacted Victorian garden parties we see on television, where two lovers exchange the most intimate glances as they properly trudge through the requisite rituals. Naked, touching and being touched, allowing oneself the unusually free expression of one's urges—it is hard to imagine any situation in which intimacy would be more at home. But sex alone neither guarantees nor is required by intimacy.

Intimacy is not mere endurance. Some couples seem to feel that they are "so close" just because they have managed to live together so long, put up with each other through so many problems, through sickness and poverty, mutual resentment and boredom. And one of them, no doubt, will be shocked and surprised when the other says, "I feel so far away from you." But intimacy, like "love," is a laudatory characteristic in our society, and so one ascribes it to oneself whenever it is remotely feasible. And having endured, one feels that one at least deserves that badge of credit. This has nothing to do with intimacy.

Intimacy is not familiarity. Feeling comfortable is not feeling intimate. One can feel comfortable alone, or with a bearskin rug, with friends, drinking partners and social workers. Feeling at home is not feeling intimate; one can enjoy that in a den before a warm fire, being greeted by the dog at the gate or the doorman at the portal. And what one *knows* about another person is not intimacy either, even if the knowledge is reciprocal. But here we enter a rather large topic and an enormous area of confusion.

Knowledge and intimacy are often thrown together, for instance in such phrases as "carnal knowledge," which may well be argued to be a confusion of epistemology, or sex, or both. The idea that *knowing* someone is either a prerequisite or equivalent to intimacy is so common that it seems like common sense. Having intercourse with someone is indeed a way of getting to *know* him or her and, at the same time, getting closer. An intimate conversation is often thought to be a revelation of secrets or a "heart-to-heart talk." Intimacy is, in particular, supposed to be the disclosure of those lesser-known, more embarrassing facts about you—your inability to hold onto friends or your incompetence with a checkbook. It is essential to intimacy that this knowledge *not* be common, for one cannot be intimate by quietly telling what everyone already knows. Thus intimacy becomes a private conversation, preferably with some sex (touching fingers and cheeks at the least), which includes the somewhat painful disclosure of embarrassing information about oneself. "I never told that to anyone before" is thus supposed to be a sure sign of intimacy and an indication of encroaching love.

Social psychologists, when they test hypotheses about intimacy, typically rely on what they can get people to *say* to one another. The results are then easily recorded and liable to only minimal misinterpretation. One set of experimenters, for example, approached various passengers in an airport waiting lounge, initiated various conversations and then noted their responses.[2] When the initial remarks were impersonal and unrevealing, the replies tended to be very much the same. When the initial remarks were calculatedly personal and revealing, however, these total strangers would sometimes make the most intimate revelations, about their sex lives, their sense of success, their fears and insecurities. Now my point is not to report or comment on the truth or plausibility of the hypotheses being tested, but rather the presupposition of the test itself. That presupposition is that intimacy is a function of, or at least can be measured by, the kinds of information people exchange. Of course there is an obvious advantage in using such precisely recordable materials, but it is worth noting that no such precision is available in measuring, for instance, the tone of voice or the shifts in posture, much less the sense of distance and anonymity that lies behind these revelations. For, as we all know, it is often far easier to confess to a total stranger (airplane passengers are notorious) than friends, spouses and lovers. But perhaps this is precisely to say that exchange of information of this nature is not at all intimacy, but something we are often willing to do only when intimacy is *not* at issue.

One of several recent books on intimacy (there have been hundreds) expresses the psychological presupposition in its title: *Sharing Intimacy: What We Reveal to Others and Why*, by Valerian J. Derlega and Alan L. Chaikin (Prentice-Hall, 1975). The book is about intimacy, or what its authors call "self-disclosure." Their sociological presupposition is what they call "the lonely society." They presume an epistemology—as opposed to an ontology—of loneliness, the view that, even if we recognize our coexistence with other selves, we have enormous difficulties knowing anything about one another (Chapter 2). The problem seems to be our difficulty in "having someone to

[2] Zick Rubin, "Lovers and Other Strangers," *American Scientist*, Vol. 62, 1974.

talk to" and our response, accordingly, is to "share secrets."
In fact "sharing secrets" becomes the essence of "self-disclosure," and most of the book is about the propriety, desirability
and risks of sharing such secrets with strangers, friends, husbands and wives. It is what people *say* that is important,
though to be sure there are other aspects of their behavior and
other features of their situation which may be relevant as well.
Sharing secrets lets us know that our problems are not unique.
Sharing secrets is a way of "gaining feedback," "reducing uncertainty" and "putting our problems in perspective." Making
friends and falling in love alike are based on "getting to know
each other" and intimacy, as the sharing of secrets, is the key.
In fact sex (particularly in the "inexpressive male") seems to
have at most an instrumental role in intimacy, that is, something to talk *about* and a "medium of exchange for intimate
information."

Intimacy is not knowledge, or familiarity, or comfort. Love
and intimacy can always *use* knowledge, familiarity and comfort, of course; they may even be presupposed to a certain extent, but the nature of intimacy itself is to be found elsewhere.
What we *know* in love, as well as what we say, is vastly overrated. Intimacy may include the exchange of secrets, but it
need not. Indeed, one embarrassing implication of that theory
is that two people who are sufficiently well known to each
other and perhaps to the public at large (two "celebrities,"
for instance, or a psychiatrist and his or her patient) would
have no room for intimacy; there would be nothing left to exchange. But the very opposite seems to be the case. It is their
*privacy* that is intimate, not the exchange of information. And
if the exchange of embarrassing information were the main ingredient in intimacy, it would follow that those of us with the
most embarrassing information to exchange would be the most
intimate, with a veritable wealth of love to go around. But indeed the truth seems to be very different. The exchange of embarrassing secrets may make me momentarily vulnerable but

this is just as likely to *end* my sense of intimacy as to enrich it. Having shared my secret with you, blurting it out in a moment of carelessness, I now wish you would just disappear. And that, I would suggest, is hardly the mark of intimacy.

Perhaps it is true, as we have been reminded for so many years and in so many sermons, that "the flesh is weak" and "to err is human." But is love therefore to be confused with mutual confession and compassion? Is the basis of love embarrassment? The shameful do not make better lovers, whether or not they make better patients or confidants. Love is a sharing of strengths as well as weaknesses, and our conception of intimacy is too bound up with only the latter. There are, of course, emotions of mutual degradation, but love is not one of them. There is a sense in which intimacy involves knowledge, but knowledge and vulnerability are not themselves intimacy.

### Sex as Language

*Sex isn't something you've got to play with; sex is you. It's the flow of your life, it's your moving self and you are due to be true to the nature of it. . . .*

D. H. LAWRENCE, *Collected Poetry*

Many of our most intimate moments are spent in silence. Silence, of course, can be awkward, but it can also be "pregnant," particularly in the midst of a longing gaze, when talk of almost any kind is a breach of intimacy. This is nowhere more obvious than in sexual desire, when talk tends to become mere chatter, a veil which at one dramatic instant is pulled away by silence. It is evident too in sex itself, looking and touching, and after, with that calm sense of closeness already achieved. It is sometimes said, by those who use sex as protection *against* intimacy (and as a masquerade for it), that sexuality involves turning the other person, and perhaps also oneself, into an "object." But in intimacy just the opposite is the case; the distance required by "objects" is broken down completely. We

are two sensuous subjects, not pure consciousnesses, much less
souls, but "embodied" lovers, feeling our bodies and each
other's body and oblivious to the usual daily distinctions between what's yours and what's mine, what's body and what's
mind.

Sex itself is not intimate, I have insisted, but it is nevertheless our primary vehicle for intimacy. This is not a natural
necessity. Most animals do not experience anything like intimacy as they mate, and many people in many cultures would
find our notion of intimacy foreign to themselves as well. Sex
as such is underdetermined, in the sense that it can be made
into a great many different types of activities—merely instrumental, a means to pregnancy or a release of tension, an assertion of privilege, a male "right" to his wife that is closed to all
others—or it can be symbolic in a grander sense, as an expression of mythological proportions, "the flow of your life," according to Lawrence, or the enactment of the cosmic process,
according to Rollo May. What sex is *not*, even in this most he-
donistic of cultures, is mere *pleasure*. Sex is a *language*, in
which we express our "deepest" feelings for one another. Love
is by no means the only emotion so expressed, even between
lovers. Sex is a non-verbal language, in which nothing is (verbally) explicit or need be actually *said*, but in which we therefore find it often easier to express what we will not say, and to
find expressed what we will not easily hear.

Sex is our vehicle for intimacy, first of all, because it is an essentially *private* activity, in contrast with speech, which can be
broadcast to millions all at once. And even sex in public (kissing and cooing in the park, for example) is almost belligerently
exclusive, visible to others but shutting them out absolutely. It
is the essence of intimacy that it be relatively rare, and sex provides this rarity, in part because of our insistence that it be a
private activity, and in part because of the restrictions and
taboos we impose upon it. But at the same time sex is the language of romantic love, in part because it is the common de-

nominator of virtually all peoples in all cultures, and thus opens up the possibility of romantic choice to virtually everyone. This raises an innocent paradox: that love and intimacy employ sex as their primary language because it is both universal and rare, because everyone has it but every time it is considered unique and special.

To say that sex is a language, a (for the most part) silent, non-verbal language, is to allow ourselves to understand why sex is so important, not only in love, but in the expression of a great many other emotions besides. The standard "liberal" view of sex as pleasurable activity (the only restriction being that it be "between consenting adults"), makes it all but impossible to understand why this activity should be so important to us, so devastating when we fail or do without it, so exhilarating when it goes well and is obviously so much more than merely enjoyable. (Indeed, in the Freudian view of sex as pleasurable release or catharsis, it is not even obvious why we need to bother with other people, since we can "release" ourselves alone.) It is important if not obvious too that sex need not involve genital intercourse, but might indeed include any mutual bodily activities and expressions, including a languid look across the room and playing "footsies" under the dining-room table. But every move is a gesture filled with meaning. Sex as a language cannot be taken lightly, cannot be "casual," whatever our superficial moralizing might be. One cannot make a sexual gesture devoid of its meaning any more easily than one can say something in English, e.g., "It is cold," and not mean by it that it is cold.[3]

Because sex is a language it can be "spoken" well or badly, awkwardly or expertly, and the emotion expressed will get through better or worse depending on this. Technique im-

[3] But I can say, "It is cold," as a signal in a plot, for instance, and not mean that it is cold. So I can even have intercourse—e.g., in a Masters and Johnson experiment—and not, in this special case, mean anything by it either. The meaning is there perhaps, but I do not mean it.

proves articulation as well as pleasure, but too much emphasis
on technique blocks expression altogether, like a memorized
speech in a casual conversation. The very fact that two people
kiss or have intercourse is itself immensely significant, of
course, but every gesture and movement within that context is
significant too. First of all, it signifies, in a very strong sense,
*being* together, and it is not a mere matter of misunderstanding when one person says (afterward) to another, "I
thought you agreed that this was just for fun." But sex is not
just an expression of togetherness, a symbolic gesture of shared
identity. It also involves the complex expression of many of
those interpersonal privately defined roles which make up that
shared identity, and it is here that the connection between
love, sex and intimacy becomes most apparent. In silence.

Our most crucial roles together rarely have to be spelled out.
And when they are, it may often be a shock or surprise. We
sometimes trust not what's said but what's displayed, particularly where affection is concerned. But we also feel a lover's
hesitation, a hint of avoidance, as well as vulnerability or dependency, long before these are ever expressed in words, even
before we are conscious of it. Some roles defy intimacy: treating the other person as a confessor or acting like a confessor
oneself can do this. Causing pain in sex can, but need not always, have this effect. Other roles are easy vehicles for intimacy—simple play, baby talk, touching or allowing oneself to
be touched slowly, gently. But no gesture automatically initi-
ates a role; it all depends on the context and the intention.
Play can be avoidance; baby talk can be just silliness. A slow
soft touch may be simply a step in a back rub as well as an excuse to "open up" completely. But then, a good Russian idiom,
enunciated on the streets of Los Angeles, may not have a
meaning either.

Sex is the vehicle for love and intimacy only in so far as it is
mutually understood and accepted. The most loving touch is

still an act of aggression when it is unwanted, unexpected, totally unsolicited. On the other hand, a brutal lunge or a painful pinch can be fully an expression of love, so long as it is a matter of mutual desire and expression. Sex consists of shared symbols as well as symbols of shared identity. Sadism itself is almost never an expression of love, but sadism with a masochist may well be. Indeed, the most common complementary roles in love and in sex are those of domination and submission, often alternating with an emphasis on an underlying sense of equality, all as a matter of gesture and almost never actually stated. Sexual "positions," which the guidebooks prefer to treat as a mere matter of "variety," are indeed gestures of great importance. "Who's on top" has much to say about the relationship itself, and some of the most crucial roles in love are expressed in just this way. The "dominant" position is also a symbol of dominance; so is "submission." Switching roles frequently is a way of emphasizing equality. Some couples find only one position comfortable, making rather obvious (though they may never acknowledge it) at least one set of roles that composes their identity. Some couples far prefer positions of equality (lying both on their sides, for example); others eschew intercourse altogether, because of its symbolic significance, the male "inside of" the female, "invading" her. But there is nothing right or wrong about this viewpoint. Symbols mean what they are believed to mean, and for some couples this is what they mean. And there is nothing "natural" or "unnatural" about such views either, in so far as there is nothing "natural" about symbols and their meanings.

Touching itself represents intimacy to us precisely because we are so cautious about it. A salesman's slap on the back or a co-worker's pat on the butt is not intimacy but intrusion, and it is because we so guard our bodies that sex itself remains a matter of personal privacy and so significant. The genitals remain the key to sex for most of us just because, not as a matter of nature but of custom, they are so rarely even visible much less touchable by other people. We can easily imagine it otherwise. Indeed, promiscuous people may well develop a sense of intimacy which largely ignores the genitals and emphasizes instead some part of the body and activities which are generally neglected: fingertips, face or even feet perhaps. Again, it is the symbolism that counts, the mutual roles that are acted out silently that constitute the heart of intimacy and the expression of love. Every touch is an assertion, and where and how is meaningful in terms of the role(s) in which it plays its part. A single touch can represent control, domination, even vulnerability, all at once. There are positions and actions which clearly symbolize vulnerability, "openness" and trust (although it is important to point out that this is obviously not the only way to express vulnerability and trust; as one of my critics has pointed out,[4] opening a joint checking account may be a far better expression of trust than any sexual openness). There are fancy ways of making love that represent co-ordination to a remarkable degree, plain and simple ways of making love that represent simplicity and tradition, outrageous ways of making love that represent eccentricity, daring, mutual creativity or rebellion. There are ways of making love that are explicitly subservient, self-consciously noncommittal, openly devoted. One might (if so inclined) chart all of these explicitly, in a sort of "how to" book of positions for the non-verbally inarticulate. But expression is whatever makes itself mutually understood, and a book of translations would be appropriate only in the most bizarre of circumstances (perhaps for Robert Heinlein's peculiarly "groking" creature in *Stranger in a Strange Land*, though he seems to have been successful enough without it).

Sex is central to intimacy as its medium of expression, though one can easily imagine or find cultures in which this is not the case. Intimacy in turn is central to love as that set of

---

[4] Janice Moulton, "Another Sexual Position," *Journal of Philosophy*, 1976, in response to my "Sexual Paradigms" in the same journal, 1974.

essentially private and personal roles through which we build a shared identity, although one can imagine and find societies which do not distinguish the personal from the public as we do, and consequently will not have either our concept of intimacy or our conception of romantic love. One might imagine romantic love without full-blown sex, without intercourse and heavy petting, perhaps, but one cannot imagine romantic love without some form of caress, if only with eyes and the touch of two fingers and an occasional kiss. Intimacy tends to be vulnerable, not because it is intrinsically confessional or an admission of weaknesses, but because it is essentially devoting oneself to roles and investing oneself in an identity which another person can snatch away, without warning, or with a clumsy statement or gesture, even a critical look. While we're playfully cooing, you can at any moment turn serious and "adult," reducing my remaining moment of childishness to mere foolishness. And as I act out my own sense of insecurity or trust or submissiveness or mock aggressiveness you can at any time raise the curtain on my private performance, by laughing at me, chastising me or, worst of all, dismissing me. It is not that our intimacy is itself built out of embarrassments, but intimacy as strictly private and personal roles and identity is by its very nature easily embarrassed, even if it is not in itself in any way embarrassing. There is nothing intrinsically embarrassing about sex, from which it does not follow that public performances are not shameful, including even public talk about it. But if we want sex to be a continuing vehicle of intimacy—which is to say, if we want to keep our conception of sensual sexual intimate romantic love intact (and this is always an open question)—then sex too will have to be kept under wraps, which is in no way to say a "dirty little secret," much less "repressed." But what romantic love, sex and intimacy share in common, and what allows them to function as they do in our lives, is precisely this common yet in each case unique sense of privacy, this completely familiar yet in every couple original expression, using gestures and organs equally available to every one of a billion-odd couples, in every case signifying something quite special.

# LOVE AND THE TEST OF TIME 21

## ("DIALECTIC")

*It is very romantic to be in love. But there is nothing romantic about a definite proposal. Why, one may be accepted. One usually is, I believe. Then the excitement is over. The very essence of romantic love is uncertainty.*

OSCAR WILDE, *The Importance of Being Earnest*

Nowhere is our all-or-nothing attitude to love more evident than in that peculiar slogan, "Love is forever." It may have an impressive metaphysical ancestry, in Plato, St. Paul and the whole of Christianity, but in a plain matter-of-fact everyday interpretation it is not only false but absurd. Love comes to an end. Sometimes abruptly, sometimes quietly. Often it starts again, and not infrequently it actually lasts a lifetime. But no love has the assurances of eternity; all love is fraught with ups and downs and uncertainties, and even the marriage contract has its temporal escape clause—"till death do us part." We all know love to be risky, traumatic, a ragged road with cataclysm possible at every turn. So why do we say, "I'll love you always"? Sometimes, in the thrill of the moment, we even believe it.

As in other all-or-nothing dramatizations of love, such as "Love is everything" (that is, it is at times extremely important to us) and "You're the most wonderful person in the world" (I'm enthusiastic about you), "Love is forever" is an overly extravagant expression of an important emotional truth. It is a child's word—the Greeks called it "infinity"; it means "uncountable," a *refusal* to see the end, open-ended desire and continuity. Whether or not love is going to end, that ending is emphatically not built into or even allowed in its experiential structure. (One might contrast such emotions as hope, fear and the thirst for vengeance, whose end is essential to the emotion.) Couples beginning to live together or entering into marriage are loath to discuss legal agreements about what will be whose if they break up. Making contingency plans ("if it doesn't work out") is considered in poor taste, as well as proof that one isn't really serious. Love projects itself into the indefinite future, not forever, but as far as one can see—though sometimes this is not much more than a year or a month or two, or even a week or so. Love needs that opening. Many other emotions do not. Love is a process, a *dialectic*. It takes *time*. And not to give it the time it takes is indeed to be that much less in love.

Time is the test of love. Love that does not last is mere "infatuation," no matter how intense, how dedicated, how indistinguishable from "the real thing." Indeed, there may be no other difference between the two.[1] Of course the amount of time required to prove the "truth" of love varies from generation to generation; most of my friends seem to consider eight or nine months sufficient, some of my students a few days, my parents and their friends nothing short of a lifetime. But the point to ponder is that we do consider time as a test, since it is not so for most other emotions. One would not dismiss anger or jealousy if it lasted only five weeks, or even five days. Indeed, one can get truly angry even for a minute. ("I'm glad I got that out of my system.") Yet the idea that love could be

---

[1] "Infatuation" is therefore not the name of an emotion at all, but a retrospective judgment about love. It is like the word "counterfeit," in that counterfeit money might indeed be indistinguishable from the real stuff, but nevertheless it is judged to be worthless.

satisfied the first time we make love ("I'm glad I got that out of my system"?!) or that love could be complete in a single moment—no matter how "marvelous"—is unthinkable. Thus the troubadours confused the beginning of love for its end, and Don Juan is a problem not because he loves for only a week, but because, what's worse, he knows this in advance.

### Love and Death

One of the bases for our civilization has been the idea of love. The idea of love was founded on our loving a mortal person forever. This brought us to terms with the idea of death. It is a way to face death. That is what makes it tragic and dramatic and precious—

OCTAVIO PAZ

In contrast to the idea that love is "forever," that time is the test of love, the same tradition has promoted the dramatic connection between love and death. Octavio Paz suggests, as Plato did twenty-five hundred years before, that love is a way of *facing* death, a means to immortality. But in literature it is one of our favorite clichés to *end* a romance with the death of the lovers, thus saving the author the almost impossible task of spelling out how they lived "happily ever after" without passion fading away or getting lost in the clatter of domestic responsibilities. How would one have continued *Romeo and Juliet*, or written a sequel to *Tristan and Isolde?* But this literary device is not to be confused with the sometimes tedious exigencies of life, and the connection between love and death, for most of us, is again one of those all-or-nothing dramatizations which leads us to falsify and demean our own experience. Few of us are ever asked, much less expected, to die for love. And we are practical enough to look with pity, not admiration, at some young lover who dies of despair by his or her own hand. But this does not make love any less—perhaps only

more circumspect, more in perspective. But again, this dramatic exaggeration of the life-and-death importance which we
ascribe to love has its germ of truth, not only in showing once
again the remarkable significance this emotion has in our lives,
but also in proving how closely love and identity are linked to
our very existence, so that cessation of love is often equated
with death. But moving from metaphor to real love and life,
we have to do what Romeo and Juliet did not—understand
how love continues, day after day, how the dialectic of
love goes on, the stuff of which comedies, not tragedies, are
made.

When Denis de Rougemont published his classic if tenden-
tious *Love in the Western World* some forty years ago, he tried
to capture both "love is forever" and the love-and-death connection in a single theory, and with a single distinction. He distinguished what he called "conjugal love"—essentially based in
a marriage and supported by the grace of God—and "romantic
love," which he considered pagan, irrational, anti-social and essentially destructive, even fatal. Not surprisingly, Romeo, Juliet, Tristan and Isolde appear as paradigmatic examples of romantic love, and he takes their premature demise to be not a
literary but an emotional necessity. Romantic love, which is intrinsically unstable, has no other possible end, unless, of
course, it simply fades away and ends in disappointment, the
less than dramatic but perhaps still tragic experience of us less
than fictitious everyday heroes.

I think De Rougemont overstates his case, but he has recognized something quite essential which his many critics often
prefer to ignore: that romantic love is not only unstable—or I
shall soon say "metastable"—but a poor preparation for, even a
threat to, the stability of marriage. Romantic love is not the
anteroom to marriage but, in an important sense, its opposite
(which is not to say that they are not complementary). As
Kierkegaard argued in *Either/Or*, marriage is responsibility,
romantic love is irresponsibility, the first a bedrock of civilized

society, the latter a rebellious emotional attachment. I think that De Rougemont is right in pointing out the essential difference between a relationship which is based on obligations, expectations, the mores of society and, in marriage, a contractual "commitment" and a relationship that is based wholly on the contingency of an emotion. Now granted, in our day the distinction between love and marriage has broken down considerably; few people still see marriage as a lifetime necessity which they *cannot* ever get out of, but marriage (and often living together too) includes commitments and obligations which love does not. It is based on the *expectation* of staying together, while romantic love includes only the desire and hope. Although there may be some time when the two emotions are almost indistinguishable, the essential experience of each is distinctly its own.

It is the contingency of romantic love that concerns me here; "working out" a relationship need not have anything to do with love. Indeed, one thinks of Rodney Dangerfield's classic line: "We sleep in separate rooms, we have dinner apart, we take separate vacations—we're doing everything we can to keep our marriage together." Romantic love is essentially a tension. Marriages can be happy; romantic love must be exhilarating. This is not to say that one cannot have both, but it would be naïve to suppose that two forces moving in opposite directions "naturally" belong together, "like a horse and carriage." Marriages are made "forever," ended ideally only by death. Love, on the other hand, lasts but from day to day, week to week, an exquisite contingency which, like all uncertainties, chooses death as its metaphor. But it is a metaphor, like "happily ever after," that conceals more than it reveals, and hides the essential relationships between romantic love and time.

## *Love and Time*

> "Love me forever, if only for tonight."
>                                        —ANON.

Of course we want love to last. But here we may find one of
those curious sleights of hand that Nietzsche once diagnosed
as the "great philosophical errors," confusing cause for effect,
wishes for causes. We begin by assuring each other that love
will last. Soon we are taking love's lasting as the test of love
and then it is no longer the desire but one of the structural
components of love, love as a state which if real endures. But
love, we keep insisting, is not a state.

We say love is forever but celebrate love for the moment.
Indeed, lovers are notoriously reckless in the conception of
time, in their impatience, in their view of the future. The moment is everything. But then, to confuse matters even more,
we say, "I wish this moment would last forever." But it is the
very nature of a moment *not* to last; that's what makes it a moment. So there seems to be confusion at the very core of our
conception. We treat love as a state when it is rather a process,
and treat love as a moment which might last forever. But love
is neither of the moment nor forever. Love essentially involves
a sense of time—indeed time comes to be defined by the relationship—but we do not need to refer either to the specious
present or to unimaginable eternity in order to understand
this.

To say that love takes time is to say that it is never just "for
the moment"; love always has duration; because it is a process, it always looks forward to the future and back to its past.
Love looks to the future, in fantasies of marriage, babies, a trip
to Boston next summer, for it is in future plans and possibilities that our shared identity (like our individual identities)
is largely determined. Our mutual expectations are as essen-

tial as our mutual admiration of one another, and here too the dialectical complexity of love becomes apparent: you tell me that you want to become a great musician, and I adopt your ambition as my own. You get insecure and have your doubts, but I'm now the one who urges you on, and indeed I have come to take your sense of the future as so much a matter of my identity that your loss of interest in it can be extremely damaging to my sense of my own identity, and thus to our love as well.

The future is not an infinite expanse of moments (an archaic view of time in any case) but a series of hypotheticals and contingencies ("what if . . .") whose significance fades asymptotically. Quite the contrary of love being concerned with the infinite, much less lost in the moment, it is rather absorbed in the immediate future. Sometimes it is the next ten seconds that seem to mean everything to me, or the next five hours, the next two days. It is the anticipation of your touch, expecting you to call, waiting for the movie to end or the bill to arrive. It is being hardly able to wait until we get home, or enjoying this weekend as if it were followed by an abyss, and preceded by one as well. Indeed, one sure way to threaten love, though inviting assurances, is to push such abstract questions as "What will happen when we get tired of each other?" and "What if you get bored with me?" Or even, more positively, watching old couples and hoping to be like them. Indeed, not only do such questions break the delicate webbing that ties the present to the immediate future—by stretching it too far—but they may even help bring about precisely the feared possibility that they seek assurance against. Love is not so much moment by moment as it is step by step. And in love as in Keynesian economics, "the long run" is often least important, and least real.

Love also refers to the past, sometimes in an obvious and all-consuming sense, for instance, in love that has gone on for years. The sense of a shared past can act as an anchor, to hold love together through an extremely troubled present and not

very promising future. At least for a while. But even the beginning of love looks to the past, in a most curious way, desperately trying to weave together a temporal identity that has little basis either in past or present. "You mean you went to that
Allen Ginsberg reading too? I wonder if we saw each other
then, perhaps even bumped into each other in the aisles?" It is a
frivolous enterprise but an essential one. If love is the temporal
process of forming a self-identity, then the past is as essential
as the present and the future, just as prone to fantasy (in this
case retrospective interpretation) and just as much of an ingredient in the sense of a shared self emerging from two seemingly wholly separate selves. But because love takes time, it
takes whatever time it can get, even creating time from random moments and memories. If life is art, then even short is
long. (*Si vita ars est, ergo donc brevis longus est.*)[2]

### Dialectic

The essence of our relations with others is *conflict*.
                                JEAN-PAUL SARTRE

Love is a process, a dialectic, a movement—toward what?
Toward a shared identity, the creation of a shared self. But
this is complicated by the fact, which we have not yet
sufficiently emphasized, that this goal is impossible, unachiev-
able, even incomprehensible. Two selves cannot become one,
not when they start out so differently—with different origins,
even from different cultures, with different tastes and expectations. And yet this does not mean that the goal is impossible to
work for and to want even desperately, to *yearn* after. For this
indeed is the famous *languor* of love, the play of contradictions
reinforcing each other.

The paradox of love is this, that it presupposes a strong
sense of individual autonomy and independence, and then

---

[2] The pun is from Gayatri Spivak; the Latin is from Jon Solomon.

seeks to cancel this by creating a shared identity. But this cannot be, for no sooner do we approach this goal than we are abruptly reminded of our differences. Perhaps you dislike a movie I love, or maybe I'm bored or insulted by one of your friends. Even in the most trivial differences, we are thrown back to our individuality, wondering how we could possibly "work" as a couple. But then, as we move apart, the self we have already formed together pulls us back; the separation is too painful; we have too much at stake, too much together, too much to lose. We *want* this, whatever the differences. Love is this process, not a state of union but a never ending conflict of pushing away and pulling together. In some couples the dialectic is wholly obvious, in that curious alternation of love and hate and sweet sex and battles and reconciliation that leaves other people looking on in perplexity. For others it is a subtle wave motion of relative independence and dependency, never so violent that either becomes a matter of desperation. But whether dialectic is violent or rather a soft fluctuation, it is alternatively adoration, minor annoyances, passionate joy, indignation, childish play, guilt, euphoria, shamelessness, shame, delirium, resentment, gratitude, indifference, gaiety, need and solitude, too easily summarized, after a few months or years, simply as "love," when in fact it's been a hundred other emotions besides, all as a part of love.

Because love is a process, it takes time. Because it has a goal, we can say that love is "going somewhere" even if that goal is ultimately impossible, and even if, in another sense, love has nowhere to go (Chapter 7). To say that an affair "isn't going anywhere" is to say that the possibility of a shared identity now appears to be impossible, though one can, of course, be mistaken. It is important not to assume, however, that progress toward a goal is necessarily "growth"—in the current laudatory term—an improvement, a betterment or "expansion" of self. Sometimes it is clearly the case that progress in a relationship involves individual degeneration or stagnation. Sometimes, the

cost of shared identity might well be the withering of an autonomous and admirable self, or both individual selves. Our romantic mythology aside, romantic love is not guaranteed to
make us better people, more creative, less violent or any of the
other grand consequences that are supposed to flow from it.
Indeed, the tension that keeps love alive may be severely damaging to other facets of one's self, depending not only on the
intensity of the emotión but on the specific roles that the lovers
adopt along the way. But luckily, it is not usually this way.

At first, particularly when two people have just met, shared
identity consists almost wholly in fantasy, in projection into
the future and a kind of ignorant idealization. Through time
together, shared efforts and enjoyments—most importantly the
various roles that constitute intimacy, including, presumably,
sex—the self that is formed comes to be less based on fantasy,
more on matters of fact and mutual recognition of real virtues,
needs and foibles. The excitement can cool as well, but it need
not, for it is a cynical view indeed that makes the thrill of love
dependent on fantasy and novelty alone. Because love is a
dialectical tension, it survives over time not only in its erratic
and never completed progression toward shared identity but
also in the sporadic counter-assertion of individual identities,
in which we push apart and challenge those bonds but at the
same time test and help strengthen them. Thus love continues
by creating conflicts and differences as well as similarities, and
the motive for doing so is not only the assertion of one's
differences vis-à-vis one's lover but continuing the dialectic as
well. Thus one becomes "the sloppy one" in part so we have
something to fight or tease about, in part to assert our
differences from, as well as to define, each other. The same
differences and conflicts that at the time seemed to be proof of
our incompatibility and the beginning of a breakup turn out to
be precisely the movement that keeps us together.

Differences and conflicts have as much a place in creating
the new identity as in threatening it from within, and here es-

pecially we can understand love as a dialectical process over time, not necessarily growth toward a goal but a dynamic equilibrium of tensions alternatively created and resolved, always with a sense of difference and contingency, but never losing that sense of identity that is no longer only one's own. Here too we can understand the role of such "negative" emotions as jealousy—which can be one of the most fatal threats to any relationship—as another way of preserving that tension, a simultaneous and extremely painful recognition of both the independence of one's lover and the powerful bonds of identity—now appearing perhaps as "possessiveness." But in small doses it is a force for cohesion as well as bitter conflict, and although jealousy itself may last only for an instant, it may be the violation that reminds us how much we value a relationship we may have come to take too much for granted.

### Metastability: Master and Slave

METASTABLE (chemistry) chemically unstable in the absence of certain conditions that would induce stability, but not liable to spontaneous transformation.

RANDOM HOUSE DICTIONARY

Dialectic is tension, but a certain, distinctive progressive tension that supports and creates as well as threatens and destroys. One can imagine two dancers or wrestlers, pressing against one another with more than sufficient force to knock the other down, but because their force is balanced and properly directed the net result is that they hold one another up. Two teams of children in a tug of war lean back on their ropes so that they would surely fall down if each were not pulling just as hard in the other direction. Indeed, it is the most grievous crime for one team to suddenly let go, thus releasing the tension and letting the other fall into the mud. And unromantic as the examples (and the ones to follow) might be, they are good illustrations of the mutually supporting but at the same time opposed tensions and conflicts that make love as a process possible. Indeed, the idea of love as a simple stable "union" is as banal—and as false—as it sounds. Love is a struggle but, as in dance, a struggle that can be both beautiful and inspiring.

The fact that love is balanced tension explains why it should so often have the *appearance* of a state—sometimes for years. But love is always to be understood as what Jean-Paul Sartre calls *metastable*. It may have all of the appearance of stability, but the violence of the forces in balance are such that, should there be a single slip, a momentary imbalance, an ill-considered comment or careless act, that stability shatters into disaster. A homely example is the familiar experience of carrying hot coffee across the room. Four friends are visiting, and we are making the hazardous journey from the kitchen to the living room, five cups of near-boiling java and a small pitcher of milk balanced on outstretched arms. If all goes well, the tensions will disappear in a sigh of relief and the dangers be soon forgotten. But we know what happens at the slightest spill or loss of balance: one drop of hot coffee on tender skin causes a reflex action, perhaps only a minor twitch, which spills much more coffee, which makes us drop one of the cups; we instinctively grab for it and then—total disaster.

Love is like this too. We literally play with fire, evoking in ourselves and each other the most intense passions and extravagant expectations which we encourage with an uneasy sense of confidence. At first one can say almost anything, for nothing is at stake. Soon only the most precise answers are allowed, and only the most exact movements. Lovers are completely tolerant, but only within those delicate boundaries. (It doesn't much matter how much sugar is in the hot coffee.) One can become practiced as a lover as a host or hostess, and become adept at managing the dangerous tensions, keeping them in balance, avoiding or correcting those disappointments or discourtesies that all too easily lead to disaster. But the tensions and the dangers are always there. Unless of course one decides to play it safe by letting love cool until it is no longer capable of causing any pain. But then, unfortunately, it will be too tepid to enjoy as well.

Because love is always metastable, apparently in a state of rest but always bustling with tension and prone to disaster, it also tends to *move*—by breaking down barriers and allowing a relationship to expand its scope—but sometimes to degenerate too, causing new wounds and insecurities that keep a couple off balance for weeks. But it is the movement itself that is most important, not its direction; indeed it is only at the very beginning of a relationship—or at the very end—that the image of a direction to love even makes sense. It is the tension and the balance and the movement that constitutes love, the conflicts and accidents as well as the happiness. The idea of a real unity—as Aristophanes suggested—is only an abstract ideal. Love is this shift of needs and tensions, mutual fantasies, plans and ideals *within* the structures already formed by the ideal of shared identity. Dialectic is as often a switch as a progression, indeed it is sheer movement without an end—like quarrels without a point—that characterizes romantic love, not at all the ascensions into heaven that are preached so tiresomely and the "happily ever after" that ends our fairy tales.

The fairy tale or fable that seems to me to best illustrate the nature of dialectic is a parable that the German philosopher G. W. F. Hegel proffered in his *Phenomenology of Spirit* (1807). It is Hegel with whom the term "dialectic" is most often associated, and Karl Marx, for one, took it directly from him. The parable is called "master and slave," and although Hegel intended it as a general statement about a certain kind of interpersonal relationship, it can be adopted precisely—and has been, for example, by Jean-Paul Sartre—as a model for the dialectic of love. The story is simple: two people who are essentially equals (this is important) meet each other, size each other up and engage in a battle. What they are fighting for, Hegel says, is not riches or territory or peace or greed or selfishness or any of the other aspects of "human nature" that philosophers and political theorists have imagined, but simple *recognition*. Hegel calls the battle "for life and death," but we can say, less violently, that it is a quest for *identity*. Imagine two people on a first date, each trying awkwardly to impress and attract the other, not because one wants anything further from the other—let us assume they do not—but because each wants to be thought well of, as a good person, as intelligent, as interesting, as if (and it seems this way at the time) one's conception of oneself depended upon the recognition of this single stranger. But since each is looking for recognition from the other, each may be all too likely to ignore the needs of the other. So empty compliments turn into teasing, and teasing turns into an argument; the attempt to be charming becomes defensive—too much praise of oneself, too much belittling of everyone else. They are offended; they try to be civil. Or they are nervous, well on the way to being depressed, but they wait, hoping for some magic "click" that will end this awkward struggle and start another. So they start a fight. Or lose themselves at a party, or,—more often—begin a sexual struggle, not so much out of desire as desperation. Sex provides the magic. Sometimes it becomes a way of seeming to lose oneself in an activity that is sufficiently overwhelming or familiar or both that the tension seems to have ceased, or at least becomes a far more exhilarating form of tension. Sometimes sex is magic in quite another sense, introducing the end of that civility that covers up Hegel's life-and-death struggle to allow a full outburst of indignation, an abrupt end to a "date" that wasn't going anywhere anyway—or something new to talk and argue about, which may end in frustration and irresolution but nevertheless marks the beginning of a tense and passionate affair. (Then again, some people do just manage to "have a good time.")

The struggle itself is just the first step in Hegel's little story; the best part comes in its aftermath. In Hegel's parable one person wins, one loses; the winner spares the loser in return for his subservience. The analog in love may not at first seem clear, but Jean-Paul Sartre works it out in some detail in his *Being and Nothingness*. Back in the days when sex was a man's demand and a woman's defeat, the identification of winners and losers, masters and servants was rather straightforward. Today it is not. But in a thousand subtle ways we recognize what it is for someone to "make a point" or lose one. Consider a couple beginning a quarrel. The point of the quarrel doesn't matter; there may not even be one. They are struggling for recognition, to be recognized as needed, perhaps, or as having carried the lion's load of the relationship. But here the notion of winning and losing makes perfectly good sense, whether or not sex is part of the battle, its cause or, often, its resolution. And it is here that Hegel makes his most exciting observation—namely, that winners and losers are always in a precariously unstable way; the winner, now faced with an awesome responsibility and the dependency of the other, finds him or herself even more dependent in return. The winning spouse in a marital quarrel breaks the other down to tears, wholly dependent on the next response, hoping desperately for an apology, or "I didn't mean it." He or she is racked with guilt and anxiety, no matter how angry a moment ago. The relationship is in one's hands, and everything now becomes focused on the defeated other. The loser, on the other hand, finds just the reverse: that this position of seeming dependency is indeed a position of tremendous power. It is the loser who feels free to think about something else, to reconsider the relationship and think, perhaps, that his or her self-esteem might well be better served elsewhere. The victor becomes the dependent one, the loser the more independent. But this state can't last either, for as that independence is asserted, as the "master" gives in to his or her anxiety, the roles are once again reversed, and the dialectic moves again—though not in any direction, perhaps even forever in a circle. It is this constant movement, expressed in as well as punctuated by sex in particular, that keeps the excitement of love alive.

The picture of love as a life-and-death struggle is overdramatized, for certain, and Hegel is quite clear (as Sartre is not) that this is not all there is to human relationships. But it is a model of the dynamics and dialectics of love that is more instructive than the idealized image of love as unperturbed and calm emotion, mixed with hostility only as a sign of "human weakness" and torn apart by our "tragic inability to love." Love itself is conflict, but a conflict which can be as constructive as destructive. Two people can never become one (though Hegel at times seemed to think so) and yet, as Aristophanes so rightly pointed out, we desperately want to do so. And in that impossible desire is the essence of love, a constant struggle between our sense of individuality and our sense of a "union." But this sounds more negative than it is. Perhaps the Hegelian-Sartrian parable is too brutal to capture the often tender and extremely enjoyable means we employ to carry on this conflict, but the battle for identity, sometimes indeed involving the sense of winning and losing and dependence and independence, is what love is ultimately all about.

Movement takes time. How much time? Certainly not necessarily a lifetime, much less forever. Some people can find in an evening of intimacy what others can't do in a year. In fact what we mean by "a good lover," our recent sexual technical fetishism aside, is predominantly the ability to inspire that sense of intimacy and familiarity quickly. For some people, intimacy seems to take nothing else *but* time; it is not so much an effort or an activity as mere presence, time spent together. For them, love indeed may require years and, even then, end with the tragic impression that "we never really got to know one another." But whether love takes a week or a decade, this much is clear: love is a process of transformation, a sometimes violent alteration of self that is always torn between our ideologically all-pervasive need for independence and autonomy and our equally all-pervasive obsession with romantic love and shared identity. And this takes time, whether the tension is developed through a gentle tender wave motion of alternative attitudes and identities or in the violent twists and turns of our grade B romantic novelists. Love takes enough time to allow for that famous *yearning* that Aristophanes quite rightly put at the very core of love, that impossible desire to be (re-)united in equilibrium with one's sense of oneself. It cannot be found in a moment; it may not last forever. But in between the moment and eternity, there is for love all the time in the world.

# BEYOND
# SEX AND GENDER  22
## (LOVE AND FEMINISM)

*"Love. Being in love. Yuck!" Val poured more wine in their glasses.*

*"Val hates love," Iso explained, a wicked smile on her face. Mira blinked at Val. "Why?"*

*"Oh, shit." Val sipped her wine. "I mean, it's one of those things they've erected, like the madonna, you know, or the infallibility of the Pope or the divine right of kings. A bunch of nonsense erected—and that's the crucial word—into Truth by a bunch of intelligent men—another crucial word. What the particular nonsense is, isn't important. What's important is why they did it."*

MARILYN FRENCH, *The Women's Room*

Is romantic love unfair to women? So it has been charged. There is an argument currently gaining wide acceptance, as evidenced, for example, by the enormous number of readers who have recognized themselves in Marilyn French's *The Women's Room*, which would undermine everything we have argued here, if it is sound. The argument, which I will call for convenience "the feminist argument" (see Chapter 8) says essentially that romantic love is a cultural concoction whose purpose is to delude women into rationalizing their own subservience.

The feminist argument is extremely persuasive, far more so than the murky pious praise and the alleged "need for love" that have been the topic of so many predominantly male theoreticians and theologians from Plato and St. Paul to Rollo May. The argument begins with the realization that romantic love, which has so often been promised to women (by men) as the key to happiness, is a myth, an illusion, a fraud. It does not, as promised, change one's life, turn the drudgery of housework and motherhood into joy, much less "forever." But not only that. It is the myth itself that has this as its ulterior motive; it is an illusion whose deconstruction reveals a political purpose. Love was invented by men as an instrument of a kind of culture—which might be summarized as "capitalist"—in order to "keep women in their place," or in any case isolated and dependent on men, and if not happy, then at least hopeful of love and complacent about their socially inferior but infinitely useful occupations. By preaching that love is always good and desirable, it is charged, men have convinced at least most women that love is more important than politics and power, thus limiting the competition to themselves. By teaching that love is "everything," men have convinced many women that it is also worth any sacrifice and, like generals in their luxurious tents behind the battle lines, they have succeeded in getting others to make the sacrifices without having to make them themselves. And within the realm of love itself, men have created an image of the "feminine," such that the virtues a woman finds or creates in herself for the sake of love are directly at odds with the virtues required for success in the world—soft, yielding, quiet, accepting versus hard, aggressive, outspoken and critical. A man can be sexy in pursuit of his career; a woman is sexy despite of or in contrast to hers (unless, of course, sex is her career). To be in love, for a woman, is to be submissive, and therefore, even within the relationship, disadvantaged and powerless, second class and degraded. And if the lover or husband also insists on praising her effusively, worshiping the ground she walks on or putting her "on a pedestal," that is just so much worse, for he is disguising the fact that, even while being worshiped, she is becoming the willing victim in her own political oppression.

This is not the cynicism of neo-Freudian male reductionists: "romantic love is nothing but sex," etc. It represents the personal outrage of a million minor tragedies, of an enormous number of women, only some of whom would identify themselves as "feminists" and few of whom would be able to articulate the precise mechanism by which they have been systematically shut out of power or what this has to do with love. And yet, though I disagree thoroughly with the conclusion—that romantic love as such is the machinery of oppression—there is so much in the feminist argument that we have already accepted:

· that much of what we believe about love is demonstrably false or obscure, mere mythology and pious illusion;

· that love indeed is not "everything" or "the answer" nor is love always good or desirable;

· that love often provides private compensation for public impotence or anonymity;

· that love is a cultural creation in a male-dominated society and so—we may reasonably suppose—it was indeed "erected by men," presumably not to their own disadvantage;

· that love consists of personal roles which, more often than not, cast the woman in the more submissive and subservient position.

There can certainly be no argument against the claim that the promise of romantic love has long been used against women, by way of compensation for political impotence, as an excuse to keep them in the home (and away from the public positions of power) and as a ready rationalization for social inequities in everything from politics ("women are too emotional") to changing diapers ("women are naturally better at that sort of thing"). And indeed there can be no objection to the charge that the "feminine" role in love makes it difficult for a woman to be both romantically desirable and successful in the male-dominated world of money and power. So what, you might well ask, is left of love to defend?

What fails to follow from these persuasive premises is the conclusion that romantic love itself is the source of inequity or an obstacle to equality between the sexes. It does not follow from the fact that there is much in love that is illusory that love is an illusion, nor does it follow from the fact that love is a cultural artifact that it is simply artificial, a "fiction" or a manipulative ploy. It does not follow from the fact that it was (probably) invented by men that love is disadvantageous to women (a man may have invented the wheel and the toothbrush too). It does not follow from the fact that romantic love is often used to reinforce submissive and subservient women's roles that those roles are intrinsic to romantic love as such, and, most important of all, I want to argue that these supposedly "feminine" roles have no essential connection with women and no essential place in love.

If, as the feminist argument charges, romantic love *required* in its structure a division into distinctly male and female roles, strictly corresponding to what has traditionally been called "masculinity" and "femininity," then I would agree that love and the loveworld constitute archaic emotional structures that we had better leave behind us. But if, as I have argued in a preliminary way in Chapter 15 and will argue more thoroughly now, romantic roles are fundamentally sex-neutral and presuppose a significant degree of equality, then the much-abused neo-Victorian crypto-caveman scenario of macho "me-Tarzan" and passive submissive lovingly house-cleaning Jane is not at all a paradigm of love but at most one of its less likable historical curiosities.

### The Argument Against Nature

The key to the feminist argument is to be found in an initial attack against "nature," not against the birds and the bees, that is, but against the word, and what has been done with it. "By nature"—that is, as a matter of biological fact—women have vaginas and uteri instead of penises; women tend to become pregnant, have children and nurse them. Women tend to have smaller frames and more predictable emotional cycles. The innocent conclusion is that men and women are different "by nature." But then the argument runs wild. It is argued that women are "naturally" more passive, men more aggressive. It is "natural" that women should stay at home, be more emotional and find in themselves an overwhelming "need to love," nature's preparation for perpetual motherhood. It is argued that women have naturally submissive sex roles, an argument often backed up by dubious analogies to the mating habits of certain fish, a couple of birds and a peculiar species of spider. The psychologist Albert Ellis writes in *Cosmopolitan* that men are "naturally" more promiscuous and so women will "just have to put up with it," and a common argument even among feminists is that women's love is "naturally" unconditional and more "accepting" than men's because of their motherly instincts. A recent book in "sociobiology" (*The Evolution of Human Sexuality* by Donald Symons, Oxford, 1979) argues on the basis of evolution that women are "naturally" choosier than males, "naturally" more concerned with their own physical appearance, "naturally" less combative, and "unnaturally" concerned with orgasm, which is "a by-product of selection for male orgasm."

Against this horrendous tradition of genetic fallacies and casual extrapolation from some detail of nature to grand hypotheses about "human nature," the feminist argument rightly objects that virtually everything about men and women worth our attention, apart from those concerns peculiar to gynecologists, urologists and designers of toilet fixtures, is not a matter of "nature" at all but of culture. This is especially true of romantic love. In her book, *If Love Is the Answer, What Is the Question?* Uta West rightly comments that "we no longer have instincts; what we have instead, is *myth*." It is an overstatement, but no matter. Romantic love is indeed better understood as a myth than as natural instinct, and the differences between men and women are part of that myth as well.

This might be a good place to develop that distinction which has become immensely important in recent literature but is often confused or ignored in more volatile arguments on the subject. The word "sex," in addition to referring to that complex of physical desires, feelings, activities and processes that we call "sexual," also refers to that very distinctive set of biological differences that allow us to distinguish "the sexes," male and female. But "sex" in this second sense must be distinguished in turn from "gender," which involves differences in roles and behavior rather than in physiology. The contrasting terms here are "masculine" and "feminine," not "male" and "female." All of this is typically tossed together in a set of simple equations: that males are masculine and have distinctively ("natural") male sexual desires, and females are feminine and have distinctively female desires, which may or may not (depending on the theory and the period) include sexual desires. But whether or not gender has a natural (biological) basis in sexual (physiological) differences, gender is essentially a cultural category, and so, for the most part, is sexual desire. Sex itself may be biological, of course, but to say that sex is biological is not to deny that we *make* sexual distinctions and that *what* we make of them—like racial differences or differences in height or facial features—is a cultural matter.[1] And to say that gender is a cultural category is to make quite explicit the sug-

[1] A difference, the current French philosopher Jacques Derrida calls it, a difference whose only difference is to "differ," i.e., to *make* a difference.

gestion that genders differ, along with their significance, from culture to culture, even to the point at which a culture might well come to expect what we call feminine behavior primarily from males, and what we call masculine behavior primarily from females. Or a society might come to deny the relationship between sex and gender roles altogether, in fact do away with gender roles and relegate sexual differences to the oblivion of utter unimportance. This last possibility is now commonly celebrated as "androgyny," and we shall talk about it in some detail later in this chapter.

The feminist thesis, now recast in more specific terms, is that sex differences are—or should be—a matter of indifference. Gender roles, which typically function in such a way that women are considered less capable, more emotional and therefore unable to wield power, are wholly a matter of cultural creation, artifacts, like electric can openers and putt-putt golf carts, and consequently both unnecessary and wholly dispensable. But at this point it is important to slow down the feminist counterargument long enough to emphasize that cultural creations are not therefore easily dispensable or unnecessary; some are essential to the structure of a particular society. And whether or not sex and gender distinctions are now dispensable, it does not follow that romantic love is so easily done away with, unless romantic love in fact depends upon those gender roles, which is what I shall deny. Indeed, my point is that romantic love is both sex- and gender-neutral, which means that love between lesbians or between male homosexuals is just as much romantic love as love in the traditionally heterosexual married couple.

As far as sex is concerned, what love requires is sexual *expression*, not the efficacy of species preservation, and this is just as possible between unreproducing lovers as it is between fertile and baby-ready protoparents. Indeed, it has recently been argued, by Masters and Johnson, for example, that homosexual couples—both male-male and female-female—tend to be more expressive and consequently more mutually satisfying in sex precisely because they are free from the traditional sex models. It is true that, even where there are not male and female roles (in a homosexual couple) there is nonetheless a tendency to bifurcate into masculine and feminine gender roles, one dominant and aggressive, one submissive and more accepting. But, first of all, this should only confirm our distinction between sex and gender (without leading to the conclusion that homosexual couples are thereby "trying to be like" heterosexual couples) and, second, it should not be supposed that dominance and submission, or any number of other complementary roles in sex and love, are the same as masculine and feminine gender roles. Comedy teams tend to bifurcate into complementary roles too, but not necessarily by sex or gender. (Every couple needs a "straight" role sometime.) But the main point, of course, is that romantic love does not require any couple, hetero- or homosexual, to distinguish themselves by either sex or gender roles. Love is shared identity and mutual expression, and there is nothing about shared identity—including reciprocal sexual identity—that requires male and female or masculine and feminine roles. Indeed, a man who feels that he has to assert his "manhood" in his personal relations is rightly suspected of being *less*, not more, of a lover, and a woman too eager to be dominated by men should quite rightly wonder, not about love, but about the ease with which she accepts the role of passivity. There is nothing in the structure of love as such that requires or even suggests that women ought to be cast in submissive "feminine" roles and men ought to act aggressively "masculine."

I have argued at length that romantic love does indeed serve an important function in our society, one not easily replaced. But at the same time I have argued that love is not necessary, that other functions in our society meet the need it serves, sometimes equally well; yet it does not follow, because it is not exclusively needed, that it is not needed at all. Indeed, when one looks at the distant utopian solutions proposed by some of the feminists, romantic love seems far more preferable, at least more practical, and far more easily improved than replaced. Uta West rightly criticizes one of these utopian fantasies—the all-female lesbian society—as simply shifting the abuses of romantic love from one domain into another. Her own neo-Aristotelian solution—friendship *cum* sex or "balling buddies" (an odd as well as vulgar locution)—seems to ignore rather than deny the emotional connotations of *any* sexual relationship, treating sex as essentially release and recreation. Shulamith Firestone, on the other hand, proposes a grand posthistorical fantasy à la Marx and Engels which, like their own "classless society," gains most of its appeal from its utter obscurity. And then there is the more common tragedy of resignation, refusing to give up what one knows to be a fraudulent hope and rejecting it at the same time.

What makes the feminist argument particularly viable at this particular time in history is the fact that, in only the last generation, the linkage between women and biology, the easy equation between sex and pregnancy, marriage and love has been thoroughly broken, by pharmaceutical breakthroughs and corresponding changes in custom. Women are no longer, to use the common phrase, "trapped by their biology." Neither are they subject to the vast array of fallacious arguments about what's "natural" and "the difference between men and women" either. For even where these arguments are not fallacious they have now lost the premise on which they have always been based. The "natural" differences between men and women, suddenly, make no difference at all.

There is an innocent sense in which biology remains at the basis of love, of course. Romantic love is essentially sexual, and one cannot imagine sex in any sense between disembodied spirits. But no particular sex, size or shape of the requisite bodies is required by love—only that there *be* two bodies, sensuous, expressive bodies that can do whatever needs to be done.

There is nothing essential to romantic love that requires the requisite bodies to host genitalia of the "opposite" sexes; in fact, there is nothing about romantic love—or sex for that matter—that absolutely requires genitalia at all. Genital sex is not the exclusive or ultimate expression of love. Genital sex is not the purpose of love either, as biological reductionists are prone to believe. None of the roles that make up romantic love are firmly bound to genital sex, nor to heterosexual genital sex. Romantic love is utterly neutral with regard to biology; however sexually obsessed we may be, there is nothing "natural" about it.

### Love and Power

Even if romantic love is utterly neutral with regard to sex (that is, male and female and what most prominently distinguishes them), it does not yet follow that it is similarly neutral with regard to gender. Indeed, what would become of our romantic literature without *her* soft and dutiful gaze, waiting for *him* to return from the battle and give her a hard and possessive embrace? But in our no longer warrior society, in which the day's battle is more than likely a screaming telephone battle with the local tax office, we can switch the above pronouns all that we want, delete as well the adjectives "soft" and "hard," dispense with the roles as well as the sexes. Yet it is part of the history of romantic love, and so part of the feminist argument as well, that masculine and feminine gender roles have played a large part in this emotion and, consequently, in our respective gender identities as well.

Many years ago, in one of the more virulent classics of the genre, Shulamith Firestone argued in her *Dialectic of Sex*[2] that

[2] A book easily maligned and too easily dismissed *ad feminem* as "fanatic," on the basis of its venomous prose and bewildering contradictions as well as its sometimes silly Marxism and a relentless diatribe against men—as "robots," "sadistic manipulators" who are, of course, "incapable of love" and "oppressors." The arguments, however, are often insightful.

it was precisely the "liberation of women from their biology," not now but several generations ago, that brought about the distinctively male invention of romantic love:

> Romantic love developed in proportion to the liberation of women from their biology. . . . Male supremacy must shore itself up with artificial institutions or exaggerations of previous institutions (p. 165).

Romantic role models, she argues, the gender distinctions of "masculine" and "feminine," are developed *in place of* the no longer essential distinction between male and female. Gender depends not on nature but on culture; thus the question, *for what purpose*, and *for whose benefit*, has gender been created? The answer is not long forthcoming.

> Romanticism is a cultural tool of male power to keep women from knowing their condition. It is especially needed—and therefore strongest—in Western countries with the highest rate of industrialization (p. 166).

Romantic love is thus to be understood in terms of *power* and, so viewed, the main difference between masculine and feminine gender roles becomes obvious. The argument, interestingly enough, is traced to Freud. Freud is usually considered the nemesis of feminism, but Firestone rightly credits him "as having grasped the crucial problem of modern life; sexuality" (p. 49). But where Freud takes sexuality to be a psychobiological problem, Firestone sees it as a political problem. Where Freud mysteriously talks about the powers of the libido, Firestone talks concretely about *power* itself. And where Freud talks murkily and unconvincingly about penis envy and castration fears, Firestone substitutes the tangible fact of family power relationships, the all-powerful father and the privileged sons (p. 53). Penis envy becomes privilege envy, and Firestone quite plausibly suggests that the young girl who is said to envy her brother's curious genitalia is more likely feeling deprived because she is not allowed to play her brother's rough-and-tumble games. And with this switch on Freud, the theory can begin: romantic love is the extension of this power game into adult life, a more subtle way of depriving a woman of "male" roles and at the same time flattering her as a "lady." Promise her anything, but offer her only love.

What Firestone is arguing, from Freud, is what Freud and many neo-Freudians prefer to ignore—the institutional nature of romantic love and its functional role, not only in the individual psyche and the family but in the power structure of society as a whole. Firestone's argument is that, now that female sexuality as such is of much less importance for survival, the institution of romantic love serves the function of introducing femininity as a matter of emotional significance, as a way of continuing archaic male-dominated institutions and power structures. Femininity, in a word, is *impotence*. Masculinity is *potence*. And to reinforce the roles, femininity is isolated in the home, as soon as possible, while masculinity gathers further power in the market place. Women, in turn, find themselves seeking approval—the test of success in their feminine roles—entirely from men, while men gain their support and approval as well in a variety of friendships and business or professional relationships.

There are a number of arguments that run together here, all with the same conclusion but quite different all the same. First, it is said that romantic love has been foisted upon women as a way of perpetuating archaic and distinctly inferior household roles, once based upon biological necessity, now simply so that men can retain their traditional dominance outside the home. Second, the argument is that the privacy of romantic love and its marital aftermath is such that it keeps women isolated from each other and wholly dependent upon the approval of men, thus reinforcing their archaic and inferior positions within the home by making them the only possible source of personal self-esteem. Third, there is a kind of proper

suspicion that, since romantic love was obviously invented by
men, they did so to their own advantage, in order to perpetu-
ate women's roles. And, fourth, it is argued that romantic roles
as such are essential to love and cast women in submissive, inferior positions.

I have already agreed with the first of these arguments,
that romantic love has been *used* as a way of continuing to encourage women to retain once biologically necessary roles that
are now unnecessary. But it is clear that our society in general,
not only feminists, is becoming fully aware that the once easy
equation between sex and gender, the identification of the biological necessities of tribal life and the cultural niceties of Victorian courtship rituals, is no longer viable. The next step is to
remove the supposed necessity of gender identity from romantic love as well, which is just as archaic and now unnecessary
as the biological complementarity of the sexes.

The isolation of women and the exclusively male-dominated
world of power are starting to break down, extremely quickly
on any reasonable historical scale, and this changes at least one
of the key connections among romantic love, gender identity
and power. Much of the power that was once the exclusive domain of males had to do not only with the fact that they had
power but with their variable sources of recognition and approval as well. Men were not solely dependent on women for
their sense of self-esteem as women were entirely dependent
upon men. But now, as women aggressively find themselves
friendships and alliances—even to the extent that a current
popular argument maintains that only women are even *capable* of friendship—and are beginning as well to find professional, political and other sources of self-esteem, this source of
power is opening up to them as it is to men. Thus in this sense
it has become evident that it is not romantic love or gender
roles as such that determine one major traditional source
of asymmetrical women's dependency, but an entirely distinct set of inequities which might be summarized as un-

equal access to approval and self-esteem. This isolation of women is now coming to an end—I would argue. (Even the reactionary countermovement, the "total woman" syndrome, has the ironic outcome of helping to bring about the public visibility of women speakers and "women's issues," thus destroying this sense of isolation.) Romantic love, consequently, no longer remains a woman's sole source of self-esteem, a burden which, in any case, no single emotion could ever be expected to sustain.

The argument that romantic love was invented by men, as popular as that may now be, is as much paranoia as history. And in any case it is very bad history. If one considers Plato a male author of *eros*, what is most evident is that he used this conception not as a way of casting women in inferior roles but of dismissing them altogether, as not worthy of love. Women were inferior, yes, but not because of love. If we follow the scholars and date the origins of romantic ("courtly") love in the chivalric spirit of twelfth-century France, we might attribute the "invention" of romantic love to the wandering knights and their poet accompanists the troubadours, but regardless of who "invented" love, it is clear that the women who were loved were more than willing to co-operate, since the new role of "the feminine" was not a form of oppression but of liberation for them, the first step in the individualization of women as well as men, the first recognition that a woman, any woman, was more than a household convenience. She was no longer merely an object for interfamily barter, a mother, a mistress and, literally, a possession.

It is often argued, for example by Firestone and more recently by Linda Nicholson, that romantic love is essentially a product of capitalism, a creation of industrialized market society. This is clearly not true. Shakespeare gave a rather complete description of romantic love in his sonnets, well over a century before the Industrial Revolution in England. Indeed, romantic love appears on the European scene centuries before the first versions of capitalism and, in so far as there is any parallel at all, this is not due to the rise of a market economy but instead due to the presupposition of capitalism—namely, the idea of individual autonomy and the severing of feudal ties according to which every person was locked into a rigid system of obligations and allegiances. Linda Nicholson argues, for example, that the market society destroyed the old conception of women as "creatures before God" and began our current capitalist insistence on evaluating people according to what they're "good for," but the truth seems to be that under feudalism women in particular were "worth something" only according to what they were "good for," and it was with the rise of a less regimented and household-centered society that individual worth "as a human being" came to mean anything at all.

Love may or may not have been "erected by males," but it does not follow and is not true that they did so—if they did—to continue the subjection of women. But this leaves the fourth argument, and to my mind the most crucial—namely, that romantic roles, in which the woman is essentially submissive and inferior, are built right into the structure of romantic love. Even if we reject the now outdated biological arguments, even if it is true that the isolation of women is no longer the issue it used to be, and even if romantic roles were once—eight hundred years ago—a liberating influence, it can be charged that the straitjacket of "femininity" is today a source of oppression and a still powerful psychological rationalization for the continuing exploitation of women, in the name of "love."

### Beyond One-Dimensional Love
### ("Androgyny" and More)

My answer is that "femininity" and so-called feminine roles have nothing essential to do with love. But before I argue this, I want to consider briefly an argument that would seem, if successful, to make this answer unnecessary. One feature of romantic love, which has been often neglected or distorted in current controversies, is the essential *privacy* of love and the loveworld. There can be no conception of romantic love, I have argued, without the crucial distinction between public and private, and a personal sense of "who I am" over and above—in fact sometimes opposed to—my social status and public image. But this means that, in so far as masculine and feminine roles are part of love, they need not enter into public life at all. The roles one plays in love, and the roles one plays in public life, need have no essential connection. Thus one answer to the feminist argument is that we can and should indeed do away with our concepts of femininity and masculinity in the public sphere, but not therefore in the personal sphere. But this answer is not sufficient, and for at least three reasons. First of all, distinct as they may be, it is difficult to imagine that they would not affect each other, and that a change in public status would have no effect on one's personal self-conceptions. Second, this would still be disadvantageous to women, in so far as *attracting* a lover, as opposed to already living with one, requires a public display of romantic availability which makes the woman's public role thoroughly schizoid. There can be no exclusive relegation of love to the personal, except in very restricted cases, and then only after the relationship has been initially formed. And, third, even if such separation were possible, it would still relegate the woman to subservient status *within* the relationship, however powerful her roles in public. It is therefore the concepts of femininity and masculinity themselves that must be rejected.

There are at least three ways of doing this. Two of them have become popularly known under the camp word "androgyny." The word is often confused with "bisexual"—which is only one of its variations—but in any case I tend to agree with feminist poet and author Mary Daly when she writes that "androgyny makes me think of Farrah Fawcett and John Travolta scotch-taped together." The first form of androgyny (or

"androgynism") insists that masculine and feminine characteristics exist together in everyone, and so it is unnecessary, the
argument goes, for everyone to feel that he or she should
develop only one set of sex-bound characteristics. In the public
sphere, the argument is appealing, since what it says, in effect,
is that everyone has the same potential and so should have the
same opportunities. Its effect, in other words, is to deny the
difference between men and women and to provide a single
ideal of rights and potential for all, which leads one author,
Joyce Trebilcot, to call it "monoandrogynism."[3] In the personal sphere, however, the same view leads logically to the
idea of bisexuality; if we each have essentially the same masculine and feminine characteristics, then it would follow that
we each also have the same masculine and feminine desires.
This sounds like Freud's well-known bisexuality argument, but
it isn't. For Freud, this was a sexual matter, a fact about biology; for the monoandrogynist, it is a matter of cultural potential, not biology at all. But here we see a problem with this simple view too; as a theory about *potentials*, it slips too easily
between the idea that the various roles that we call "masculine" and "feminine" *can* be developed in everyone (whether
or not they should be) and the idea that these roles are *already*
lurking somewhere inside of us, waiting to be developed but,
alas, in our society only one of the roles ever is, frustrating the
other. But the recognition of the cultural origins of these roles
ought to lead us to a more radical conclusion, not that they are
"there in everybody" but rather that they are unnecessary,
unreal; they do not exist except in so far as we *will* them.

The second form of androgyny is more radical in just this
sense; it denies the simple duality between masculinity and
femininity and emphasizes the wide variety of gender roles,
including any number of combinations of the two "pure" extremes, masculinity and femininity. In effect, this breaks down

[3] "Two Forms of Androgynism" in Vetterling-Braggin, Elliston and English,
eds., *Feminism and Philosophy* (Littlefield Adams, 1977), pp. 70–78.

the extremes as well and refocuses our attention on particular traits and roles rather than on the monolithic extremes, and opens up the possibility of a large variety of roles which are neither, traditionally speaking, masculine nor feminine. (Because of its pluralism, Trebilcot calls this "polyandrogynism.")

But this second form of androgyny or androgynism suggests a third possibility, which escapes the man-woman etymological orientation of "androgyny" altogether by dismissing masculinity and femininity as essential roles, particularly where romantic love is involved. What we have been allowing without comment for too long is the idea that these two roles define, if not all, at least a large part of our romantic tradition. In fact they had no place in Plato; there the crucial distinction was one of age and experience, the lover as teacher, the beloved as pupil. The notion of masculine-feminine may have played a significant part in courtly love, but the notions of chivalry and attractiveness were matters of historical context, and not necessarily essential to the concept of love as such. And as one looks at the structure of romantic love—apart from the grade B novels—divisions according to sex and gender have had very little place, even where sex itself is concerned. Indeed, romantic love consists of roles, private roles which are only occasionally or coincidentally played out in public. But the point now to be made once and for all is that few of these roles have anything to do with sex or gender and, in so far as they do, it is not *because* they are male or female or masculine or feminine roles but only because they contain roles that are usually associated with sex and gender, such as domination and submissiveness, aggressiveness and passivity. But what happens in love is that these roles are continuously redefined, and whatever might be expected on the masculine-feminine model, what we actually do in love is something quite different. Indeed, this leads to the unexpected conclusion that masculinity and femininity are, in fact, public roles, and not private, and that love requires the overcoming of these roles rather than the realization of them. Indeed, as soon as one begins to list the huge gamut of roles through which we are intimate with one another—not only the thousand varieties of sex that need have nothing to do with gender, but cooking, talking, walking, dancing, looking, scratching, fighting, driving cross country, feeding the squirrels, confessing, celebrating, crying, laughing, knowingly nodding to each other in a room full of people, sharing the events of the day, consoling one another in defeat, studying German, staying in bed on Sunday, reading the funnies, bitching about the weather, whispering and occasionally whimpering—the emphasis that puts so much stress on a single set of asymmetrical roles, "masculine and feminine," becomes nothing more than embarrassing. Indeed, people who are too caught up in their "masculine" and "feminine" roles are not infrequently, after the initial attraction, disappointing lovers. This has nothing to do with sexism but only with boredom. How can you build your life around a one-act actor? How can you identify with a movie poster?

Beyond sex and gender means beyond *androgyny* too, beyond that one-dimensional set of man-woman identities that too many bad movies and sado-masochistic Freudian fantasies have set out for us. Love is a multiplex of personal roles of all kinds, which are being continuously redefined and re-enacted, which need have nothing to do with sex or with those simple stereotypes of gender. In fact to think of love in terms of masculinity and femininity is like having a conversation in which each party is assigned in advance the same (one of two) single speech. At most, one can expect a predictable performance, instead of the "anything's possible" exhilaration of love.

### Why Blame Love?

One of Marilyn French's refrains in *The Women's Room* is, "But of course, she would never think of blaming love." It is the presupposition of her novel, the structure of the tragic parade she sets before us. Men are unfeeling and selfish jerks, women are victims, but it is love itself that is the illusion that binds the two together. It is the illusion that gives rise inevitably to dis-illusion-ment, and the appeal of that illusion that keeps women hoping for love, that single wonderful stroke that will make life meaningful.

Is love an illusion? No. I have argued at length that love is essentially fantasy, but fantasies, unlike illusions, are not self-deceptions and so not prone to disillusionment. Love has its impossible ideal, of total "oneness," but an unreachable goal does not an illusion make—unless one also believes that the goal is possible, even, perhaps, easily achievable. Our conception of romantic love does indeed include a number of tragic illusions—the idea that love if "true" will last forever and make life over in a flash, for instance—but these are detachable from the emotion itself, which is not an illusion but a perfectly ordinary, if extraordinarily delightful emotion. If love often fails to "work out," then perhaps we have to re-examine what we think we are "working for"; but it is our expectations, not love itself, that ought to be revised or rejected.

The danger of confusing love with illusion is more than the personal unhappiness it causes; its cost also includes creating a serious obstacle in the public fight for women's equality. Even if one assumes that the battle for equality will entail antagonism with men on a public level, it is sheer folly—if it is also unnecessary—to carry that antagonism into intimate relationships which, despite certain utopian hopes and radical experiments to the contrary, may well be indispensable in our society—at least for the present and the foreseeable future. The argument goes beyond this too, for if, as I have argued, romantic love actually *requires* a sense of equality, then love provides, rather than works against, the ideal of feminism. Historically, romantic love (and Christian love too) were powerful forces in breaking down the old hierarchies and roles. But

today, too, that conception is still at work, in spite of the continuing overemphasis on sex and gender roles and despite the
fact that too many feminists see love as the problem, instead of
as part of the solution. Indeed, here as elsewhere in politics,
projecting one's personal disappointments onto the world as
cynical "realism" is not the way to win adherents. Romantic
love between men and women, from its very inception, has always been the primary vehicle of personal and, consequently,
social equality. It has always been "feminist" in its temperament, whatever mythologies have sometimes been imposed on
top of it. Romantic love and feminism are neither incompatible
nor antagonistic; in fact I would argue that, for the present at
least, they should not try to do without one another.

# WHAT'S SO GOOD ABOUT LOVE? 23
## (LOVE AND SELF-ESTEEM)

*After seven years of marriage Pierre had the joyous firm con-*
*viction that he was not a bad man, which he had come to feel*
*because he saw himself reflected in his wife. In himself, he felt*
*all the good and bad inextricably mingled and overlapping.*
*But in his wife he saw reflected only what was really good in*
*him, since everything that was not absolutely good was rejected.*

TOLSTOY, *War and Peace*

We began this book with a question, not out of cynicism but rather curiosity—why is love so important to us? If love is one among many emotions, each of which consists of its own self-defining meaningful world, why have we so singled out love, romantic love in particular, as "the meaning of life" and "the ideal of human existence"? We can't imagine without criticism a person dedicating his or her life to anger or envy (though many do), but we not only imagine but celebrate those who live (or give) their lives for love. Why? Why do we think, as Walker Percy puts it, that "the only important, certainly the best thing in life, is ordinary sexual love"? (*Lancelot*, p. 12).

What is so good, so praiseworthy, so admirable and exhilarating about love? It is often said that love is "good in itself," "intrinsically good," even the standard by which other values are measured; but this isn't an answer, first, because it is clear, even in our romantic society, that love will not excuse *every-*

*thing*, that love is not *always* desirable (for example, when one is already in love with another person). Second, I would argue along with a great many philosophers (John Dewey, for example) that nothing is "good in itself"—not pleasure, not life, not sex, not even happiness. (God, perhaps, is "good in Himself," but nothing follows from this about us.) And, third, we have already covered considerable ground in showing that the desirability of romantic love can be explained, can be accounted for in terms of both the place it fits in our society in general and its internal definitions of self and identity. In this chapter, what I would like to do is to bring these explanations together as an answer to the question, "Why is love so important to us?" In other words, "What's so good about love?"

The first part of the account is cultural, and we have stressed throughout this book the importance of appreciating the social preconditions and presuppositions that are necessary even for love to be possible. In particular, there must be a high degree of mobility and individuality, such that the more "natural" bonds between members of families and communities are systematically severed, sending individuals "out into the world" to "find themselves" and each other. And there must be a general distinction between the social public roles an individual plays and the personal private life he or she leads, with a stress on the personal and private as the realm of a person's "true" identity. Thus we can begin, in a very general way, to explain the cultural significance of romantic love by pointing to the interpersonal gaps that are perpetually created in our society, waiting to be filled, and the need for relationships which will give form and structure as well as content to our personal as opposed to our less personal public lives. But we should not make too much of this "external" cultural account. It explains, as too many theorists fail to explain, the socially created "need" for love and its cultural peculiarities—not as an ideal of "human nature" but rather as the invention of certain kinds of societies. But preconditions and presuppositions only provide us with the framework within which love finds its place. Given the interpersonal gap to be filled and our emphasis on personal rather than professional relations, our alleged "need" for love could just as well be filled with friends and extended families. The special significance of romantic love does not follow from the fact that there is a definite place for it in our society, for it is a place that can be filled by other, less exclusive and less complicated emotions as well.

One might argue that what love provides that friendship and extended family do not is intimacy, sex too perhaps, but this seems to me to be wrong on several counts. First, it is an emasculated view of friendship and family too, perhaps, that assumes from the outset that these cannot be intimate, at least. Secondly, it remains to be seen what is so good about intimacy, just as we need to pull together our answer to the question, "What is so good about love?" And, third, however good that might be, it seems to me that discussions in terms of *need* are in any case mistaken. If we need romantic love and intimacy, these are *created* needs, and then the question simply moves one step further along—why are they worth creating? What do they provide for us, in addition to the fact that they fill a gap in our social lives which might be just as well fulfilled by staying with our families, moving in with an uncle and aunt, forming new friendships at work or "just hanging out with the boys/girls"?

The key to our answer, which we have kept hammering away at for the last dozen chapters, is SELF. It is sometimes said that love is "selfless," but this would indeed render love a mystery, for what would then serve as its motivation? But the essence of love, we have argued, is precisely the formation of self, a shared self, and here, in the realm of self-identity, we shall find the answer to our question.

Self-identity is the structure of self; the value of this struc-

ture, on the other hand, is called *self-esteem*. Every emotion
forms its own self-identity—in anger as self-righteousness, in
resentment as the oppressed, in envy as the deprived and in
faith as the faithful. Every identity gives life a certain meaning
—as unfair, offensive, competitive, hopeful and so on—but not
all meanings are of equal value. Some meanings, one might
say, are *de*-meaning. Others tend to maximize self-esteem,
roughly, "how good we feel about ourselves." This in no way
implies any lack of consideration for others or any desire for
their disadvantage, unless the emotion itself is antagonistic or
competitive, as in hatred or jealousy. In love, in particular, the
maximization of one's own self-esteem goes hand in hand with
the maximization of the lover's self-esteem, since, as we have
argued, they involve one and the same shared self.

The reciprocity of romantic love explains not only its importance as an interpersonal bond but its value for self-esteem as
well. Whereas many other emotions tend to be antagonistic or
competitive, romantic love intrinsically includes mutual reinforcement and encouragement. Emotions such as anger, resentment and jealousy, which turn another person into an
offender, an oppressor or a trespasser, tend to maximize one's
own self-esteem (which they do quite effectively) but only at
the risk of setting someone against us, who in return is anxious
to knock us off our high horse, humiliate us and substitute for
our self-esteem his or her own. In love, since this sense of self-
esteem is constituted mutually, it is entirely in the other person's interest (even in unrequited love) to think well of us
and encourage us too. It is a simple but powerful difference,
and in this difference the significance of romantic love becomes apparent to us; it is the one emotion (or at least, one of
a very few) that enlists other people as wholehearted support
for our own sense of worth, in return for which they earn our
support too. And since the world—the loveworld—within
which we carry out this mutual support for self-esteem is by its
very nature an essentially private world, within which no one

else's opinions are even allowed, the mutual maximization of self-esteem can indeed be astounding, virtually without limits —at least for a while.

## The Psychology of Self-Esteem

The literature on self-esteem tends to be split into two warring camps, ever since Freud argued quite clearly that love was an attempt to assure self-worth through what he called "identification." On one side of the dispute it is argued, for instance by Freud's disciple Theodor Reik (1944) and more recently by the social psychologist Elaine Walster (1965), that romantic love is an attempt at compensation. This means that people with low self-esteem, who are "down" on themselves, are more likely to fall in love than those whose self-esteem is not so threatened. On the other side, such theorists as Abraham Maslow (1942), Carl Rogers (1965) and Alfred Adler (1926) have argued that people with "high" self-esteem are more capable of love than those with "low" self-esteem. Of course there are reports of patients by the hundreds and experiments by the dozens to support both theses, but here as elsewhere in the social sciences one might be wise to consider first British philosopher Peter Geach's warning, that "no experiment can clear up a confusion of thought." For it is evident even in this brief statement of positions that it is none too obvious what is being argued, what is meant by "self-esteem" or what is meant by "love."

In one sense, the apparently conflicting claims about love and self-esteem are about two completely different phenomena; the tendency of "low" self-esteem people to *fall* in love is quite different from the alleged ability of "high" self-esteem people to *be* in love, that is, to sustain a more or less long-term relationship with a minimal amount of neurosis and dependency. Moreover, a reading of much of the literature on love and self-esteem shows the correlation with "low" self-esteem people to be not about love at all but merely about "romantic liking" (Walster), mere "attractiveness" (Dittes, 1959) and "acceptance" (Sheerer, 1948). Seeking approval and becoming infatuated are both much less than love, and except for the psychoanalysts (Reik) there is virtually no mention of "identification," the earmark of love, in any of these authors. This leaves us with a rather limp set of hypotheses: (1) that people who feel down on themselves are more likely to seek approval from others and (2) that people who feel good about themselves tend to sustain better relationships than those who do not.

The intricate connections between love and self-esteem are not going to be captured in such crude correlations. First of all, as Elaine Walster has correctly argued against her colleagues, such talk about "high" and "low" self-esteem *people* ignores the obvious—that we all fluctuate in our sense of self-worth by the day and by the hour.[1] Second, although it may make sense as a kind of convenient generalization to talk about "feeling good about oneself," our self-esteem, like our identity, is context-dependent, and it is a common enough experience that we find ourselves extremely self-critical in one social or personal context immediately before or after feeling extremely good about ourselves in another. Tolstoy's Pierre is a classic example; after a life of dissipation, whores and scoundrel friends, several political and religious conversions and his stint as a prisoner of war under Napoleon, he comes to see himself through Natasha's eyes, not to the exclusion of all of these other identities, but by way of escape and compensation from them—or so, at least, Tolstoy tells us. His self-esteem, in other words, concerns that self which he now identifies with Natasha, not self in general—if there could possibly be such a simple monolith in such a complex character.

[1] In her experiment she "produced" low esteem in her undergraduates by giving them a personality test from which they emerged "immature"; she then had them asked out on dates (hardly a test of love).

Within this context, however, does it make sense to talk about love and self-esteem as the psychologists and psychoanalysts do, in terms of compensation (love for low self-esteem)? To be sure, a person unsure of him or herself will be far more receptive to the approval of others, but *loving* them is another matter. Furthermore, one might render up the hypothesis that self-esteem virtually *always* goes up when one falls in love, whether or not this is also complicated by problems of rejection or anxiety and subsequent collapse of self-esteem. Indeed, the structure of love is such that it *begins* with the recognition that mutual identification and reciprocal support are improvements over one's present solitary or in any case loveless identity, but it does not follow that low self-esteem is the precondition of love, as Reik suggests. It may be true that someone who feels sufficiently "down" on him or herself will be literally "hungrier" for love, but an increase in self-esteem is always a potential motive for emotion, and this is true of "high" self-esteem people as well as "low," in our best moods as well as our worst. But as a mutually reinforcing relationship it also follows that the liabilities of one personality will inevitably become liabilities for the other as well, and when two insecure and self-contemptuous people form a romantic identity, it is easy to see how their reciprocally inflated self-esteem is prone to collapse. Two relatively strong personalities, on the other hand, need not spend so much energy in mutual support, since each is already capable of holding up his or her own identity. Thus the psychological correlations reported in the literature are two not very significant manifestations of a much more complex set of emotional structures and tendencies.

But all of this is still too simple; to talk about self-esteem, even so qualified and relativized to contexts and relationships, and mutual support and reciprocity, in the formation of shared self-identity and heightened self-esteem, is to ignore the huge variety of mechanisms for mutual self-esteem that we find in romantic love, which are by no means to be reduced to the simple psychological catch-all, "seeking approval." Romantic reciprocity can be parasitic, symbiotic, a question of simply providing a context, or a challenge, or competition, or mere association, as well as identification, approval and sheer shared enthusiasm. To think of any one of these processes as the sole source of mutual self-esteem is to turn the fascinating complexities of romantic relationships into an artificially one-dimensional exchange that would not even work in a grade C novel. Which does not, of course, lessen its popularity as a psychological theory.

### *The Sources of Self-Esteem*

Self-esteem, we should emphasize, is not the same as what one *thinks* about oneself, though no doubt this will always be both a factor and a reflection of self-esteem. But a person who accepts an ideology of oppression or egalitarianism or class superiority may well think quite differently than he or she actually feels about his or her self-worth. Thus what a person says about self-worth must be taken critically too, and what seems far more important are such indirect indications of self-esteem as the extent to which a person feels compelled to make excuses or apologize (Sheerer). Neither does self-esteem mean self-acceptance or high regard for oneself; a Christian martyr, if we may borrow an example from Nietzsche, might have remarkably high self-esteem even as he despises himself; indeed it is his self-contempt on the one hand that is the source of his remarkable self-righteousness on the other. But of course one can find another martyr for whom martyrdom is indeed an expression of and a reconfirmation of his sense of self-contempt and inadequacy, whether or not this is frosted over with self-congratulation and righteousness. And since people in love quite often act the role of martyrs ("self-sacrifice" and "devotion" and all that), the comparison is not out of place. The moral, however, is that there are no easy tests or dependable platitudes on this extremely delicate topic of self-worth.

Self-esteem is often summarized, as Pierre summarizes it, as the feeling that one is a "good" (or at least "not bad") person. This is not always the case. In our rebel society, in which criminals are often our folk heroes, "bad" can become a curious word for virtue, and a person's self-identity and self-esteem may well turn on seeing oneself as "the baddest" or even as "evil." (Certain witches and gang leaders come to mind.) But this makes it clear that self-esteem, like self-identity, does not pertain to some omnipresent entity called the self as such but rather to the various roles and qualities that constitute our sense of self-identity. And these roles and qualities might be almost anything whatever, surely not necessarily "good" or desirable from someone else's point of view. One person finds his or her identity in cruelty, seeks a partner who will tolerate that cruelty and finds his or her sense of self-worth heightened accordingly. Another seeks a submissive identity, free as possible from responsibility and defined as much as possible by the status of *victim*, finds a suitably oppressive partner and, in degradation, heightens self-esteem. But if this is so, in what sense can we talk about "high" or "low" self-esteem at all, if self-esteem can be raised in degradation or by sadism and, we might add, can be lowered for some people as soon as they find themselves in a position of respect or responsibility? Our answer, again, is in terms of self-identity; this is a role that they will *work* for, a role that they *want*, a role that they will *choose* from a number of alternatives, including its seemingly more savory opposites. One might point out that wanting such roles betrays a serious problem in self-esteem to begin with, at least in some cases. But what this shows is not that self-esteem cannot be elevated by degradation or lowered by responsibility but only that, once again, self-esteem is not a simple singular attribute but a complex sequence of senses of self-worth which may in many cases play off against one another, as our identities do too. But the point of romantic love is precisely to try to simplify this complexity and narrow down the sequence of senses to what usually at least begins as a more manageable set of identities, with one person, selecting out those identities and roles whose fulfillment seems most desirable, whatever *we* (looking in from the outside) might think of them.

Some of the mechanisms of self-esteem to be found in romantic love are not so romantic at all. For example, romantic love typically begins with a *challenge*, an appropriate conception of "courting" in terms more usually reserved for games and war, "winning" and "losing," making a "conquest" and strategies such as "playing it cool" or "playing hard to get." Marilyn French, for example, in her book, *Bleeding Heart,* is obsessed with this paradigm, which may indeed have its place in the initial phases of love, but as one among many metaphors and mechanisms and not as the definition of love itself. But though this sense of challenge is not itself sufficient to explain the mutual reinforcement of love, it does provide an initial impetus, an opening appreciation for the affections and approval of the lover and the first requirement that one must think somewhat well of oneself if one is to play this sometimes most serious game at all. But the challenge soon ends and love begins. Or, if the only source of self-esteem turns out to be the challenge itself, love soon ends as well.

A second and more enduring source of self-esteem in love is the simple fact of being admired or approved of by someone whom we admire and approve of in return. This is not, as some cynics might suggest, merely a matter of tit for tat, "I'll say something nice about you if only you'll say something nice about me." It is true that our estimation of others tends to increase remarkably when we find that they think well of us, but it is hardly ever true that our estimation of others, and consequently the importance we attribute to their estimation of us, lies wholly in the fact that we expect their approval in return.

But notice too that this source of self-esteem is not peculiar to loving and, indeed, is sometimes more effective when it is not part of love. Being complimented by a stranger is often far more of an ego boost than the now familiar compliment of a friend or lover—thus giving rise to "Arenson's Law of Marital Infidelity," that mutual approval is subject to the law of diminishing returns, and self-esteem is boosted less and less by those from whom we come to expect praise and approval as a matter of course. The law has a corollary too, that rejection and disapproval from those we love is far more devastating than rejection or disapproval from any stranger or mere acquaintance. But this, of course, serves as a source of inhibition and fear, not as a source of self-esteem. On the positive side, however, diminishing over time or not, mutual admiration and approval, though far from providing the whole story, are obvious sources of self-esteem.

To a certain extent, love raises self-esteem by mere *association* with another person whose virtues or accomplishments we admire. This need have nothing to do with their approval or admiration of us in return. The man who feels good about himself because he is with a brilliant woman is a clear example of such association, and the woman who feels good about herself because she is with a famous artist is another. Notice that this source of self-esteem, like the others, is not peculiar to love and might well be true without it. Notice too that this source presupposes nothing in return, though presumably the lover too has his or her motives for sharing the virtue so enjoyed by the other. Again, this is just a small piece of the picture, but it is obviously another source of increased self-esteem, through association with another person who has virtues that we ourselves may not have. (Again, even in unrequited love.)

A much stronger source of self-esteem in love that is easily conflated with the last is *identification* with the other. In association, one claims some sense of worth by being *with* the other person; in identification, one comes to claim the other's virtue as in some sense one's own. A friend of mine who is a mediocre violinist fell in love (and is still in love) with a woman who is an outstanding concert soloist. He *shares* her sense of pride and accomplishment, indeed feels (and she agrees) that it is partly his own, owing to his constant encouragement and support. This source of self-esteem is accordingly far more central to love than the others we have mentioned, because it is the first to presume some sense of shared self, virtues held in common, self-esteem that is not only reciprocal but shared. Indeed, what is crucial to my friend's sense of esteem is the fact that he does share his wife's sense of accomplishment and at no time wishes that it were his own instead. To do so would be envy, the very antithesis of love, for in that competition and opposition the sense of shared identity is inevitably lost.

And yet competition itself may provide a source of self-esteem in love. A classic example would be the old Spencer Tracy-Katharine Hepburn movies (*Adam's Rib, Woman of the Year*) in which they play lovers always at odds, in which their mutual appreciation of each other and their sense of self-esteem is boosted by regular competition with each other. This is not the same as the "love as war" or "love is a game" metaphor we first discussed, for it is not their love itself which is the subject of the competition. This is crucial. In so far as love itself is a matter of competition, it is not yet wholly love, for it is the distinction between selves rather than their identity that is primary. But in so far as love and shared identity are already established to a certain degree, competition in other matters can be a powerful source of increased appreciation and self-esteem —and perhaps, an antidote for Arenson's Law as well.

In the same way, the *idealization* of the other person in love raises one's own self-esteem, for in rendering one's lover ideal one is, if indirectly, idealizing oneself by implication as well. What must be true of me if I am loved by the most wonderful person in the world? I too must be quite wonderful, no? Thus

Pierre sees himself reflected in the eyes of his wonderful wife, who is all virtue, and so he too, at least in her reflection, is all virtue too. It is an innocent deception that serves an important function in a society that praises humility and discourages us from praising ourselves—namely, it allows us to congratulate ourselves indirectly, through our lovers. But perhaps too it is just this sense of "being used" as a vehicle for self-praise that leads many women, in particular, to complain about their men "putting them on a pedestal." Indeed, what they are really doing is putting them behind a mirror.

### Love, Roles, Virtue and Identity

The sources of self-esteem listed above are collectively significant, but even all together they do not begin to tap the tremendous resources of romantic love and self-esteem. These "superficial" sources may be obvious, but they have therefore been overemphasized by many theorists just because they are so obvious. What is much harder to describe, and almost impossible to measure, is the extent to which self-esteem is boosted in love by the complementary roles that we are able to play with one another, the identities we are able to assume in private, often at odds with or the exact opposites of the roles we are called upon to play in public or family life. A man who has an inferior job as subordinate during the day compensates by acting the confident lover with his wife; the businessman harried with responsibilities enjoys a submissive role free from the burdens of control with his lover; the tough and success-ful businesswoman retreats from her daily need to be "busi-nesslike" and totally independent into a relationship in which she can act wholly the child, all emotion and playfulness. Here the sense of shared identity lies not merely with some specific quality or accomplishment, which one lover shares with the other. The identity lies in the often asymmetrical playing of roles, in which one declares the self he or she would like to be

(if only in contrast to other roles). And self-esteem follows
from the playing of these roles, whether or not one would consider the role itself virtuous or in any sense an achievement.
In a society where we tend to think of our "real selves" in
terms of such private and personal roles, finding someone, in
love, with whom to play them provides an all-important, perhaps the most important, source of self-esteem.

Perhaps most complex of all is the extent to which certain
virtues are themselves created within the relationship. The key
word here is "virtue," not simply a role or an identity—which
in themselves are value-neutral. A virtue is by its very nature a
source of self-esteem, but what is peculiar to most or at least
many of the virtues is the fact that, while one cannot simply
designate oneself to be virtuous, there is no settled factual
basis for virtue either. Virtue is constituted by the agreement
of other people. Examples would be courage, honesty and,
more generally, "being a good person." Whether one is courageous or not depends upon what is expected of one by others,
and to what extent one satisfies their expectations. No act is in
itself courageous, whether it be facing up to a marauding griz-
zly bear (which might just be considered foolish), or standing
up for one's convictions (which in a conformist society would
be considered merely anti-social behavior). And so it is that
within small groups the virtues are defined with but minimal
reference to standards that hold for other groups, and within
the smallest of groups, namely, a two-person relationship, virtues are defined by just the two of us. If only you believe that I
am generous or trustworthy I am, and if only you believe that
I am a "good person" I am that too. And in this context (whatever one thinks of it), we can see how important the personal
privacy of love can be for our conception of ourselves, in terms
of not only the roles we play together but the virtues we define
for each other as well. And what counts as a virtue, too, might
be wholly within our private domain. Thus kinkiness, wick-
edness, silliness, slovenliness, bitterness and coquettishness

may not be virtues in the public domain, but we all know cases in which, within the confines of a relationship, they take on the aura of cardinal virtues, sources of pride as well as mutual admiration.

In addition to shared roles, identities and mutually created virtues, there are shared values and attitudes toward the world, shared enjoyments and happiness. Any value shared is thereby reinforced; an enjoyment shared is thereby approved as indeed "enjoyable." Happiness shared is thereby less likely to be mere foolishness. Thus one of the more obvious but by no means "superficial" sources of self-esteem is this sense of shared values, attitudes, joys and happiness. Loving someone is often said to be "wanting to share one's happiness"; one might also say that wanting to share one's happiness—or, for that matter, the lover's happiness—is itself a powerful reason for loving. Happiness shared is happiness made more real.

In addition to the various identities and roles that combine to form a relationship, there is an all-encompassing identity in being "a couple," which may in some cases be more important than all of the others. Pride in one's (shared) self *as a couple* involves attributes not applicable to either person alone, for example, "having been together all of these years." Indeed, people who take little pride in themselves as individuals may both take pride in their relationship as such, not because of any virtues or attributes which they share with the other in the senses we have discussed but rather because of just those attributes that they have created together as a couple. Some people are incapable of identifying themselves primarily as a couple, which does not make them incapable of love but means rather that their sense of shared identity and self-esteem remains first of all a matter of individual qualities and achievements, no matter how extensively these are also shared. On the other hand, some people are incapable of taking pride in themselves as individuals but can take great pride in their relationships, which tend therefore to be the prime ingredient in their conception of themselves.

Finally, one cannot underestimate the sheer importance of *having an identity*, any identity, no matter what it is. In most societies, family place and public roles define personal identity quite unambiguously, except for occasional and usually tragic conflicts as in *Antigone,* who was forced to choose between sisterly loyalty and civil obedience. In our society, in which self-identity seems forever indeterminate, romantic love provides one of the most ready sources of self-definition, and thereby the esteem of having a self-identity, even if that identity turns out to be demeaning. It is better to be the village idiot than to be no one at all. It is better to be loved as a fool than not to be loved and better to have loved and lost than never to have loved. And in our bewilderment about the multiplicity of romantic identities and the way in which lovers so often demean one another, it is easy to miss the most obvious fact of all: that having an identity is itself what is most important. Only then does one begin to negotiate for the better roles in life. The virtue of "first love," in fact, may be not so much its innocence or its unbridled enthusiasm as the fact that it takes whatever it gets and, for lack of comparison, can consider itself wholly satisfied.

So, what is so good about love? Love provides us with identities, virtues, roles through which we define ourselves as well as partners to share our happiness, reinforce our values, support our best opinions of ourselves and compensate for the anonymity, impersonality or possibly frustration of public life. Lovers not only by mutual agreement but by way of self-interest pay heed to what is best in each other, ignore what each would like ignored, provide support where others will not and provide fantasies where reality lags too far behind desire.

Love is not "everything," perhaps, but it gives us, in this society anyway, much that we might not otherwise obtain. It gives us a source of self, in particular, which is more free—if sometimes more insecure—more variable—if sometimes more uncertain—more intimate—if often less community minded— more exciting—if sometimes more dangerous—than any other we are capable of imagining. Indeed, it is hard to see how we could reject love—in theory or in practice—without rejecting an essential conception of ourselves. We are a romantic society, and given the alternatives suggested by its critics, I would hardly prefer any other.

# EPILOGUE:

# ROMEO'S REVENGE, PLATO'S *SYMPOSIUM* REVISITED

*Hang up philosophy,*
*unless philosophy can make a Juliet.*
SHAKESPEARE, *Romeo and Juliet*

PERSONAE:
Socrates, Romeo, Agathon, Alcibiades, Aristophanes, others.

SCENE:
The House of Agathon, toward the end of the evening.

SOCRATES: [*Drunk as a boot*] Thank you, Agathon. I can see that I was indeed foolish in agreeing to follow you in praise of love. Well, I won't compete with you. You praised love in every way possible, regardless of the truth. Strange, isn't it?— how *eros* sounds so familiar—young, pretty, poetic—anyone I know? [*He laughs, bows, spilling honeyed wine down his thigh*] Phaedrus, I prefer your *eros*, old and wise, much more suitable to the present distinguished company. And, Pausanias, I like what you said about our obligations to educate and enjoy the beautiful youths. I'm glad to hear that my efforts have been appreciated around here. Aristophanes, I can see that you take love to be a comedy, like everything else, but you are simply wrong—if you were being serious at all—about love being the search for one's missing half; love is much more than that, as I shall prove to you. But now, if you'll pass the wine, I'll take my turn, in pretentious pseudo-dialogue form of course, and sing the praises of love in my own wise-ass and belligerent so-called "Socratic" way. That is, if you can stand to hear the *truth* about love. Can you?

ALL: Yes, indeed, Socrates.

SOCRATES: Good. Now, young Romeo, you haven't said a word all evening, so you'll serve as my "yes-man" for this dialogue; let's see how many short affirmatives you've got on hand with you.

ROMEO: Okay, Socrates.

SOCRATES: Good, now. [*Croons*] "Love is better, the second time around . . ."

PHAEDRUS: Come off it, Socrates.

ARISTOPHANES: Well, he said he'd sing the praises . . .

PAUSANIAS: Shut up, Aristo.

SOCRATES: Okay now, seriously. Let's look at love: Take my wife Xanthippe . . . please. Hey, there's a gadfly in my wine. Yuck! [*Throws the remainder of the cup across the table at Eryximachus*] Pass the wine again, will you? Now, Agathon, I wholly approve of your approaching the question by asking, "What is the *nature* of love?" That seems like a good place to begin our dialectic, whatever that means.

ROMEO: Indeed, Socrates.

SOCRATES: You agree, young Romeo?

ROMEO: Yes, Socrates.

SOCRATES: Once more.

ROMEO: Yes, Socrates.

SOCRATES: Well then, let me ask you whether love is of something or of nothing? By the way, where'd you get a name like "Romeo"? Anyhow, I know the question sounds unintelligible, but let me clarify it with a couple of tautologies before I hit you with my whammy. If I were to ask you if a father is the father of something, you would have no trouble answering, would you?

ROMEO: Uh . . .

SOCRATES: Of course you would say "of a son or a daughter," right?

ROMEO: Yes, Socrates, of a son or a daughter.

SOCRATES: Brilliant, you luscious young thing. And you would say the same of a mother?

ROMEO: Very true, Socrates.

SOCRATES: And would it not also be true that a brother is always a brother of something?

ROMEO: [*Puzzled*] Uh, yes, Socrates, but . . .

SOCRATES: And how about a sister?

ROMEO: You're warming up to something.

SOCRATES: Answer the question.

ROMEO: [*Impatiently*] Yes, Socrates, but what's your point? I have another engagement.

SOCRATES: So I now want to know, and I'm asking you, whether love can desire that which love already is.

ROMEO: What?

SOCRATES: That is, does the lover possess, or does he not possess, that which he loves and desires?

ROMEO: Well, that depends on what you mean by "possess. . . ."

SOCRATES: Don't be stupid, a man can't desire what he already has. Whoever desires something is in want of that something, and he who desires nothing is in want of nothing. That, in my judgment, is absolutely and necessarily true. What do you think, Romeo?

ROMEO: What does that have to do with the word "father" referring to the fact that a man has a child? Or, for that matter, what does that have to do with love?

SOCRATES: The very word *eros* means desire, don't you agree?

ROMEO: Yes, in Greek.

SOCRATES: So *eros* is the desire for something, right?

ROMEO: Right. I want Juliet . . .

SOCRATES: But if it is the desire for something, it cannot itself already have that something, right?

ROMEO: I guess so, Socrates. But . . .

SOCRATES: Look, I can't say that I wish to be rich if I'm already rich, can I?

ROMEO: No. But that's trivial and uninter—

SOCRATES: So if love is of something, it must be something wanting to a man, right?

ROMEO: Do you mean . . .

SOCRATES: Hush, kid. Now is this something that is wanted not beauty?

ROMEO: On that, finally, we agree, Socrates. Yes, she is beauti—

SOCRATES: And we have already seen that love is something which a man wants and has not?

ROMEO: Are you saying that *I* can't be beautiful because I love Juliet who is beautiful too?

SOCRATES: [*Ignoring him, addressing the rest of the table*] Then love wants but has not beauty.

ROMEO: [*Irritated*] Sometimes you say "love wants"; other times you say "a man wants"; *love* doesn't want anything: *I* want Juliet. Now what are you talking about?

SOCRATES: *Eros*, of course. Pass the wine again. Now would you call that beautiful which wants but does not possess beauty?

ROMEO: [*Disdainful*] Of course not.

SOCRATES: Then would you still agree with Agathon that love is beautiful?

ROMEO: That's a different question. Juliet is beautiful and love is beautiful but that doesn't mean . . .

SOCRATES: You and young Aristotle, always hung up on particulars. I thought we were talking about the nature of love, not just bragging about lovers.

ROMEO: [*Sulking*] Okay, Socrates. [*Impatient*] Isn't it midnight yet?

SOCRATES: Now I want you to answer one more question—is not the good also the beautiful?

ROMEO: No! Mercurio is good but he isn't . . .

SOCRATES: You're supposed to say yes.

ROMEO: No! You're right that *eros* has certain connotations of nobility, but I'm not going to let you shift the whole discussion into ethics.

SOCRATES: But that's where I'm best. I know all the arguments about virtue.

ROMEO: But not, evidently, about love. No, the beautiful is not the same as the good, even if beautiful people are sometimes good, like Juliet.

SOCRATES: You're really cramping my style, kid.

ROMEO: We're here to talk about love.

SOCRATES: Well, I don't know about you, but I'm here to drink. The idea of talking about love was the Doc's over there, to slow us down in our drinking.

ROMEO: Doesn't seem to have worked.

SOCRATES: Doesn't matter. Anyhow, where were we? Oh yes, and you agree then that, in wanting the beautiful, love also wants the good?

ROMEO: No. You cannot ignore me, Socrates.

SOCRATES: Let us just say that I ignore the truth, for young Romeo cannot be easily ignored.

ROMEO: Let's see where you were going. Okay, suppose I give you your "Yes, Socrates"?

SOCRATES: Say it.

ROMEO: Yes, Socrates.

SOCRATES: Ah. Now, if love is of the good, and the beautiful, and also, of course, of the true . . .

ROMEO: Hey, wait a minute . . .

SOCRATES: Then the lover is, in short, a lover of wisdom. And following our strange friend Pythagoras (who didn't know how he could both come and be here at the same time), we can call the true lover "philosopher."

ROMEO: Are you trying to tell us that philosophers make the best lovers?

SOCRATES: The *only* lovers, kiddo—the rest is just poking around.

ROMEO: You really are trying to argue that philosophy is love, and philosophers lovers. I don't believe it.

SOCRATES: And I've proved it. . . . More wine, please. . . . You already agreed that truth and goodness are the most beautiful things and, since love seeks beauty, what is more beautiful than wisdom, and who is more wise than a philosopher?

ROMEO: I don't believe it. Damn your philosophy; I want my love.

SOCRATES: And now I will take my leave of you, and rehearse a tale of love which I once heard from the wise woman of Mantineia, called Diotima. Of course, I won't tell you when or where this was, and you may well suspect that in doing this I'm just expressing the opinions of my scribe Plato. But in fact I am doing it so that you can't pin me down for my opinions.

ROMEO: In your other dialogues, you feign ignorance.

SOCRATES: Same idea, different technique. Anyway, here's the tale, told through me by Diotima. [*To the table, in a high-pitched falsetto voice, with a pronounced lisp, as Diotima*] "So, my dear Socrates, since humility forbids you to say this yourself, I shall speak through you, as the spirit of love, which has blessed you philosophers above all men, where the true beloved is truth, and you, poor henpecked lout of a libertine, so eagerly pursuing this truth, are the happiest of men."

ROMEO: [*Astounded*] You really are a clown, you know. A buffoon.

SOCRATES: [*With a wink*] An *ad hominem* argument, kid, an elementary fallacy. You'll go far in this philosophy business.

ROMEO: That's not my ambition. Besides . . .

SOCRATES (as Diotima): [*Assuming an extremely effeminate posture*] "Address the goddess, if you please."

ROMEO: Okay, Diotima, why then are all men not lovers, since all men seek the true and the beautiful?

SOCRATES (as Diotima): "You left out the good."

ROMEO: And the good.

SOCRATES (as Diotima): "Most men are misled by their desires and their passions."

ROMEO: [*Ironically*] You mean most men are poor lovers because they are misled by their passions and desires? I thought that love is a passion. And you already argued yourself that *eros* is a desire.

SOCRATES (as Diotima): "Socrates argued that, not me, and he's taken his leave."

ROMEO: This is insufferable.

ARISTOPHANES: But fun, you must admit.

SOCRATES (as Diotima): "Hush. I don't mean that mean-spirited desire that drives you, Romeo, so obsessed with a single beauty—and a mere *girl* at that—but that true passion, the love of wisdom, which sees through the follies of fleshy desire and the endless pursuit of a beautiful body."

ROMEO: You've been known to pursue beautiful bodies yourself, Mr. Philosopher.

SOCRATES: [*Normal voice, offended*] I'm an educator, and the beautiful learn better.

[*Guffaw from around the table*]

SOCRATES: How dare you profane a Platonic dialogue. Besides, I'm seventy years old.

ROMEO: A dirty old man.

SOCRATES: But pure in my thoughts. Let's get back to philosophy.

ROMEO: You mean love?

SOCRATES (as Diotima): "I say that love is a philosopher at all times, an enchanter, a sorcerer, a sophist."

ROMEO: I'm surprised to hear you call yourself a sophist.

SOCRATES: [*Normal voice*] That's Diotima, of course.

ROMEO: Of course.

SOCRATES: Anyway, love. (As Diotima): "Love is not mere desire, that is, desire for bodies and beauty, love is the desire to see past these fleeting desires and passions, to transcend ourselves . . ."

ROMEO: You mean to deny ourselves, and our lovers too.

SOCRATES (as Diotima): "No, I mean transcend ourselves, forget about these ugly bodies . . ."

ROMEO: You mean *your* ugly body.

SOCRATES (as Diotima): [*Annoyed*] "To see ourselves as something more than transient existence among corruption and decay."

ROMEO: "Corruption and decay"? She's only sixteen!

SOCRATES: [*Normal voice*] You just wait.

ROMEO: I will, but with Juliet.

[*There is a loud commotion at the other end of the table. A lizard fouls the tunic of Aristophanes; Plato's revenge for* The Clouds.]

ROMEO: Why do you have to pretend it's all for a "higher" purpose? Why can't you consider your desires themselves noble, without having to rationalize them? Does love need your philosophy as rationalization?

SOCRATES: I believe that they are indeed "higher." Diotima will explain it to you. (As Diotima): "And is not the possession of beauty and wisdom in love conducive to happiness?"

ROMEO: No, being with Juliet is happiness, wisdom be hanged.

SOCRATES (as Diotima): "And is it not true that all men seek happiness and the good life?"

ROMEO: I'm happy now. Besides, given the Greek word for "happiness" (*eudaimonia*), that's a tautology. Yes, whatever men seek as the good life is to be called "happiness." That's just what the word means.

SOCRATES (as Diotima): "And is not enduring happiness better than merely fleeting happiness?"

ROMEO: Well, more is better, if that's what you mean. I hope that Juliet and I can spend a lifetime together.

AGATHON: [*Softly*] I wouldn't set up a retirement fund just yet.

SOCRATES (as Diotima): "And so the love of the eternal, which brings everlasting happiness, is far better than love of mere men, which is only transient?"

ROMEO: It's a woman I love, I'll remind you, and where did "love of the eternal" come from?

SOCRATES: That is what love is.

ROMEO: Would it be fair to say that the core of your argument, Socrates, is that love is better without another person to foul it up?

SOCRATES (as Diotima): "Diotima."

ROMEO: Diotima, you do prefer the impersonal, the eternal, to the virtues of particular persons and personal beauty.

SOCRATES (as Diotima): "Mere trifles."

ROMEO: Trifles, perhaps, but they're all we've got. And they're enough.

SOCRATES: [*Normal voice, impatient*] Look, do you agree that one loves a lover for his beauty?

ROMEO: "*Her* beauty," yes. Though I know this is not the company in which to praise my Juliet.

[*General chuckle*]

SOCRATES: And that what makes one person beautiful may make another person beautiful as well?

ROMEO: Yes, but there is no one . . .

SOCRATES: So then the reasons for loving one person apply to another?

ROMEO: If beauty were the only reason for love, which it's not. Every lover is different in some respects.

SOCRATES: But they're all beautiful?

ROMEO: Indeed.

SOCRATES: Well then, the reason for each is beauty, and what you seek is beauty; do you not agree?

ROMEO: Socrates, that's the best argument for promiscuity I've ever heard. But you have no conception of love at all, which is nothing if not for a particular person, not a type, not an abstraction.

SOCRATES: Why not seek Beauty itself, instead of any one of these trifling instances? Divine beauty, unclogged with the pollutions of mortality?

ROMEO: "The pollutions of mortality!" No wonder you have such a jaded view of love. You're right, I'm hung up on particulars: Juliet, my one and only, her particular body, her particular beauty. I'm not after Beauty. I'm not after Woman. I want Juliet, nothing more.

SOCRATES: Nothing more?

ROMEO: Nothing more.

SOCRATES: But you must want something more, for what is desire without a goal, without a state of satisfaction, and why should anything satisfy you short of eternal happiness?

ROMEO: I have my goal, my satisfaction, my happiness. Love is happiness. Who needs eternity?

SOCRATES: What else could be satisfying, in the eyes of eternity?

ROMEO: But I don't have the eyes of eternity, and neither do you. A passion is satisfying because it transcends eternity, in the only way we can transcend any of your metaphysical pretenses, by being indifferent to them, by being wholly absorbed in life, by being in love. Besides, the point of desire is not its satisfaction but its prolongation. When you're happy, you don't need eternity. Why do you need it, old man?

SOCRATES: How can you choose a life of mere repetitive and momentary pleasure? There are higher desires, you know.

ROMEO: And what makes them "higher," except for the fact that they fit into your moral theories? Besides, I don't lead a life of pleasure. I'm in love. And I'm in love with Juliet. Why do you keep talking about love as an abstraction, when there is nothing more tangible and personal in the world?

SOCRATES: How can you call that "love"? A mere passion.

ROMEO: And what else could love be?

SOCRATES: I think you just want to *be* in love. Juliet doesn't matter. It's just the passion you crave.

ROMEO: But she *does* matter; she counts for everything. Even if you're right that I want the passion, it doesn't follow that it isn't Juliet I want too. And what I want even more is to be loved in return. That's just what's wrong with your whole damned theory, that you pretend to love only that which cannot return it—the eternal forms—and so you've got no responsibilities. And my family calls *me* irresponsible! You take your lovers for granted—young Agathon, for example, while you babble about "love." For me, it is the love that is everything, not the idea of love. I don't use my Juliet as a medium to the absolute.

SOCRATES: I do prefer philosophy, but . . .

[*There is a loud crash, and much shouting. Alcibiades stumbles into the table, drunk and roaring, supported by a flute girl, whom he is fondling clumsily. His head is entirely covered with flowers. (He had, we later learned, just knocked the genitalia off half the statues in Athens.)*]

ALCIBIADES: Well, what are you waiting for?

AGATHON: We've quite started, thank you, but please join us.

[*Alcibiades virtually falls on top of Socrates, dumping the heap of flowers around the philosopher's head, making it difficult for him to either see or speak.*]

ROMEO: Well, that's one way to shut him up. Thank you.

SOCRATES: Mmmmph.

ERYXIMACHUS: Hey, Alcibiades, are we to have neither conversation nor song when you come in, but simply to drink as if we were thirsty?

ALCIBIADES: Let's sing then, much better than the drivel I heard in here before. No, on second thought, I'll say my piece on love as well. I shall praise my friend Socrates here, for he is a raunchy old hypocrite and the dirtiest old man in Athens.

ARISTOPHANES: Yes indeed. He gave me fleas last week.

ALCIBIADES: [*To Socrates*] Now tell me, Socrates, you will not deny that your face is that of a satyr?

SOCRATES: Mmmph. Mmmth.

ALCIBIADES: And do you not play a marvelous flute, to charm the young girls, and do you not play your wonderful wit as a musical instrument, to seduce the young boys? And even war heroes and army commanders? [*He chuckles to himself*] And isn't your idealistic philosophy nothing more than a cover-up for your own life of past raunch and a flimsy justification, I would add, for your rotten marriage? You're always falling in love, you raunchy rascal, and you'll have rogered half of Greece by the time the law catches up with you. You should be tried for hypocrisy, you know. You lose the most noble idea at the mere hint of a fleshy thigh. And afterward you jump into a fit of abstraction the way we jump into the baths. You are indeed a lover, but hardly of wisdom. Like us, you love a good party.

ROMEO: Ha!

SOCRATES: Mmmpth!!

ALCIBIADES: [*Waxing eloquent*] Stronger than the walls of Ilium is your outrageous and self-righteous stance of ignorance, which no one can refute. Yet you battle incessantly, and will no doubt be happily chattering at dawn when the rest of us have long since given in. But then it's probably better than going home to Xanthippe, where you never get a word in edgewise. Oh, Socrates, you're a satyr, and a cocktease besides. Let me move closer to you, and hold you in my arms!

[*He passes out, on Socrates' lap*]

SOCRATES: [*Pulling the flowers off his head, looking at the unconscious Alcibiades*] Well, that's another way of being irrefutable.

ROMEO: You're being upstaged in this dialogue, you know.

SOCRATES: Well, I can't win them all. But he's right, you know, I'll bet that I am the last one left standing.

ROMEO: Braggart.

SOCRATES: No, I'll let Plato tell it for me.

ROMEO: Why not write it yourself?

SOCRATES: Because it's the face-to-face encounters I love, more than the philosophy.

ROMEO: You know that, thousands of years from now, scholars will be picking apart your arguments with tweezers, making up arguments where you leave them out and adding embarrassed footnotes about what they'll call your "pederasty."

SOCRATES: I can never find the argument myself. It's the *inter-*

*course* that I love, quite literally. I could teach you a thing or two, young Romeo.

ROMEO: Thanks, Socrates, but I have to see my chemist.

SOCRATES: You're missing a first-rate education.

ROMEO: Do you think the scholars will take notice of your lusty desires? Do you think they'll realize how much you enjoy these games, and how playful you are?—which is your own expression of love. No. I'll tell you what they'll make of you: a moral prig. They'll accept your arguments against the flesh and your repudiation of desires. They'll turn your pretense of eternity into a rejection of life itself and love besides. They'll call you a "sodomite," and a "pagan," and reinterpret you as a proto-Christian.

SOCRATES: [*Flabbergasted*] That's not possible. What's a Christian?

ROMEO: In fact, do you know what the ideal of love will be? The sexless adoration of the divine. And do you know what they'll call it? *"Platonic* love." You won't even get the credit.

SOCRATES: Should I sue? Call in one of the wasps, Aristophanes.

ROMEO: That's what happens when you keep blabbing about "transcendence." Besides, people will make of you what they want to make of you. When it suits them, you will be a pagan and a pervert. And when it pleases them, you will be the father of philosophy and the hero of the truth.

SOCRATES: But that's not fair.

ROMEO: That's what happens when you don't publish.

SOCRATES: But you're nothing but a fiction yourself.

ROMEO: I'm actually a fantasy, but—I'd rather have me as a fantasy than you.

ARISTOPHANES: [*Very drunk*] If I may interrupt you there, I've been wanting to protest all evening that none of you, particularly you, Socrates, ever seems to take me very seriously. (I suspect you don't appreciate poets, myself, but perhaps I'm just being hypersensitive.) But what you failed to take seriously tonight was my perfectly serious argument, that shows just why love is so serious, not because it is eternal but because it answers an essential metaphysical need. It's serious, in other words. Seriously. [*Collapses*]

SOCRATES: How can we take you seriously, when you present us with a fable that is so at odds with all of our established myths?

ROMEO: But they are all myths, including your tribute to *eros;* the difference is that Aristophanes' wonderful myth tries to capture the experience of love, especially that exquisite *yearning* that goes beyond sexual desire and that desperate need to be together. That's just what your famous philosophy leaves out entirely, Socrates.

SOCRATES: But how are we to understand that nonsense? It can't be the literal truth.

ROMEO: How can you not understand it? Juliet is my other half. We were made for each other. And what difference if that isn't true? Surely you must know the experience; you just don't talk about it. Indeed, Aristophanes was the only one here tonight, except me, who has understood love at all; the rest of you have just been muddling around in metaphysics. This is a poor dialogue, Socrates—you've done much better.

SOCRATES: Yeah, I know, but there really isn't much to say about love. It's not like the theory of knowledge, or the theory of justice, where you can be hardheaded and argue about precise hypotheses. In fact, Eryximachus, I think your idea of talking about love is simply dreadful, and I'm glad Plato isn't here to write it down and publish it for posterity.

ARISTOPHANES: [*Sleepily*] I have no objection to my little tale going down in history. I rather like it, in fact.

SOCRATES: Well, no one would understand what I've been saying anyway. I'll tell you what—why don't we talk about virtue for a while?

ROMEO: Not me. I'm exhausted. And I have a full night ahead of me.

ARISTOPHANES: Ciao, Romeo.

SOCRATES: If you want to redeem yourself, Romeo, tomorrow we're going to enjoy a long harangue about justice. Want to come along?

ROMEO: Not my kind of entertainment. Ciao, Greeks. [*Exit*]

SOCRATES: [*To Agathon, who is asleep again already*] Who invited him here tonight anyway?

[*Agathon half opens his eyes and with great difficulty rises to join Socrates on his couch. But then a band of revelers enters; great confusion ensues, and everyone is compelled to drink large quantities of wine. By daybreak everyone is asleep or has gone away, except Socrates, Aristophanes and Agathon, who are drinking out of a large goblet which they pass around. Socrates is lecturing to them, saying something about the need for a writer of tragedy to be a writer of comedy too. Aristophanes obviously disagrees, but is too tired to argue. Agathon nods his assent, too sleepy to understand Socrates' meaning. And when they both have dropped, Socrates puts them to bed and goes off to the Lyceum for a bath. He never speaks of Romeo again, but he vows, if ever again should anyone speak of love, that it should be far more mysterious and obscure than anything he said tonight.*]

*Index*

# INDEX